FLIGHT OF THE DOVE

To Del and Ceec,
builders of one of
Jeannette's hopes,
United Women Power—
Love to both,

Fran Elge

Flight of the Dove

THE STORY OF JEANNETTE RANKIN

by Kevin S. Giles

The Lochsa Experience
Publishers

The Touchstone Press
P.O. Box 81
Beaverton, Oregon 97075

Library of Congress
Catalog Card No.: 80-81863

I.S.B.N. No.: 0-918688-03-5

To my daughters
Heather and Harmony,
that in their aspiring futures
they can enjoy, as
Jeannette Rankin envisioned,
a world free from war.

ACKNOWLEDGEMENTS AND SOURCES

Information pertaining to Jeannette Rankin lies in the hands and minds of widely dispersed sources. The Jeannette Rankin Collection at The Arthur and Elizabeth Schlesinger Library on the History of Women in America at Radcliffe College in Cambridge, Mass., contains much of her correspondence and other personal papers highlighting her Congressional years. A substantial collection of her work in the peace movement can be found in the files of the National Council for Prevention of War in the Swarthmore Peace Collection at Swarthmore College in Pennsylvania. A small but growing collection at the Montana Historical Society Library in Helena, includes notes and papers of Belle Fligelman Winestine, Jeannette's former administrative secretary. The Society's collection of Jeannette's late brother, Wellington D. Rankin, also was useful.

The unselfish assistance of Mrs. Winestine was invaluable. Another of Jeannette's administrative secretaries, Frances Elge, offered a considerable insight into Jeannette's political motives. Jeannette's relatives — Mackey Brown, Louise Rankin Galt, Edna Rankin McKinnon and Virginia Ronhovde — were generous with interviews and personal information.

Special thanks to friend and reference librarian Lynne Daghlian Livingstone, who helped build the foundation for the book with her quick and concise suggestions for research, and to Don D. Bielenberg for creative guidance. Personal thanks to psychologist and historian Bailey Molineux, who appraised the manuscript; to professional colleague David Conley, who upgraded it with his customary journalistic intuition; to Diana Beckstrom Vashro, who contributed days of typing, and to my wife Becky, who made innumerable personal sacrifices so I could complete the work.

TABLE OF CONTENTS

FLIGHT OF THE DOVE
Preface

Jeannette Rankin's role as dissenter and feminist has been largely ignored until recent years, when the 'new woman' liberation of the Seventies has eased her ideas into vogue. Jeannette has been but a dark horse among the historically pontificated, yet for decades her message persevered: liberate women, and subsequently men, through peace.

Possibly Jeannette Rankin *was* the greatest feminist this century has seen; more objective scholars conclude she merely lived *among* the greatest. Her competition lies in Jane Addams, Coretta Scott King, Gloria Steinem, Betty Friedan, Jane Fonda, Shirley Chisholm, Barbara Jordan, Bella Abzug. Each of these women — and innumerable other strongly influential personalities — have contributed greatly to politics, music, drama, journalism, religion, social work and education.

Yet unique about Jeannette Rankin is that she attacked the roots of oppression and maintained an intense, lonely struggle as a social reformer from the raucous muckraking and suffrage days of the pre-World War I era to the final hours of the Vietnam War.

Her life passed in 1973 with much of her work misunderstood. She was a dissenter, and during times of war, protest has been confused with treason. For a fact, the news media simply never gave Jeannette a fair hearing. She emerged in the public mind a confused, angry, cynical spinster, misplaced in time and a stranger to tradition. Thus, we have been slow in realizing the value of this brilliant woman.

But her memory has stayed with us, for she has given us subtle answers to our future. Her extraordinary talent for leading people nicely to her viewpoint was only the surface of her superb strength. Jeannette thought the pervasive belief that war is glorious and patriotic was the most destructive myth in modern civilization; a volatile human aggression that wrenched apart family and friends. Her use of social democracy as a tool to end war flowered when most of her attempts at social legislation were aborted by bloated appropriations for killing and destruction.

Whether diplomacy would replace war as a method of settling international disputes became a growing source of anxiety for her in the decade before she died. In speaking of her lifelong commitment to freedom, she said: "I'm a bit more frustrated now... I worked for suffrage for years, and got it. I've worked for peace for 55 years, and haven't come close."

She was an example to millions of Americans that to protest war would not destroy democracy, and in her spartan self-sufficiency she demonstrated we can be free thinkers without the security of consumptuous living. She not only questioned the productivity of home conveniences, but she protested in disbelief the vainglorious expenditures for war. Women and children enjoyed her protection from the time she campaigned for equal suffrage in 1911, yet she argued men were no less liberated.

Jeannette Rankin was one of the great humanitarians of this age, ranking among such peace advocates as Jane Addams, Martin Luther King, Mohandas Gandhi and Henry David Thoreau. She was dedicated to love and understanding among people of the world.

If we are to learn anything from Jeannette Rankin, we must

heed her aggressive search for knowledge and truth. In her philosophy we are encouraged to seek independence by exercising our rights and responsibilities as Americans. Jeannette thought every person should find a purpose in life, believing that without clear goals people could be influenced against their will during a crisis. She had no strength or support on which to depend except what came from within herself, and yet she worshipped a great moral obligation to rid the world of war.

Jeannette was sustained in this commitment by her lucid deliberate philosophy of peace and freedom, which proved to be so strong that she drove herself to extremes. During her Congressional term in World War II she dictated a letter to her secretary, Frances Elge, bemoaning the tragedy of young boys who were killed in battle before achieving their "life's mission." She once wrote of life and death:

> *A person can be shot, but an idea cannot. Killing is the antithesis of life and negates the very possibility of growing into fullness. It is the same passion for the ideal, which a mother expresses in her love for her children, which we must achieve and maintain if we want our ideals to mature and flourish in society: self-control, compassion, honesty, integrity, and love must be conceived in our minds, incarnated through our daily actions and living, and patiently sustained in adversity. A dead enemy cannot become our friend. And — just as certainly — the ideal dies within us when we violate it.*

As a Montana schoolboy I despised Jeannette Rankin. Young boys sense no fear; war can be a splendor, a ticket to manhood. I was drunk with the glory of the military uniform and the romanticism of combat, and when I learned Jeannette twice had cast votes in Congress against American entry into world war, I thought such behavior to be unforgivably irreverent of flag and country. My youthful mind did not ponder why she may have cast votes in the negative. Even throughout my college years, when she was making rousing anti-war speeches to university audiences and witty observations about politics on national television, she was an enigma to me.

In October 1976 I met Belle Fligelman Winestine, a delightfully spunky octogenarian who had been Jeannette's administrative secretary in Congress in 1917. Mrs. Winestine spoke of Jeannette Rankin as a futuristic American whose ideas were 60 years ahead of our thinking. We struggle over the issue of the Equal Rights Amendment today, for example, yet Jeannette had said in 1916 that women who understood the power of the ballot could make far-reaching social changes that would make them as powerful as any male lobby.

Jeannette's future-oriented notions have provided historians with precious little information, however, because she was impatient with writing or discussing the past. She simply lacked the discipline to put her ideas on paper, although she produced short essays explaining her positions when she feared she had been misunderstood or ignored by the press.

Jeannette's prowess was in thinking and speaking. She was a remarkably articulate and seductive persuader at the podium, but her private thoughts are buried in her life's voluminous correspondence. Early in Jeannette's Congressional career, the press learned to be wary even of the news releases emanating from her office. In 1917, a *New York Times* reporter, hastening to file a story on a speech she was to make later that day, got a copy and hustled off to beat his afternoon deadline. At the podium, however, Jeannette discarded the speech, preferring to speak impromptu. She trusted her intuition and her quick mind more readily than a written speech, and the *Times* story was dreadfully out of step with the actual news event.

In light of her indifference to building a firm public record of her life, telling Jeannette's story promised to be a stiff challenge. She sometimes was effusive, then curt and impatient; alternately exuberant and depressed; mostly determined to obtain the goal of peace, sometimes believing such a goal to be futile; widely conscientious about her work, but speaking little about private fears and personal relationships.

Yet writing Jeannette Rankin's biography became an obsession with me, because her name invokes fascination.

I wondered how I, "a mere man," could meet the task of portraying this multi-sided woman in print, and yet I was to learn from Jeannette that we raise our own sex barriers and make our own shortcomings. When a person wonders how Jeannette, "a mere woman," battled with faith and conviction through the hogwash of sex sentiment and "woman's place is in the home" syndrome to find a forum for her ideas, we realize personal success lies in a genuine desire to find the truth.

Jeannette's truth was liberating American women and children by securing peace. In her opinion, war was a corporate function having nothing to do with freedom and independence, and it inhibited personal and social growth. Jeannette said the truth about war will expose the lies and myths that allow it to exist. We will understand that slaughter and destruction can be avoided by reasonable and honest diplomacy at the conference table. When we are persuaded to fight on foreign soil, we should demand to know why, for in Jeannette's example dissent is virtuous.

I wrote Jeannette Rankin's story because the prospect of breathing a new life into this magnificent woman is an enticing venture that profits the minds and hearts of people everywhere.

I sometimes wonder why we couldn't have reached out to touch her, to comfort her, to assure her that the contribution she had made was an honorable and lasting one. People who listened to her arguments, however, knew she expected no favors for her pleas. She made great personal sacrifices with no possibility of compensation. She simply sought the truth, and that plight proved refreshing to Americans who recognized and appreciated her exercise of democracy. Coretta Scott King observed of Jeannette Rankin after a peace march to the Capitol in Washington, D.C., in 1968:

> *She is the endurance symbol of the aspiration of American women — the symbol of the aspirations for peace of millions of us.*

Kevin Giles
Helena, Montana
Oct. 1, 1979

"There can be no compromise with war; it cannot be reformed or controlled; cannot be disciplined into decency or codified into common sense, for war is the slaughter of human beings, temporarily regarded as enemies, on as large a scale as possible."

(Jeannette Rankin speaks for legislation proposed in 1929 by the Women's Peace Union)

Prologue

Jeannette Rankin — social reformer, pacifist, feminist — thought war was a vulgar indictment of the free will of the American people.

As a student of the Progressive Era — when oppressed Americans demanded to be heard in government and spared from the economic savagery of big business — she learned we create the environment in which we live.

In the midst of reform, Progressivist Teddy Roosevelt invented the term 'muckrakers,' and as these journalistic social critics expounded sordid tales of a nation gone mad with wealth while thousands of Americans starved in ramshackle tenement buildings, Jeannette began carrying a banner for women and children. She campaigned for the U.S. House of Representatives to give these neglected Americans a voice in government, and being elected from Montana she was the first woman to sit in Congress.

The year was 1917.

The gentle Jeannette took her seat among the black coats and starched white collars of America's lawmakers. She was full of desire to prompt legislation benefiting women and children.

Then America declared war on Germany, and the onslaught of World War I wiped her social legislation from the Congressional calendar. Americans had a war to keep themselves busy, so suffrage by federal amendment, children's health and nutrition programs, birth control for women and equal pay for equal work had been stalled. The war was a godsend for critics of the women's rights movement, who had fumed the sanctuaries in their world were being desegregated, compromised and abolished.

America's first Congresswoman, however, refused to allow her constituency to be destroyed. Having been in Congress only six days, she faced the prospect of casting a vote on the issue. Should she vote for war against Germany, or should she vote for peace? Lobbyists tugged at her conscience. Vote for war, her brother pleaded, to remain politically alive for the next election. Vote for war, her suffrage sisters begged, to avoid the sentimental sob sister image that would follow a vote of dissent.

Legislate the rights of women and children, Jeannette was told, but acquiesce with the manly concern of war.

Jeannette was about to demonstrate her symbolism. As reporters furiously scribbled notes, she rose from her seat in the House chambers early on a starlit Good Friday morning and by voting against the resolution promised that never again would American women accept war as an inevitable male pleasure.

Jeannette Rankin was wed to the cause of peace from that moment. As she left Congress in late 1918, she envisioned a world movement, and in the subsequent two decades, nurtured a microcosm in Georgia, her 'center of infection' from where she hoped an epidemic could spread. Writer Katharine Anthony, when visiting Georgia, thought her companion Jeannette was a pioneer among pacifists:

> She would never buy a farm which others had cultivated. She likes to blaze trails for others to follow and plough new lands for others to cultivate. The edge of cultivation has no terrors for [Jeannette]. She would always go beyond the edge and set her plough in virgin soil.

When foreign war again threatened to rob healthy, young

American men from their cradle of innocence and hurl them into a hatred they did not understand, Jeannette was elected once more to Congress as a member of the House of Representatives.

Pearl Harbor was bombed.

Congress hurriedly voted to declare war on Japan, and Jeannette, vowing she would not allow a totalitarian regime to rule America, was the only member of Senate or House to vote 'nay' on the resolution. The horrible backlash of public sentiment toward her stand would have ruined most dissenters. But the feminist Jeannette persisted in her belief that the American woman would be liberated only when she prohibited her man from going to war.

Jeannette's peace work continued in the late Forties and Fifties, although she mostly dropped from public view. She traveled worldwide, particularly in India, and saturated herself with the teaching of Mohandas Gandhi. She re-emerged in the Sixties a free spirit, a woman who read pacifist literature as avidly as most Americans watched television, walked on a living room floor of tamped earth and Oriental rugs, and drank raw eggs for better health.

But emanating from this eccentricity was a practical purpose for living: to liberate women by abolishing war. She studied, traveled and campaigned, and by 1968 when people were rioting, petitioning and filling the streets to protest the Vietnam War, she returned to the forefront of the peace movement to lead 5,000 women dressed in black in the march of the Jeannette Rankin Brigade on the U.S. Capitol in Washington, D.C.

Jeannette found the love of war ingrained so deeply in the American consciousness that the mood of Richard Nixon's 'silent majority' of the Sixties differed little from the didactic war mania of 1917. Even during the impassioned years of the great world wars — great in Jeannette's opinion, only for the magnitude of death and destruction — the American consciousness remained unchanged. Men continued to be the dominating force, proving the gains of equal suffrage mostly had been illusionary. Neither women — nor men — were free.

This conflict proved to be the theme of Jeannette Rankin's life. She was habitually at odds with a male macho society predisposed to maintain an image of military superiority. She saw women as slaves of the war system, which created purple-hearted heroes, generated corporate dollars and enhanced a gregarious national unity for the men. Women were not free to enjoy the plunder, however, for mass market, mechanical killing violated their basic human instincts of motherhood and love.

But her beliefs were not without their sacrifices.

Her life lacked romantic love, broad social pleasures and personal fulfillment. Jeannette endured a lonely existence, fraught with disappointments. She lived in an era when dissent was considered disloyal and when patriotism was believed to be synonymous with the glory of war.

She was scorned, ridiculed and chastised by people for whom war was an American classic to be revered, tolerated and exploited, yet she refused to accept that young men were expendable as a guarantee to free living.

Such feminist, independent thinking was not in vogue in a nation where the larger share of the national budget was promised to the military shrine.

But Jeannette matured to the forces and methods of evil that had scrambled humanity in a battle of bitter competition in the *laissez faire* era of the late 19th century.

She argued stubbornly that families should not want to send children to the nightmare of combat. Too many limbs were blown away, too many coffins were buried in forgotten cemeteries, and too many men simply disappeared. She believed war was a coward's method of dealing with world problems. Jeannette wrote in regard to a bill proposed to Congress in 1929 by the Women's Peace Union:

> *There can be no compromise with war; it cannot be reformed or controlled; cannot be disciplined into decency or codified into common sense; for war is the slaughter of human beings, temporarily regarded as enemies, on as large a scale as possible.*

Jeannette maintained that war was a spurious American conviction. She hated war because she hated injustice. She could not understand why the farmer milked his cow and gave no milk to the calf. She could not reason why a mother gave birth to her son, knowing he might be swept away to the terror of war. And she was outraged that Americans worshipped with flags and guns and songs an institution where death, disease and destruction prevailed.

And for that reason the lonely dissenter turned to American women and urged them to use their political power to pacify the military minds and bring a greater sense of justice to the nation. Jeannette perceived that the real trial of women was to advance beyond the mere embellishments of social change (the hard-won right to vote, she believed, had been used ineffectively) to the abolishment of war, which would be the true liberation of both sexes.

"Go! Go! Go! It makes no difference where just so you go! go! go! Remember at the first opportunity go!"

(Jeannette Rankin's diary, circa 1902)

A DOVE AWAKENS
Chapter 1

For nearly the first 30 years of her life, Jeannette Rankin was a hapless product of the reform era, and her goals in life were not clear to her.

Born to a father of Scot-Canadian descent and a mother immigrated to Montana Territory from New Hampshire, Jeannette's childhood years on the Rankin's Grant Creek Ranch were beset by indecision and a tortured love affair with the work and interests of men. She had inherited, in many respects, the tough and colorful personality of her father, a hot-tempered, intense, powerful man who rather would brawl with his fists than argue diplomatically. But John Rankin also was dignified and shrewd, and he amassed a small fortune from the profits of his land holdings, his ranch and his water-powered sawmill.

He was a fighter, an intuitive entrepreneur who worked hard for what he wanted, and this was a trait he was to instill in Jeannette. Born in 1841 in Apin, Ontario, the fourth son of Scottish immigrants Hugh and Jeannette Rankin, he learned early in life that he could relieve the financial burden of his parents by putting himself to work, and he dropped out of school after only three grades to learn carpentry.

Joining up with brother Duncan, John Rankin set out in 1869 for Fort Benton, Montana Territory, driven by rumors about gold strikes in the Rocky Mountains. Braving the thrashing Missouri Breaks, subsisting on watermelons, navigating a river that roamed the flood plains of an empty prairie, the Rankins found themselves stranded when their boat ran aground on a sandbar 40 miles from Fort Benton. As John Rankin would tell his children, he heaved his tool chest onto his back and walked to the tiny pioneer town.

Hearing much of Helena had been destroyed by fire, the Rankins bought a team of oxen and headed south, hoping to cash in on the rebuilding. When they arrived, most of the work had been done. Helena again was a busy hub of activity. Teamsters thrashed maddened mules, the tinkle of cheap pianos echoed from boisterous saloons, and miners tapped staccato on the boardwalks with their heavy workboots.

The Rankin brothers wasted no time fretting. They moved four miles up Last Chance Gulch to a village named Unionville where gold had been discovered, and built a stamp mill to crush ore. But John Rankin tired quickly of his investment, driven by the urge to discover whether life had anything more appealing to his sense of adventure.

He traveled westward across the Continental Divide to Missoula, where at 29 he established himself as a builder: architect, logger, carpenter and craftsman. He invested in ranching and also built the first sawmill. In only a few years he figured prominently in city politics, and had mastered some of the intuitive secrets to wealth that were raising J. Pierpont Morgan, John D. Rockefeller and Andrew Carnegie to the top of the Eastern financial world.

But as Jeannette would demonstrate in the reform of the early 20th century, her father exemplified in the preceding *laissez faire* period a classic pattern among leaders. As Jeannette would work for personal fulfillment among the poor and oppressed, John

Rankin's reward was material wealth that prevented a life of economic misery. A student of geometry, he won prominence in his community when he built the Methodist Church in 1872 and constructed the first bridge across the Clark Fork River, which had divided the town.

Rankin became a rich man by Western standards, surfaced in civic affairs and was elected county commissioner in 1878, while the woman who was to become his wife was making her way west.

Olive Pickering had been teaching school in New Hampshire. "I was young and good looking and dressed well, and the school board probably knew that I needed a job, so they always gave me one," she explained to a friend.

But when an uncle named William Berry visited with tales of life in Montana Territory, where he had been a sheriff in Missoula, Olive begged her parents to let her go West. In a few days, Olive and her eldest sister Mandana left the security of Eastern living and traveled by transcontinental rail to Corrine, Utah. They rode a stage north to Missoula, where the 20-year-old Olive began teaching in a small one-room schoolhouse. Mandana, being less of an adventurer and complaining that Montana "was not a fit place to raise children," returned to New Hampshire.

Olive Pickering, however, was not shy toward adventure. Her presence into rugged, lawless Montana Territory proved she was anxious for new developments in her life, and she even became accustomed to the Indians who sat on the board fence surrounding the schoolhouse.

Miss Pickering was intelligent and had a good sense of humor, but she was no socialite. She preferred visiting with people only in her home, and was more intrigued by cooking and sewing than by politics. She did not have the spirit to be a leader, but she had the stability to make leaders. A friend described her as "kind, firm, and in a mild way domineering."

John Rankin and Olive Pickering married in August 1879, and Jeannette was born the following June.

The Rankins lived at their ranch six miles northwest of Missoula, until John Rankin had finished building a house at 134

Madison Street. The three-story house — considered the most elaborate in town — was topped with a glass-enclosed Burmese-style cupola with a surrounding walkway. The house had rare amenities in a territory known for its rugged lifestyle: hot and cold running water, a woodburning, forced-air stove, and zinc bathtub. Jeannette began school and brought gawking new friends home with her, but the Rankin children didn't regard the house as novel because they lived in it.

Summers at the ranch appealed more to Jeannette than life in town. The Rankin children thrilled at the prospect of loading their belongings into a surrey or onto a hayrack and heading into the country. The ranch was in a steep canyon, and from the porch, the family had a panoramic view of the snow-capped Bitterroot Mountains. Jeannette's imagination flourished in this free land, and she learned to appreciate the freedom for which she fought in later years.

She was a blossoming feminist, for extravagances were few and pampering was nonexistent, and the fear of failure forced her to think for herself and draw conclusions about her relationships with other people. Hard work was more than expected of her — it was demanded — and in this sense she shared an intolerant drive for feminist survival with poorer Eastern women, committed by the threat of starvation to the factory sweatshops.

As the eldest daughter of seven children, Jeannette assumed a burden of responsibility to the household that did not evaporate on a teenage girl's whim. The responsibility elevated her into an adult's world of cruel sacrifices, and she saw her mother as a perpetual baby machine. Having assumed motherly care of her siblings since an early age, Jeannette was well acquainted with the drudgery of the work. For the post-Victorian woman, marriage and family life promised to be a captive experience. Few women actually escaped this entrapment, although Jeannette hesitated to relinquish her freedom in the manner her mother exemplified.

National statistics suggested she was conforming with the trend of taking a critical look at marriage. Divorce increased from about 11,000 in 1870 to 55,751 in 1900. Jeannette, as many other women, was wondering whether marriage was the answer.

In the 1890s, when Jeannette was a precocious ranch girl, American women were freeing themselves socially, if not politically, enjoying bicycles, beaches and Lillian Russell-style audacity.

Women also were gaining a great measure of liberation in the increased labor demands of the Industrial Revolution. By tens of thousands, even women not driven by hunger hastened to avoid a life of toil at home by filling factory jobs, but the employers' reasons for hiring them often were less than humanitarian. Bosses skimped on pay, degraded working conditions, and demanded longer hours with no overtime considerations. While problems faced by the labor wing of the women's rights movement progressively worsened, other women boldly cried for reform.

In 1874, for example, women had appeared on the streets of Cincinnati and Pittsburgh to protest the liquor evil, and the Women's Christian Temperance Union was born. In 1890, when Jeannette was but 10 years old, Jane Addams had begun her Hull House social movement in an area of Chicago where crime, illiteracy and malnutrition were rampant.

But in her innocent, unknowing way, Jeannette took little heed in the social revolution of the Gay Nineties. That she and Jane Addams would travel to Switzerland only 30 years later as friends and sister feminists was wholly unforseeable as Jeannette passed her youth in the vast mountain wonderland of the Rocky Mountains, where lusty deer and elk fed in quiet meadows and creeks flowed bitter cold and clear, even in the warmth of summer.

Jeannette was a perceptive young girl. But Montana did not gain statehood until 1889, and the state was removed geographically and communicatively from the throbbing population centers of the East and Midwest.

The great Eastern cities already were crumbling from corruption, crime and poverty when Montana Territory still was only a wild, unexplored frontier. As the cry for reform resounded throughout the nation, pioneer communities in Montana were struggling with founding city governments. News was slow to reach the newborn camps and villages, and as most Montanans,

Jeannette understood little about the class struggle nationwide.

Most Montana newspapers were owned and controlled by the powerful Anaconda Company of Butte, and the editors were silent about labor reform and the women's rights movement, which enhanced labor reform. The *Anaconda Standard*, for example, boasted correspondents worldwide, particularly in the fashion centers of Paris, London and New York City, but the copper baron Marcus Daly forbade his newsmen to breathe a word of the true human sentiment that was growing among the oppressed.

Jeannette learned most about life in the East from her mother, who had left New Hampshire as a young adult, and from Civil War refugees who ranched and farmed in the Bitterroot Valley. She listened in wide-eyed wonder as the old Southerners gathered with her father in the ranchhouse parlor, spitting out tales of the war and life in the South as frequently as they spat streams of tobacco. They were rough and frank in their talk, and Jeannette was electrified by the atmosphere of it all, much to her mother's displeasure.

Jeannette was efficient in the kitchen and learned from her mother how to sew her clothes and be a good hostess. Yet Olive Rankin would reflect on her daughter's childhood that she was a daydreaming, unresponsive 'problem' child, forsaking education, religion and social life for the opportunity of political thought. Jeannette was capable and hardheaded, but restless and resentful of woman's work when it interfered with her intellectual brainstorming, or her flattering attention to her father.

John treated his eldest daughter as a son, forcing Olive to ambitiously turn her favors to Wellington, whom she dotingly called 'The Boy' until she died in 1947. Wellington was the Rankin's only son, born fourth in a family of seven children. His mother's laconic expression, 'The Boy,' conveyed blanket approval of Wellington's beliefs and activities, and Jeannette was annoyed often throughout her life that he would dare to rival her self-appointed leadership.

She was chagrined particularly that he longed to be a U.S. Senator but was personally abrasive and often deaf to the needs and opinions of the constituency he hoped to represent, and she suggested in a letter from India to her sister during the post-World War II years that she would not return to Montana to assist in his campaign because she might upstage his performance. Jeannette privately criticized Wellington's consumptuous life-style and poked fun at his devotion to Christian Science, while he accused his sister of being rash with her money and loose with her tongue.

This epic rivalry persisted beneath an exterior of love and companionship.

She was the philosopher; he the realist. He was a master in the strategy of law, real estate and money; she was the master of ideas and people. Both had been influenced greatly by their father, although each reacted differently.

Wellington had inherited his father's intuition for profit, amas-sing a fortune of nearly $10 million before his death. But he could be staid and severe in public and frequently embarrassed Jean-nette with cold humor and inhumane observations about her morals. He thought she talked too much, made promises she couldn't keep, and he was critical of her lifestyle.

Jeannette spent many summers of her life at his ranch east of Helena, Montana, and one day he brought some business as-sociates there to visit. Hoping to humor his guests at Jeannette's expense, he reportedly demanded of his sister: "Pull up your dress, Jeannette, and show my friends how bowlegged you are." Jeannette, although a hopeless manager of money (Wellington kept her informed how much money she had in her savings and checking accounts and filed her income tax returns), had the natural grace among people that had made their father socially successful.

This peculiar conflict between brother and sister had a pro-found influence on Jeannette's life.

As a child, Wellington was loved and appreciated by his sisters — an adoration that sometimes stretched to the limits of tolerance — but Jeannette was the leader of the family and assumed in many ways the care of her brother and sisters. Edna, the youngest of the Rankin children, was afraid of Jeannette and regarded her as a mother figure. Two other sisters, Grace and Mary, lived under Jeannette's rule for much of their childhood and became accustomed to obeying their older sister's commands.

A doctor visited the Rankin home one day and Edna, Grace and Mary hid in their upstairs bedroom, suspecting Jeannette had planned an unpleasant surprise for them. Jeannette climbed the stairs and ordered the girls to the living room, where a table had been prepared for surgery. A doctor waited, instruments in hand, to extract their tonsils and adnoids. Afraid to argue with Jeannette, they submitted. Another day, without warning, she took the girls downtown and had them vaccinated for small pox. "She was the decision maker — always," Edna said of Jeannette.

This initiative fueled the growing conflict between Jeannette and her mother. It was worsened by Jeannette's new awareness that she possessed all the capabilities of a woman, and a feminine demeanor, but was attracted to the politics, work and thinking of men. She consistently showed talent for activities considered taboo among the 'weaker' sex, and while still a young girl, she adopted the probing pattern of thinking that shaped her life.

One day when Jeannette was but a small child, her father brought a wagonload of machinery from nearby Missoula to lift hay into the barn. He harnessed a team of horses to the machinery and they pulled so roughly the pulley mechanism jammed. While John Rankin tried to calm the horses, Jeannette inspected the damage. The ranch hands scratched their heads in frustration, but Jeannette studiously explained to her father how to unravel the mess. He turned on his hired men in anger. "You haven't enough sense to do it yourself; you have to let a little girl tell you what to do," he scolded them.

Another time John Rankin was trying to sell a downtown hotel, but the prospective buyer refused to bargain further unless a boardwalk was built around the hotel. Rankin was a hard-nosed businessman and he refused to honor the buyer's ultimatum, but Jeannette purchased a load of lumber, and took hammer and nails to build the boardwalk. The speculator promptly bought the hotel.

Similarly, she excelled in situations requiring quick judgment and emotional detachment. Once a horse on the Rankin ranch trotted into the corral, whining in pain. Flesh on his shoulder was torn and hanging from a bad gash, and while the cowboys wrestled the horse to the ground, 10-year-old Jeannette raced to the house for hot water and a needle and thread. She expertly stitched up the wound. Another time, she calmly amputated the mangled foot of a ranch dog who had caught his leg in a steel-teethed trap, and later crafted a leather boot for the dog to wear over the stump.

Jeannette was less decisive in school.

School was no challenge to a young girl preoccupied with mind games of her own. Her brilliance could not be sparked by the dreary ritual of reading, writing and arithmetic. Although she was regarded in awe by some of her classmates, her grades were average.

Idle talk bored her, she considered athletics mostly brutal, friends could be gossipy and school was a well-worn pattern of memorization and recital. She was enchanted more with issue-related conversation.

Jeannette's membership with a social club named the Buds ended after a few years when she complained the activities were not challenging enough. She even was not content just to play with dolls, once hanging a diaper out of an upstairs window of her house, proclaiming a dress shop was open within. Eager customers discovered the shop's proprietress catered only to doll clothes, but Jeannette was shrewd enough to advertise for a wider market.

Jeannette did not turn to intellectual pursuits to compensate for inadequacies in her social life. She was pretty, lithe, popular and gregarious. She was a good homemaker, and she was conversational and resourceful. She loved to organize parties and picnics and camping trips, and on her 18th birthday her father built a dance floor on the front yard at the ranch and strung Chinese lanterns for light.

Wellington and some friends greased a pig and let it loose among the dancers. Amid that chaos they unharnessed horses from guests' surreys, most of which were rented from livery stables in Missoula, and assigned them new surreys, promising confusion and embarrassment to Jeannette's friends. She was furious that Wellington made such an incourteous gesture to her guests, but 'The Boy' was defended by his sisters.

As Jeannette passed her teen years, however, her enthusiasm for group social activities faded. She sensed a greater urgency in her life, and although she was a typical turn-of-the-century American woman in her appearance, her father's influence had made a lasting impression. She was effusive, daring and opinionated, and could be curt and cutting.

From her father, Jeannette learned to talk with men as an equal. Having no patience for charming the male ego, she neither obliged the social formalities of dating nor paid homage to the popular female role in society: marry, raise children, keep the home and let the husband handle the important affairs in everyday living. Hers was a different destiny.

A strong influence was her father's cynical attitude toward the military. John Rankin had participated in an attempted assault by the army on Chief Joseph and his peaceful Nez Perce tribe as the Indians fled a cavalry unit by slipping through the rugged Bitterroot Mountains. Fort Missoula soldiers and civilian recruits, including Rankin, confronted Joseph in a timbered valley and ordered him to surrender his weapons. Joseph returned to his chiefs, presumably for consultation, and in the black of night his people crept peacefully past the sleeping military encampment. The silent defeat was a major embarrassment to the army, and the soldiers babbled excuses while John Rankin and other civilians went home. The encampment of the military became known as Fort Fizzle.

Rankin felt shame and disgust at participating in the incident, and believed the soldiers neither had been intelligent enough to outmanuever the peaceful Joseph nor perceptive enough to understand his plight. Rankin complained to his family that the military was a joke and that the soldiers "were too stupid for words."

Jeannette absorbed these cold opinions, developing an intellectual aggressiveness quite apart from her mediocre performances in school.

Her aggression was inspired by love, trust and confidence, a positive influence allowing a sense of accomplishment and inquiry. Her relationship with her father was notable because he offered her privileges and expectations usually reserved for a father-son relationship. Jeannette learned to be gracious, enjoying a lucid and perceptive ability to ferret out the best — and the worst — in people.

Family experiences in early life may have helped nurture Jeannette's sense of justice. Unlike the person who acts to repress feelings of inadequacy, she was motivated by curiosity and the demands of responsibility, which was a byproduct of frontier living.

To the Rankins, independence was enhanced by the rewards of their labor: economic security and family happiness. The entire family shared the chore of carving a new life in the frontier, where opportunity was more than a word to people wanting to enjoy it, and frontier living demanded Jeannette be responsible for her brother and four sisters. (Philena, the second eldest child, died as a youngster).

The girls naturally learned how to clean, bake, sew, cook and care for the animals. They walked to school if the snow wasn't too deep, but their real education came from doing things at home. As Jeannette matured, she was haunted day and night by apprehension and indecision. She suffered anxiety at seeing her beloved father grow older; as the new century dawned, he neared 60. Jeannette viewed her growth in leadership as a decline in his.

She also had to contend with the rivalry of Wellington and her sisters, each of whom was developing a strong personality that threatened her role as family leader.

But Jeannette's ultimate frustration was her inability to decide her direction in life. Who was she? Where was she headed? She yearned for a greater challenge than being a housewife, which even in those days of early feminist liberation meant a life of subservience and drudgery. For 20 years, Jeannette had been her father's confidante, associate and protegee. Mixed with the subtle irony of frontier life and a demanding work ethic, Jeannette's relationship with her father had honed her personality to a fine edge.

She had learned the artistry of manhood: leadership, dissent and independence. Yet she had the beauty and domestic ability that made her an attractive prospect for marriage and mother-hood, and even deeper than her sense of social responsibility was her sense of loyalty to the family unit.

These characteristics made Jeannette Rankin.

As she matured into a young adult and finished college prepa-tory school, she felt unrest. The feeling was uncomfortable, be-cause the ranch had been a consoling place to live. Unable to convert her restlessness into decisive goals, and pursue a course of study to serve her future, she drifted aimlessly into the first class at the new state college in Missoula without realizing her personality had another side: a teeming urge to plunge into public service.

Instinctively, Jeannette struggled to complete her formal edu-cation. Was it not, after all, the proper thing to do? She admitted she was a poor student and hated school. Jeannette's mind was not captivated by the drone of a teacher in a stuffy classroom. She had a great imagination, but she couldn't find a use for it. She wrote her senior thesis on the subject of snail shells, only because she liked her biology teacher, and she was remembered by her professors as being a hardworking, but reserved student.

Sometimes Jeannette challenged her professors' wisdom. Once she was assigned to read publicly Alfred Tennyson's "The Charge of the Light Brigade," and she responded, "This is hideous. I can't read it."

Yet she was frustrated with indecision about her future, which compelled her to write frantically in her diary after she graduated in 1902 with a bachelor of science degree in biology: "Go! Go! Go! It makes no difference where just so you go! go! go! Remember at the first opportunity go!" Her outburst echoed that of reformer

Teddy Roosevelt, who suggested: "Get action, do things, be sane, don't fritter away your time; create, act, take a place wherever you are and be somebody; get action."

Jeannette's dichotomous personality was the beginning of a lifelong pattern.While failing to see the value of formal education, her sense of justice embodied a natural inclination to try to better social conditions. She was to become a fighter like her father, instilled with his sense of civic accountability.

John Rankin lusted for education, and while he had not demanded excellence from his children — often hustling them off to the ranch before the spring term had ended — he was determined they should not be restricted from the free exchange of ideas.

As the gaiety of childhood matured to the seriousness of adulthood, Jeannette realized she had special qualities not conforming to society's idea of womanhood. She was, in some respects, a man in a woman's body, and looking back, she was not sure why. Her sister Edna, 11 years younger, grew up with the impression that Jeannette was restless and unhappy, possibly inwardly resentful that she was not denied the task of caring for her brother and sisters. Jeannette's fitful mood became especially apparent after 1904, when John Rankin, at age 63, died of Rocky Mountain Spotted Fever.

His death only heightened Jeannette's sense of futility. She was nearly 25 and had left school confused and lethargic. Teaching jobs in a rural school near the Rankin ranch and at Whitehall, a small town near Butte, ended in frustration because Jeannette was not inclined to make the best of an atmosphere she had found boring as a student. She returned to the comfort of her family, where she helped her mother cook for the cowhands and filled her free time with reading.

While Jeannette floundered in Montana, the political climate that would awaken her to social reform was growing gloomier.

Laissez faire capitalism was raping America. The new industrial order was based on steel and oil. The United States in 1870 became the world's largest steel producer, and Andrew Carnegie became the most powerful steel baron of all time. John D. Rockefeller did for oil what Carnegie did for steel, and the Standard Oil Company was founded in 1872. Investors enjoyed a ballooning prosperity, and by 1892 more than 4,000 millionaires controlled America's financial future. Cities grew without planning, with a minimum of control, guided by industrial enterprise and private greed.

More than five million immigrants had arrived in America in the 1880's, double the number of any other decade. The cities were swollen with Italians, Austrians, Hungarians, Poles and Russians. They sought a new life of opportunity and yet propelled themselves into dire poverty. First they fought the system to survive. Then they fought each other. The pregnant crush of the cities became ripe for corruption.

The birth of social Darwinism brought a new philosophical order to America, which meant the strong survived and built an aristocratic order while the weak were swallowed in the wake.

Capitalists believed politicians who tried to govern economics would upset the balance of the monetary system. In a reversal of political thought, the new conservatives gave economic and material meanings to the ethical and idealistic concepts of 'liberty,' 'opportunity,' and 'individualism.' Democracy was identified with capitalism, liberty with property, progress with economic gain and the accumulation of capital.

Because the nation's goals now were identified with wealth, many new injustices were condoned beneath the guise of the new conservative terminology: democracy, liberty, equality. The swaying of public opinion to the new philosophy of America insured wars could be fought for personal economic profit.

The women's movement encountered a stormy political climate, despite more than half a century of arduous work at every level of society. Industrial growth had placed thousands of women in jobs, but the quality of working conditions had plunged. Corporations were bleeding the economy in the name of social progress. They became larger, and combined into trusts, which became more belligerent and unfeeling of the common

American. The time was ripe for change. Reform became more than just an ideal. Men — and women — rose to the task.

Jeannette Rankin — isolated, obscure, perplexed, restive — decided to travel to Boston in the winter of late 1904. Wellington, a law school student at Harvard University, was dangerously ill, and Jeannette packed a suitcase at once and departed on her first Eastern trip. Accompanied by a friend from Missoula, she stayed in Boston for six months. Socially, the visit was a wonderful experience. After Wellington got stronger, the girls dated some Harvard men and even considered enrolling at the Massachusetts Institute of Technology. With tickets compliments of Montana Sen. Joseph Dixon, they rode the train to Washington to attend the inaugural ball of President Theodore Roosevelt.

But the gaiety of upper-crust living held little fascination for Jeannette after she had seen the filth, poverty, disease and human misery of the Boston tenement slums. Here was squalor of the worst sort, so unlike the vast resplendent peace and beauty enjoyed by people in the Montana Rockies. Jeannette had been taught that hard work earned material success. But in Boston many thousands of people lived in misery daily. Were they lazy, incompetent or apathetic?

Jeannette returned to Montana suffering ambivalence about her experiences in the East. She had tasted the sumptuous lifestyle of the Eastern Establishment but she had seen the decaying neighborhoods that weren't supposed to exist in a society that boasted of freedom and justice.

Jeannette was no fool. The imperiled future of the Indian nations, for example, had convinced her that the distribution of human rights was based largely on aggression. Wealth and material possessions had cut a line of class struggle through American society. Boston had been a mere dramatization of this human conflict, and Jeannette's pervading sense of justice could not condone what she saw.

Jeannette exhausted the next two years toying with halfhearted pursuits as an apprentice seamstress and with a correspondence course in furniture design. She read more than ever, absorbing opinions and ideas about economics, politics and philosophy. She seldom sat down without a book or magazine in her hands, reading mostly about causes, ideas, news, politics and current affairs. Much of this intensity was prompted by her feeling of futility about what to do with the world.

Eventually her listlessness and depression invited poor health, and she decided to take action, as she had promised in her diary several years earlier. Planning to visit an uncle, she boarded a train for San Francisco in the winter of 1908, unsuspecting of the new direction in life awaiting her.

"One lone woman, who, unluckily, has not been able to ensnare a man."

(Rep. James Lissner speaks of Jeannette
Rankin in the Montana Legislature)

JOINING THE REFORM MOVEMENT
Chapter 2

Jeannette Rankin slept in a crowded passenger coach decorated with faded maroon velvet curtains and tarnished brass handrails as the Northern Pacific train careened through moonlit, snowy mountains. Sporadically the engineer tugged the whistle rope, startling her to consciousness. Her inflammatory rheumatism caused her considerable pain, and despite the welcome warmth of the dimly lit coach, she dozed fitfully.

Jeannette was haggard from a sinking confidence and skeptical that she could find a worthwhile project in which to invest herself. The journey had failed to brighten her dusky mood, and when she stepped off the train in San Francisco she hoped a few weeks by the sea would revive some optimism.

But it was a walk to Telegraph Hill one frigid afternoon rather than to the sea that changed her life. Jeannette climbed the steps of a settlement house, curious about the world within its battered walls. Inside she found women and children — mostly Italian — scampering about, seemingly driven by an inspiration. In talking with Elizabeth Ash, a trained social worker who managed the settlement, Jeannette learned she was witnessing the heartbeat of the movement — a movement with desperate needs.

Ash raved about reform, with its multifarious approach to social change, and asked Jeannette if she was willing to volunteer a few days to child care. Jeannette agreed, and stayed four months.

The tender heart of the hardy Montana ranch girl was saddened by the plight of the destitute women and children. Struggling to overcome their triple handicap of being immigrant, female and poor, the mothers endured countless hours of English and political lessons at the settlement. Jeannette learned the women suffered from the oppression of bigoted and antiquated laws and a total lack of legal protection, and she was impressed that they sought better lives for themselves and their children by battling their oppressors.

In a matter of weeks, Jeannette became a serious student of the reform movement. The futility she had experienced in Montana had been forgotten. Here were people who shared her fledgling ideas about political justice, and who readily accepted her empathy for their cause. Timidly at first, Jeannette attended hearings on child labor laws, factory working conditions and wage legislation. As she was swept into the movement at Telegraph Hill, she began to gain a fundamental understanding of the need for social reform legislation.

Her eagerness to learn broadened to the flood of commentary in magazines such as *McClure's, Colliers,* and *Harper's Weekly,* and from the pens of muckrakers such as Jack London, Ira Tarbell, Frank Norris, John Spargo and Jacob Riis. Jane Addams, who had been toiling at Hull House in Chicago for nearly two decades, had the most notable and productive influence on Jeannette, advocating female involvement in social problems to encourage an upswing in the quality of life in America.

By the end of her Telegraph Hill experience, Jeannette was hopelessly addicted to reform. Her languid, indecisive approach to life had vanished; she was fired with the prospect of contributing to this growing campaign and alive with ideas repressed since she was a young girl.

As a child, when she considered training to be a nurse, Jeannette had lived in the shadow of humanitarian causes. They had not surfaced, however, in free and independent Montana, which except for growing labor troubles in Butte and Anaconda, had not encountered the class struggle found in older, more populated states.

Jeannette hurried to seek practical training, and spending money her father had earmarked for education, enrolled in the New York School of Philanthropy in the autumn of 1908. The school was considered the foremost social work institution in America. Brother Wellington was finishing his final year at Harvard's law school, and while he labored with torts, Jeannette got her first taste of retorts.

The school was a microcosm of the intellectual revolution inherent in early Progressivism. Jeannette found herself in a challenging academic world, yet only blocks away were the slums of New York City's Lower East Side where pathetic social problems could be studied and debated by brilliant teachers.

Among the faculty were Louis D. Brandeis, one of America's leading lawyers and economic intellectuals; Florence Kelley, founder of the National Consumer's League that represented women in industry, and Booker T. Washington, the black leader and educator. Edward T. Devine, the editor of *Survey* magazine, was guest lecturer for that academic year, and as the other teachers, his lessons embraced the concept of 'environmentalism,' meaning oppressed Americans could revolutionize the economic system with encouragement and teaching from informed leaders. This philosophy was not advocating socialism; in the concept of Progressivism, democracy would remain intact but the powers of the Constitution would be exercised to the fullest extent.

While the average middle-class American woman was discouraged from reading anything more suggestive than the Sears and Roebuck catalogue, Jeannette was being primed with books on human misery and the economics of civilization. The school bitterly rejected Herbert Spencer's concept of social Darwinism, contending the notion of survival of the fittest was a philosophy offered by the rich to the poor to preserve wealth. Jeannette's teachers insisted Progressivism would destroy the misconception that public laws were fair and beneficial to all Americans.

In this spirit Jeannette contemplated Simon N. Patten's *New Basis of Civilization*, which argued that misery and poverty could be eliminated by a more efficient society in which the consumption of goods and services is increased dramatically to distribute wealth.

She was influenced by Patten's claim that American society was manipulated in its ideas and socio-political environment by economics, a view that would take root in her criticism of war profiteering three decades later. In a letter to her sister Mary, who was apprehensive about such apparently socialistic ideologies, Jeannette wrote:

> *There is nothing horrid about studying social problems. One dear man in a lecture spoke of Saint Simon N. Patten, and that is the way all of the school feel[s] toward him. The reason political economy has been so useless is that so many writers have taken the theories of old writers such as Adam Smith, Mill and Malthus and tried to fit them to present conditions or to fit conditions to false theories.*

The curriculum was blunt and intense, making the school an undesirable place for a faint-hearted optimist. Among Jeannette's lectures was one entitled 'Misery and its Causes,' and despite being a young woman from Montana who had enjoyed happiness most of her childhood, she satisfied the course requirements with zeal.

Jeannette studied labor disputes, criminal sociology, social reform, racial progress and the theory and practice of charity organization. Although she confided to Mary that she expected to fail because she was competing with "such well trained college girls," by the end of the academic year she had earned two A's and eight B's in 14 courses.

Jeannette got practical experience when she was required to work in the night police courts under the supervision of Maude Miner, the chief probation officer of New York City's Magistrate

Court. The work was dangerous for an unescorted woman, and Jeannette discreetly concealed a billy club in a velvet party bag with draw strings. To openly carry a weapon was an affront to her femininity, but she was smart enough to be scared.

Her most notable impression of human misery, however, was not influenced by the bleakness of her professors' economic outlook or the morbidity of inner city crime, but by the tragic living conditions she witnessed while studying the needs of deaf children in the Jewish-Italian district of the Lower East Side.

"I took the dearest...sweetest little boy to an orphan society," she wrote her mother. "He was about three years old and the mother had two younger. The father is missing. If I had been near home I'm sure I would have wanted to keep him. He was so full of joy and life. The mother didn't mind losing him. She just waved her hand and said, 'By-by.' "

After encountering these morose tales of woe in four months of field work, Jeannette began to comprehend that man was master, and she figured the evidence of this malediction could be found in the strata of society from poor to rich. The impoverished woman was harnessed, sometimes literally, to the sewing machine in the sweatshop or to the production line in the factory. The woman confined to cramped tenement quarters with ailing, hungry children wondered if her husband was hustling the streets for money and food or drinking away the future in a shabby tavern. Middle-class and affluent women popularized the Woman's Club, which purportedly lobbied for juvenile law and child labor reform.

But nearly one million American women who belonged to woman's clubs were so notoriously ineffective in their mission that a writer for the *Ladies Home Journal* blasted:

> *Until the woman's club shall show a more intellectual conception of its trusteeship, I insist that the woman's club up to date has been 'weighed in the balance and found wanting.'*

Only a daring minority ventured into public life in the first decade of the new century. The average American woman was expected to raise the children, oblige her husband, and indulge in no ballyhoo likely to embarrass her family. Jeannette cast a more adventurous portrayal of the American woman. Popular magazines of the period depicted women her age as being engrossed with romance and family life. But Jeannette eluded the amorous gestures offered by a younger man as she nursed him back to health, and waited impatiently to intervene in the agony of a nation crying for reform.

Rapidly the theories challenging her mind at the School of Philanthropy meshed with her thoughts about political justice and she became notably independent.

Hundreds of women dedicated their lives to the thankless missionary chores of the Salvation Army; Jeannette, having no impressionable religious instruction, sought a different role. Thousands of women rallied to shut the saloons by outlawing liquor; Jeannette being only a social drinker but having no hate for men who drank, resisted joining their ranks. Millions of American women labored for financial relief or the rewards of home and family; Jeannette, being of independent spirit, felt the desire to crusade.

After graduating as a qualified social worker in the summer of 1909, she yearned to put her knowledge to use, saddened by what she had seen and experienced, but more determined to fight the causes that had bred it.

With the words of her sterling professors arousing her idealism, Jeannette returned to Missoula thrilled with the lure of reform. She quickly embarrassed the sheriff with a campaign to segregate women from men in the county jail, but found little support for her plan to establish a public bath house for loggers, tramps and other people who had no place to get clean.

Frustrated with her first defeat, she took a job with the Children's Home Society of Spokane, Wash., as a home finder. Finding decent foster homes for orphans was nearly impossible. Children were traded like cattle; once Jeannette placed an orphan with a family who immediately decided they didn't want him. The boy was returned to the orphanage, where he wept in Jeannette's office. Incidents such as this made her job intolerable, and she transferred to an orphanage in Seattle, which did little to relieve her disgust of the system.

Finally, disdaining the lackadaisical, yet widespread, approach to child care — that children should be shelved instead of loved — Jeannette gave up the challenge. She contemplated the possibility that the most potent reform would not be accomplished from struggling within the institutions, but by influencing the laws that governed them. Much of her dislike of institutional work, she admitted, was having to be a detached observer of the plight of defenseless, unloved children.

The year was 1910. The advent of the Progressive Era was affording a lucid look at the nation's problems, and Jeannette continued to be swept along in the reformist fever.

Progressivism was a virile animal. It was hungry for willing, determined young workers who would sow the seeds of dissent and awaken Americans to the delirium caused by industrialized labor. As the first hint of a human rights movement in the new century, Progressivism was instigated by a coalition of farmers, laborers, women and statesmen, all of whom thought the government had abandoned the working class in favor of the industrialists.

The Progressives — somewhat an outgrowth of the Populists — advocated a participatory democracy, including among their standards simple democratic measures such as the initiative, referendum and recall.

Jeannette saw merit in such a philosophy. The tough academic principles she had studied at the School of Philanthropy had stimulated her thinking, yet her short experience in street work had been unrewarding. Her mind was racing now, envisioning the prospect of a greater contribution to reform.

Jeannette enrolled at the University of Washington in Seattle, intending to prepare for the arduous work of pushing social legislation. That the American woman who ventured into politics was considered a freak or a fanatic by more conventional observers was of no consequence to Jeannette; her father deliberately had neglected to teach her that petticoats should not be mixed with politics. The moment had arrived for women to explore politics, and few women existed who were as able, articulate and astute as Jeannette Rankin. But initially she played a minor part among a multitude of thousands.

One evening she spotted an advertisement in the university newspaper asking for volunteers to hang posters promoting equal suffrage. Her insatiable curiosity could not let the advertisement go unanswered, and soon she had collected a bundle of posters to distribute in the neighborhood.

In bold lettering, they exclaimed: "Roosevelt when Governor of New York in a message to the New York legislature urged woman suffrage." The significance of this message did not escape Jeannette, who saw a relationship between women having the power to vote and the miserable social conditions she witnessed on both coasts.

Jeannette tacked the posters on every store facade and empty wall or board fence she could find. But she scored a major victory for female assertiveness when she managed to place one in the window of the neighborhood barber shop. The American barber shop was a sacred male domain, where a man retreated to the comfort of a leather reclining chair to read the *Police Gazette* amid the smells of frothing shaving mugs, cigar fumes and bay rum. While most women wondered what their husbands did when they went to the barber shop, they were afraid to ask, and refused to stray near such a place. Jeannette, however, just walked through the door with a poster and told the startled proprieter she was going to hang it in his window.

A Washington suffrage leader was impressed with Jeannette's audacity and asked her to join the state's campaign. Spring quarter at the university was nearly finished and Jeannette was going home to Montana for the summer. But she returned in the fall of 1910 and went to work in a small logging town named Ballard, under the tutoring of Emma Smith DeVoe of the Washington Equal Suffrage Association.

Jeannette thought her efforts were mostly fruitless, having rented a lecture hall and hired a speaker for only a 15-member audience, but her superiors were impressed and Jeannette climbed the ladder into the hierarchy of the organization. The women struggled for more than two months, and suffrage passed by a margin of nearly two-to-one.

Jeannette's role in the campaign was relatively minor, but for the first time in her life she had blended her humanitarianism and her awareness of social problems with a knowledge of how to employ change. She learned quickly, convinced everything that was wrong with America was related to big money and inefficient government. Backing suffrage in Washington taught her that women promised to revolutionize government without over-throwing it.

Jeannette thus had found a key to change more productive than working among the specific social problems found in state institutions. She had tasted a method of campaign organization that could be developed and used in other states. Furthermore, suffrage offered her the privilege of genuine leadership because its success depended on the extent of hard work and initiative committed to it. Jeannette had disliked working in the orphan-ages, being impatient with the policies and procedures she believed negated change, but she was comfortable with the free lance spirit of suffrage.

The bright and able women Jeannette met in Washington state helped her formulate a blueprint for the future. She could see women as the force in social reform, using the vote to protest the decadence touching their lives.

Jeannette was not another Carry Nation, neither assimilating alcohol or religion with the suffrage issue, nor battering the morals of her opponents with a proverbial axe. But she recog-nized that women had to live with laws they had no voice in making, and she was certain they offered a special regard for the welfare of children that men did not.

That Jeannette had not experienced childbirth made no differ-ence in her ideas about the welfare of children. In being a surro-gate mother to her younger sisters, she had learned the value of adequate protection and love.

Jeannette was, in 1910, no more of a visionary enthusiast than other Progressives, who saw only the immediate inequities of American living and were unaware their movement would be nudged out of prominence by the bully of world war. She was only a student of social change and unsuspecting of her forth-coming rise to fame.

With the celebration of the Washington suffrage victory foremost in her mind, Jeannette rode a train home for Christmas. She prowled Missoula department stores for gifts and strung popcorn on the tree in the Rankin living room. But her holiday was short-lived.

She learned a suffrage bill had been introduced into the Montana Legislature, and the state Equal Franchise Society — the chief sponsor — needed a speaker to support it. Jeannette hesitated at the prospect of addressing an all-male legislature, but then boldly announced she would accept the task. Being stub-born, determined and a bit naive, she promised the hopeful suffrage supporters she would reverse the trend of joking and sarcasm that traditionally accompanied a suffrage bill.

While Montana men felt little animosity toward freeing their women, the idea was new, and in the opinion of many, such a gesture was premature. On a bright February day, Jeannette was driven to the Capitol from her Helena hotel, an intense uneasi-ness about the speech making her flinch at every jolt in the road. A speech by a woman was unprecedented. What could she say to keep the people from laughing?

Meanwhile, the Capitol was bustling with people excited at hearing a woman speak from the legislative podium. Wearied by a long winter of weather stories and political slapstick, news reporters came to life at this germane twist to the news and began battering out leads for the morning editions.

A churning sea of faces flooded the rustic chambers of the House of Representatives, where Jeannette would speak, and the hubbub echoed in the hallways that cradled the huge room. The day was briskly winter, but the galleries were crowded, hot and uncomfortable, and the bright gowns and handsomely frothered hats of the women seated among the legislators on the floor gave the House chamber a touch of life it had not experienced.

Bouquets of flowers embellishing the room contrasted strangely with the snowswept landscape outside. Each of the legislators had contributed 50 cents for purple violets ordered from San Francisco, a gesture some men had intended as a patronizing ploy but most had considered as a tribute to the woman they were about to hear.

Men shuffled nervously. Smoking was banned, spitoons had been removed and swearing was forbidden. Senators refused to attend as a formal body but adjourned business and most of them attended anyway. The atmosphere was condescending and the suffrage advocates were worried. This was a giant step for suffrage in Montana. If Jeannette's speech was mocked, the women's rights movement would be stalled for years until the passing of time forced a more studious attitude among legislators.

At 2:30 p.m., Jeannette walked into the House chamber and was escorted to the rostrum by five of Montana's leading suffragists. She waited nervously through two flattering introductory speeches, and then approached the podium. A surge of whispering feathered the room.

People had expected a mannish, elderly woman; instead they saw a slender, attractive woman, with frank, dark hazel eyes and sumptuous brown hair. Jeannette appeared younger than her 30 years, and a green velvet dress conformed nicely to her body.

Although Jeannette had become accustomed to addressing unsympathetic audiences in the Washington campaign, she was troubled as she stared at the people who were the blood of Mother Montana. Among them was every extreme of life: faces of affluence and faces of despair, faces of trust and faces of suspicion. Jeannette had memorized her speech, but she panicked suddenly.

"Will they believe me?" she asked herself. "Do they know who I am?" The hushed audience returned her stare, unknowing that Wellington, a recent graduate of Harvard, eagerly had employed his oratory skills to coach his sister with her speech.

Forcefully, but apprehensively, Jeannette began by noting she was born in Montana, and the room exploded in applause. Could the speech be this easy, she asked herself? Further justifications for her presence followed. She was a taxpayer, and she was not inclined to complain about any of the laws of the state:

> *It is not for myself that I am making this appeal, but for the six million women who are suffering for better conditions, women who should be working amid more sanitary conditions, under better moral conditions, at equal wages with men for equal work performed. For those women and their children I ask that you support this measure.*

Jeannette explained Montana women had no desire to step down from the high pedestal on which Montana men had placed them. But she pointed to the need for women in lawmaking and government, evidenced by national statistics showing 300,000 women had been victims of the white slave traffic.

With a steady fury, she reminded her listeners that women were asking for the same principle for which men fought in the Revolutionary War. She stuck to the belief that taxation without representation was tyranny, and demanded to know why a mother should be expected to nurse her child through typhoid fever, without the benefit of laws that would obviate conditions that gave her child the disease.

The speech reflected Jeannette's deep suspicion of the priorities of government without female representation. Already, she had an understanding of human rights more universal than the problems women experienced in Montana.

Having seen the pathetic lifestyles of New York City's poor, the decadence of the Boston slums, the language problems of San Francisco's Italian immigrants, the clash of men and women in Washington state, and having read the literature of muckraking journalists, Jeannette knew what many people didn't: aside from tradition and ignorance, a concerted effort existed to prevent women and children, blacks, immigrants, the poor, the ignorant and the illiterate from enjoying the civil rights they deserved.

Suspecting that Montana government was capable of ignoring

human rights issues — and subsequently preventing social reform legislation — because it was manipulated and coerced by the
Anaconda Copper Mining Company, Jeannette stressed suffrage
was not an issue to be decided by the lawmakers, but an issue to be
decided by the people they represented. As she concluded her
20-minute speech, she asked the representatives to vote to submit
the suffrage question to Montana voters at the next election.

Her words were weighty enough to toss the House of
Representatives into a bitter debate. One suffrage supporter
asked why the issue should be subjected to wit and humor, and
opponents countered with oaths of prejudice, ignorance and
sensationalism. Jeannette was labeled "one lone woman, who,
unluckily, has not been able to ensnare a man."

Jeannette, however, had ensnared something more valuable
than a single man; she had gained an army of women. Although
the bill was defeated, the margin had been narrow. Montana
women lost a skirmish, but they acquired a leader. The press,
although usually quiet about such matters, vaulted Jeannette into
the forefront of the suffrage arena, lauding her earnestness and
sincerity. Women across Montana wrote Jeannette, chiding her
for not asking them to participate in her address to the Legislature. They represented a potential statewide organization, and
Jeannette filed their names for later use.

While Montana women and other American suffragists fought
their battles, a disaster in New York City pointed to the need for
renewed vigor in the reform movement. On March 25, 1911, the
lives of 146 Jewish and Italian immigrant girls were lost in a fire
that ravaged the Triangle Shirtwaist Company in downtown
Manhattan. The factory had operated for years in violation of city
fire codes.

America reacted to the fire with horror. Women had leaped to
their deaths from eight, nine or 10 stories above the ground, after
finding fire exits obstructed or jammed shut. Others who had
been knocked down and trampled in the panic or who clawed at
stuck doors were incinerated.

Ironically, New York had possibly the most sophisticated

suffrage machinery in the nation at the time of the disaster, but the industry lobby was strong, being supported by the pool hall antics of the city bosses. People wondered whether the disaster could have been avoided if New York women had gained the vote earlier. Reform was considered a logical extension of the ballot, and most of the employees in New York City's 'sweatshops' were women.

The summer after the fire, Jeannette Rankin found herself working in the shadow of the very borough where the disaster occurred. The chairwoman of the Manhattan Borough of the New York Woman's Suffrage Party — Harriet Laidlaw — was searching for a worker who could meet the challenges the district presented. Minnie Reynolds, another New York suffrage leader, suggested that since Jeannette's "singularly sweet personality" found no suffrage work too commonplace, difficult or disagreeable, she was the woman for whom Laidlaw was looking.

New York suffrage politics was new to Jeannette because the strategy was modeled after the machine politics of the city bosses, unlike the rural barnstorming in Washington state. Learning how effective the assembly and election districts had been for Tammany Hall, Carrie Chapman Catt of the National American Woman Suffrage Association (NAWSA) developed an organization that reached to the precinct levels of America's largest city.

The plan found Jeannette walking the crowded, canyon-like streets, within a few miles to the north of Ellis Island, where immigrants seeking opportunity filed through the nation's doors into a new land. A few miles to the east was the vast tenement district where the new horizons for many of the immigrants darkened, but where Jeannette, offering hope for reform in the suffrage package, hustled support.

Most of Jeannette's work was done on the street, where she asked a passerby to listen, and then another, until a curious crowd gathered. Although a difficult way to build a movement, this approach offered her direct contact with the people who would decide the issue, taught her the rewards of building a grassroots organization, and taught her confidence in expressing her beliefs.

Her altruistic commitment to the cause found favor with her superiors. Harriet Laidlaw paid Jeannette $300 for six months' work, but the reward for Laidlaw and her colleagues was much greater; they had discovered the value of having Jeannette Rankin work for suffrage.

At 31, Jeannette had all the attributes of a good leader. Youthfully energetic, implacably determined and insufferably thorough, she was fearless in knocking on doors that might be slammed in her face. Nor was she intimidated by the vitriolic tongues of liquor lobby allies or street toughs who showered her with obscenities and ridicule. Raised in a family where she was a competitor with her brother Wellington, she did not have to overcome the downtrodden self-image afflicting many Eastern women.

Some women were embarrassed to be advocating suffrage, having been taught thoroughly that women were inferior to men.

This myth had been upheld even by Edward Clarke, a Harvard medical school professor, who warned in *Sex in Education* that because women were endowed with smaller brains and less formidable physiques than men, their health would be impaired seriously if they were exposed to the stress of higher education. Such rhetoric proved substantially harmful to the self esteem of women, but Jeannette had been taught to believe all Americans were equal by the Constitution and she felt no remorse in saying so.

She believed that to think men would grant women their rights without social pressure was myopic. Moreover, she deviated from the philosophies of suffragists such as Anna Howard Shaw and Susan B. Anthony, who openly and deliberately drove a wedge of disunity into the women's movement by chastizing the immigrant community. They were angry that foreign-born men had constitutional priority over native daughters such as themselves, and in their condemning speeches they alienated voters who had strong nationalistic ties.

Jeannette agreed with the reasons for their bitterness toward the immigrant vote, but she was disconcerted that they were willing to alienate a third major political bloc (the liquor lobby and the conservative anti-suffragists were the other two) by complaining publicly of the influence of immigrants instead of working quietly behind the scenes to compromise it. While suffragists angrily pointed out that large numbers of black men and immigrant men were illiterate but could vote, while educated, articulate, native-born women were considered second-class citizens, Jeannette considered herself fortunate that Montana had few immigrants when women were trying to win suffrage there.

She disagreed with her suffrage sisters on several matters of policy, but felt obliged to keep quiet about some of the nefarious ventures of her more radically outspoken contemporaries, who Jeannette thought often misconstrued public opinion. Jeannette avoided controversy in the interest of unity, and in substituting hard work for political bickering, she quickly was swept to the top of the national suffrage network.

In the summer of 1911 the California Equal Suffrage Association appealed to the national organization for an ardent, vigorous worker to join its central committee. In a demonstration of sharing that depicted the sacrifices New York was willing to make for California, Harriet Laidlaw temporarily relieved Jeannette from duties in the less hopeful Empire State campaign to help eke out a victory in the West.

Progressives in California concentrated their work heavily in rural areas, anticipating a smashing anti-suffrage vote in the cities by pro-liquor forces. Jeannette scooted among towns without sleeping in the same bed twice. Ballot manipulation in San Francisco and other cities hampered the efforts of the suffragists, but their work in rural California proved enough to win.

The picture was not as promising elsewhere.

Jeannette was sent to Ohio and Florida, where strong contingents of anti-suffrage forces and inefficient, top-heavy state suffrage organizations made success nearly impossible. Her work in Michigan was wasted when liquor interests were suspected of withholding vote tabulations and then readjusting them to defeat suffrage by a suspiciously narrow margin.

Jeannette learned to endure the sanctimonious drivel she experienced among anti-suffrage leaders everywhere. She thought she was justified in her beliefs, and the sensation of confronting established opinion was something she could accept, having a natural inclination to distinguish between right and wrong. Modesty was not a virtue among suffrage workers, particularly because the woman who was a listener could not do much talking. Jeannette disguised her raw militancy with a gentle femininity, but in the rough-and-tumble world of political advocacy when her patience was strained and her humor exhausted, she was capable of being rude and obtrusive.

Her only reward for working long past exhaustion and losing her voice from shouting duels was the personal gratification of a winning vote and hasty thanks from her superiors before going to the next battle.

Jeannette found her work compelling, despite tedious lecturing and traveling. She moved from state to state, helping women organize, making speeches, building confidence and establishing coffers of support for future campaigns.Although Jeannette suffered bouts of depression when things went poorly, her only response was to work harder. She became field secretary for the National American Woman Suffrage Association in 1913 and directed an overwhelming victory in North Dakota.

Through the forum of the Progressive Era, suffrage became a keen issue. Too often, the caustic tongues of leaders of opposing factions had clashed, creating an unprecedented and serious disharmony. Suffrage no longer was a joke, and the impending seriousness forecast trouble, which came during a March 1913 rally in Washington, D.C.

Scheduled for the day before Woodrow Wilson's inauguration to the presidency, the march was the brainchild of Alice Paul, who headed the NAWSA's Congressional committee. Paul and her lieutenants thought a grandiose display of support for suffrage would impress Wilson, the first Democratic president since Benjamin Harris left office in 1893. Ironically, the parade was planned to be the most overt gesture ever made by American suffragists, while the committee had been allotted a pitiful yearly budget of only $10. NAWSA leaders figured women would not be granted suffrage by federal amendment until it first was won in a majority of states. They depleted the budget for Congressional lobbyists accordingly.

In the most elaborate parade of its kind, 5,000 marchers representing most states queued on Pennsylvania Avenue in sections of men, black women, immigrants and state delegations. The parade was rowdy and colorful, with an aura of heritage that spanned America's young history.

Jeannette Rankin lined up with the Montana delegation. The women were dressed like Indians, and when the girl who was supposed to portray Sacajawea of Lewis and Clark expedition fame didn't show, Jeannette's sister Edna — fair-haired with blue eyes — dressed in white buckskin to play the role.

The parade started in an orderly fashion at the Capitol and was to proceed past the White House to Consitutional Hall. Only minutes later, trouble began. The police had dreadfully underestimated the number of officers needed for crowd control (Later they were accused of doing it deliberately). The marchers fought their way from the start and took more than an hour to make the first 10 blocks. Half a million spectators poured from the sidewalks into the street, forcing the marchers to squeeze through a small channel. Women were insulted, spat upon, pelted with cigar stubs and thrown to the street.

The rowdiness of the march pointed to a new fervor sweeping the country. The women's rights issue had succeeded in engulfing a broad coalition: men, immigrants and black women joined the white suffragist stalwarts. The rifts among the factions continued to widen but the plea of thousands of people was heard.

While Jeannette had been stumping nationwide, her concise arguments for suffrage in Montana had been remembered. Nearly two years after she had delivered her speech to the state legislature, Gov. Samuel Stewart persuaded legislators to support the suffrage amendment as part of the Democratic Party's reform package. With only two dissenting votes in each house, Montana's men were given a referendum to decide whether their women should have the right to vote.

The state needed a leader to inspire Montana women to action.

Jeannette quit her job as field secretary for the NAWSA in 1914 and traveled to Butte, Montana. She resurrected the card file of names she had started three years earlier, and began commanding the campaign at once.

The task facing Jeannette was intimidating. She had to organize women of a wide and sparsely populated state to persuade the men to let them vote. To find a way to blanket the far-reaching farms and rural communities and to neutralize the liquor industry, anti-suffragists and corporate politicians was beyond the comprehension of many. Pessimists said no woman alive could accomplish such a feat in a short 10 months, but they had not encountered Jeannette Rankin.

> *"Never mind if you do not convert the multitude.*
> *Others will follow after you who can complete the job.*
> *Try and not be selfish in the work, leave a twig or two*
> *of laurel for someone else...."*
>
> (Letter from suffrage sister Mary O'Neill)

MONTANA'S POLITICAL DEBUTANTE
Chapter 3

With a coterie of brilliant women at her command and the decade's 'new woman' ideal ripe in her image, Jeannette set out with sheer determination to elevate the status of Montana women from serf to citizen.

The forthcoming emancipation of American females was evident even in Shredded Wheat Company advertisements proclaiming that consumers who bought its products exemplified the liberated woman. Yet in 1914 Jeannette Rankin faced the responsibility of nurturing in Montana the dream to reality, and she joined other feminists in the spirit of unity. This avant-garde passion among women was no more evident than with Jeannette, who resisted the urge to experiment socially for the greater freedom of political expression.

She was Montana's 'girl next door,' a lovely political debutante with a mystical, homegrown charisma. She was known — a familiar face among Montana's plain people — yet unknown, possessing the blushing, secretive capabilities to surprise and taunt. Montanans loved this mysticism, and as president of the Montana

Equal Suffrage State Central Committee, Jeannette swept across Montana like a prairie wind, leaving few people untouched by her influence. "Why not Montana?" she asked in a circular urging men to give women the ballot. She said Montana bordered two suffrage states. Women in nine Western states and Alaska could vote, and four million women could vote for President. "Women in our organization are from all walks of life, every political party and every religion and faith," her circular said. "We unite on one point: We all want to vote."

News reporters called Jeannette a prophet. Her disciples called her electrifying. Scholars conceded she was astonishingly energetic.

This youthful social reformer blazed the suffrage trail. Everywhere she stirred press and people, awing her contemporaries with her ability to be both a charmer and a firebrand. Using curious tactics she extended even to the children, Jeannette perpetuated unrest about the standing of women. "Ask your father," she told children, "why they won't let your mothers vote."

Friends were convinced Jeannette could charm the winds of change into even the most adamant woman hater. In the words of Mary O'Neill, press secretary of the Montana Equal Suffrage Association, Jeannette was a whirlwind worker, a young woman with the temperament of those who suffer and conquer, who inspired trust with her sincerity and unselfish work. Jeannette did not wheedle, cajole or influence through sex, as the anti-suffragists said, but she campaigned as a respectable woman who considered herself intelligent enough to partake of the rights in a nation boasting rhetorically of freedom and justice.

Who was this suffragist, who wooed children to tell their dads to let their mothers vote, who made company bosses drip tears of frustration into what they thought would be their last shot of Irish whiskey, who united people from the fields and the pulpit, from the mines and from the kitchen, for a singular cause: to win the vote for women in Montana?

Leading magazines sent prestigious journalists to Montana to find out. Peter Clark MacFarlane of *Collier's*, for example, followed Jeannette in her escapades and watched in surprise as she single-handedly tried to sooth the whimpers of mothers and children who had no civic voice in creating the conditions in which they lived. Tenderly, sweetly, she dug for truth, and staked her reputation that it could be found in the voice of women.

Wrote one reporter: "Let her get started, and she is as ardent as Sylvia Pankhurst [a militant British suffragist]. You would put her down as a determined 'men-you-just-have-to-do-it' and 'we-won't-take-no-for-an-answer' suffragist." Jeannette, however, rejected the militant image. "We do not need militancy over here," she avowed. "We are getting the vote without resorting to violence."

Jeannette was a champion of the common people; afraid of no one, she lectured outside pool halls and saloons, chatted amiably at teas and drove to the most distant homestead if she suspected she would gain even one vote. As she barnstormed across Montana — preferring direct contact with the working class rather than the forums of the press and the city lecture hall — her broad smile and slender frame became a familiar sight everywhere.

Before the campaign was finished, Jeannette had traveled 9,000 miles within Montana, had made 25 speeches in 25 days, slept in her car if she wasn't lucky enough to find a bed, talked with women in their kitchens on remote farms, and interrupted romping picnickers to give her spiel.

Often her automobile became bogged to the axles in the mud of unpaved roads. She rode trains that climbed to steep elevations in mountains filled with spring snow, where the passenger coaches became cold and drafty. If Jeannette wanted to read at night, she sat on stiff furniture in a hotel parlor lit by cantankerous pungent oil lamps. She often was isolated from family and friends and relied on benevolent farmers and ranchers to provide her supper.

Yet Jeannette's grassroots stumping was her campaign philosophy in its purest form, for she had learned in her national suffrage work that county-by-county, community-by-community organization was necessary, especially in a democracy where the masses are the government.

Whenever possible, the personable 34-year-old Jeannette extended her organization to the precincts, handing responsibility to the most inexperienced people. Her vitality, enthusiasm and sincerity made these people want to help her. Such success spoke well of Jeannette Rankin, who in a few years had risen from the doldrums of a confused social worker to the visionary natural high characterizing people working for a cause. Employing a firm practical sense of justice for living things, she beckoned people to her side with an eagerness to negotiate reform by allowing as many Montanans as possible to make choices about their welfare.

Although Jeannette's role in Montana suffrage started with her speech to legislators in 1911, other Montana women had attempted to win the vote since before the growing social freedom of the Gay Nineties. Suffrage campaigning had been a desultory effort, however, with only haphazard attempts to convince lawmakers that women should have the right to vote. Political equality clubs lived and died as frequently as green leaves passed away into autumn.

People weren't opposed to suffrage so much as they were unfamiliar with it. Women had been scarce in Montana until the turn of the century, state government was young, and issues were fresh. What Montana needed was a leader who could stir up enough discontent to make suffrage a viable political issue. The challenge was stiff, if an opinion by a Carrie Chapman Catt organizer meant anything. Helen M. Reynolds, who had sent a flood of pro-suffrage letters to Montana in 1896 with poor response, wondered sarcastically whether Montana women were an inferior race to take such little interest in their own freedom.

She clearly would have enjoyed meeting Jeannette Rankin, who in the summer of 1912 became the leader of a temporary state central committee composed of women determined to win the right to vote.

They had no constitution, bylaws or membership lists, relying on the sisterhood of their cause to bind them together. Jeannette and her workers canvassed the state, establishing suffrage clubs and appointing a representative in each of the 50 counties to pressure local politicians to meet the demands of their constituencies.

Jeannette recommended in her campaign tactics that women force questions about suffrage on aspiring young politicians, and when the candidates spoke positively, to applaud loudly and wildly. Suffrage quickly became a popular issue among Montana politicians.

After the precincts had been organized, Jeannette went to every delegate of the Republican, Democratic, Progressive and Socialist parties and asked for their support. Feeling the pressure from the precincts, they acquiesced. Using all the power her grassroots organization could muster, Jeannette toured Montana between national assignments, encouraging massive letterwriting campaigns to legislators and the governor, urging support for suffrage when the Legislature met in January 1913.

The Montana central committee met for the first time on the same day the Thirteenth Legislature heard opening remarks from Gov. Stewart, and with no joking or discussing, the lawmakers passed the suffrage resolution by a vote of 100 to four. Jeannette and other members of the central committee cheered from the galleries at the final vote. But under a curious provision in the state constitution, which granted voters an election year to study the resolution before it was placed on the ballot, they would have to wait nearly two years to relish a final victory.

From flag-draped fair booths and scholarly lecterns, from the hood of her Model T Ford on dusty rural streets, and sometimes even from horseback, Jeannette informed women of the danger of living at the command of laws they had no power to change and at the influence of men they had no power to elect or replace. She invaded courthouses, opera houses, dance halls and union halls, and spoke from the stage at moving picture shows. Her common theme in speeches to women was their inability to control political prejudices affecting their home.

This controversial tone aroused the ire of some women of the pampered upper crust, who complained suffrage would unseat them from the pedestals on which Montana's men had placed them. But instead of alienating women by drawing comparisons among social classes, Jeannette bonded women by reviewing the perils of caring for a family without the protection of political representation.

Wrote Mary O'Neill, in advising Jeannette to deliver a speech she had made in Livingston before the state federation of woman's clubs:

> *You will know what I mean, but do give them all the dope you can about the influence of the women in behalf of the CHILDREN and appeal to the higher standard of MOTHERHOOD and truer home life as you did at Livingston, but even more so. That's the gush that gets to a public and the public is what we must reach and convince. That speech of yours at Livingston will do more to make suffragists than all the purely intellectual guff we might give them in a whole hundred years.*

Jeannette's personality enabled her to enlist support for her cause while radiating an intense femininity that subdued people wanting to oppose her. She was, in her discreet aggressiveness, one of Charles Dana Gibson's aloof Gibson Girls: sometimes brash, always witty, suggesting a stirring sensuality to others by her very presence in plain 'woman's work.' Newspaper editors fearing a hardened, Carrie Chapman Catt-type of campaigner marveled at Jeannette's womanly charm and her brilliant success as a conversationalist, although regarding her manly forcefulness with distrust.

She had succeeded in proving a woman did not lose her femininity by mixing in politics, but she was careful not to offend men by suggesting women wanted part of their domain. She argued the right to vote would provide the opportunity to enhance the home environment, not ignore it. "It isn't right that we should be denied an expression of opinion in our own laws," she said.

In echoing Progressive thought, Jeannette envisioned a host of social reforms forced by women with the power of the ballot.

Among them were better working conditions for women, more food and safety inspectors, and more child and maternal welfare programs to offset high mortality rates. She feared the Industrial Revolution had endangered family unity, enabling women to invade factory jobs and other industrial work without the benefit of government social programs to aid in the regulation of the family. She was angry no protection was given to children who worked long hours under perilous conditions.

Jeannette was certain voting women could force the federal government to enact health, welfare and labor legislation securing shorter working days, child labor laws and the inspection of dairy products. In demonstrating her principles, Jeannette suggested women could force the Montana Legislature to clean up the state orphan asylum to make it a model of womanly influence and a laboratory for the study of social problems.

An orphan asylum, Jeannette was convinced, was a microcosm of all the social ills found in industrial society.

The syphilletic child represented the problem of prostitution. The fatherless child introduced the problems of occupational disease and disaster, enforced idleness and desertion. Children raised by incompetent mothers introduced neglect, industrial indoctrination and abandonment. Unmarried mothers and feeble-minded children represented the appalling cost of social rehabilitation.

Such comprehensive examination of social problems was not widely supported, but Jeannette envisioned extensive social change as a natural development of equal suffrage, and was prepared to make startling advances for womanhood. Although her observations might have been premature, her solutions proved practical and were blueprints for social change decades later.

Less enthusiastic than Jeannette were millions of American women who preferred to wait until the drastic changes became socially acceptable before they partook of the freedom the changes presumably offered them. While thousands of women worked for suffrage, better working conditions and prohibition, a great many more resisted social reform, fearing they would lose their traditional niche in society.

Repeated attempts at taking a suffrage referendum to the ballot, the influence of the Progressive and Socialist parties, a relatively minimal interference of the industrial and liquor lobbies, and the swing from agrarian society to urban industrialization helped make suffrage in Montana a popular issue.

Montana women were unfettered by the social bonds that dominated women of the East, and Montana men were accustomed to having women share in the work imperative of living in the West. In combining this freedom of thought with the leadership of Jeannette Rankin, who was adept at dealing with people who disagreed with her, Montana was ripe for suffrage.

In the giddy spoils of being the state's leading female dissenter, Jeannette got plenty of proposals for marriage — her talent for lemon meringue pies was nearly as renowned as her talent for getting votes — but she preferred the love of the cause for which she worked. Whether she was hated or loved, she was on the mind of almost every Montana cowboy, miner and honyocker who had heard the tale of her dramatic deeds or was crooned to neutrality by her campaign catechisms.

Jeannette was an advocate for women but a warrior among men, and those Montana males not terrified by her firm dissenting disrespect for an undisputed male kingdom in politics were flustered into passion by her subtle sexual strength. Observed Congressman Tom Stout: "Jeannette Rankin is one of the most successful campaigners that I ever knew...by the charm of her manner and the force of her arguments."

She toiled tenaciously, asking nothing of her colleagues that she did not do herself, and to many people she became a folk heroine, sacrificing her money and energy unselfishly. So tenacious was Jeannette in her efforts to keep the campaign at full speed that her close friend and tutor, Mary O'Neill, wrote from suffrage headquarters demanding Jeannette delegate more of her duties.

In her reckless passion to flip the world like a flapjack, Jeannette collapsed into bed each night from exhaustion. She lost weight and her youthful face became aged and tormented from the strain. O'Neill cautioned her to avoid trying to accomplish six months work in 30 days, but Jeannette pushed on relentlessly, dragging her tired body from bed dawn after dawn, her eyes fixed dreamily on that distant goal: suffrage in Montana.

"Never mind if you do not convert the multitude," the motherly O'Neill consoled. "Others will follow after you who can complete the job. Try and not be selfish in the work, leave a twig or two of laurel for someone else who must come after."

Jeannette, however, had no intention of leaving work undone.

Alice Roosevelt with her flappers, cigarettes and social delinquency had characterized one perspective of the 'new woman,' causing her father to cry in despair, "I can do one of two things. I can be President of the United States, or I can control Alice. I cannot possibly do both."

Jeannette, with her petitions, banners and Progressivism, demonstrated the other perspective.

She was addicted to political revolution, although only by change from within the democratic system, and as many other reformers of her age, she rejected clothing fashions, smoking and bizarre social behavior as a means to liberation. Jeannette was stoical about the lure of sex and apathetic about business, the theatre and sports.

The socially liberated woman exhibited the desires of sex and passion, while the politically liberated woman sublimated her lust in an intense love affair with reform.

The sexual revolution forced these groups to polarize and Jeannette already was past the popular marriage age when she awoke to the possibility that she had missed her cue for romance. Her commitment to social reform was a subtle statement of her personal loneliness, yet had she satisfied her sexual desires she would have compromised her independence from men.

Jeannette spoke little of her personal life, prompting suffrage sisters to eventually forget she had one, and in the thrill of the fight for the ballot she buried speculation about her motives for such unselfish public dedication.

Accolades meant little to her, but achievement meant victory and honor for all Montana women. Jeannette was tied to her campaign by the smell of victory, and this attitude won merited national attention in New York newspapers, which remembered Jeannette's work on the streets of Manhattan. She capitalized on her distinction and persuaded the national interests to join her team. Among her schemes was to bring James and Harriet Laidlaw to Montana in support of the campaign.

James Laidlaw was president of the New York Men's League for Equal Suffrage and his wife Harriet had been Jeannette's supervisor in the Manhattan Borough of the New York Woman Suffrage Party.

These affluent dissenters were Jeannette's secret benefactors, for while she liked to tease the anti-suffragists that they were supported by corporate money, the Laidlaws poured cash into the Montana suffrage treasury.

Jeannette was indebted, and when the Laidlaws came to Montana she toured with them. While the suffragists preferred to fund their campaign through gimmicks such as 'self-denial' week — when all worldly luxuries were exchanged for a contribution — Eastern financial support was necessary to allow Jeannette and other full-time campaigners to make the dramatic personal sacrifices needed to win.

With a political reporter from the *New York Evening Post* accompanying them, the Laidlaws arrived in Billings in late February 1914 for a six-day whistlestop tour. Jeannette rode on the train with them to Helena, Butte and Missoula. In those few days, the Post reporter was won by her quick wit and clever tongue, disarming him of his desire to write a tough, unglamorous profile of Montana's leading suffragist.

"Everywhere there have been very pretty exhibitions of affection toward this 'native daughter' whose Montana traditions and pioneer parentage are well known," he observed in a full-page article. "The adage about being a prophet without honor in his own country was not exemplified."

Jeannette was immensely popular among the working class, her only enemy being the nebulous form of government called 'the system,' which she thought ignored the needs of the American people. In demanding equal rights for women and children, she appealed to the fairness of youthful Montana, and she was loved for it.

She was not confronted with threats and physical abuse experienced by suffragists in other states, although a political boss once tossed a glass of cold water in her face. Her hazel eyes were frosty with rage as she promised the smirking politician that Montana women would vote him from office forever. He shouldn't have smiled, for masked in Jeannette's genteel upbringing was the volatile temper of her father. John Rankin would have pummeled the man unmercilessly with his fists, but Jeannette promised to destroy him with the vote of women.

Such rage surfaced only when the strain of campaigning exceeded the limits of human endurance; Jeannette preferred gentle and persuasive campaigning, but she could be tough.

She deliberately tarnished the image of the liquor industry and the anti-suffragists, for example, which were the two most menacing enemies of suffrage in Montana.

The 'antis' comprised unorganized conservative women and the organized National Anti-Suffrage Association. The propaganda of both groups was based on the premise that suffrage would disrupt home life and force women and children into the street to be 'political.' Employing many of the arguments later used against the Equal Rights Amendment, the 'antis' dragged moral and religious themes into their arguments, which were threaded with emotionalism and misinterpretation of fact.

Predictably, the 'antis' clashed with Jeannette in Helena when she debated Mrs. J.D. Oliphant, an imported 'anti' from New Jersey. The meeting was packed by liquor men and the din was horrible. Oliphant spoke first and was given a deafening ovation. Jeannette's lieutenants begged her not to step onto the stage to present her views. She brushed past them and began her argument, but her talk was smothered in a chorus of boos.

The liquor wholesalers, saloonkeepers and their financial affiliates were subtle but more threatening opponents. Fearing the clout of the Women's Christian Temperance Union if women got suffrage, the liquor interests actively opposed the vote, appealing to Eastern associates for money to help in the fight.

The liquor interests were organized into the Montana Protective Association, which published the *National Forum*, the mouthpiece for its cause. When Clara Markeson, an anti-suffrage worker, met in Butte in early 1914 with the publisher of the *Forum*, Jeannette found an opportunity to use the opposition to her advantage.

She capitalized on Markeson's visit by suggesting in the *Montana Progressive* that the anti-suffragists were in collaboration with the liquor industry. Markeson was appalled that she publicly was reported to be in the company of men of such reputation, and her embarrassment and the subsequent decline of the 'antis' gave a decided boost to the suffrage campaign.

A third group, sensing the popularity of the suffrage issue but working to compromise it, was the mighty Anaconda Copper Mining Company, which controlled most of Montana's newspapers and many of the seats in the state legislature. Afraid that industrial reform would be a byproduct of suffrage, the company waged a quiet campaign, resigned for once that public opinion had drained the power of its propaganda machine. Jeannette had no love for the company but paid it little attention; the company reciprocated by being subjectively silent about her reasons for suffrage.

The Montana campaign climaxed in September 1914 with a state fair parade led by Jeannette and Dr. Anna Howard Shaw, and followed by female buglers, suffragists wearing yellow jackets, and small boys whose hatbands read, "I want my mother to vote." Banners streamed and onlookers yelled support from hotel windows, as the procession of people, horses and automobiles wound its way to an auditorium for a rally, only a city block from Helena's gold-rich Last Chance Gulch.

The rally was noisy and contagious, with new National American Woman Suffrage Association president Shaw reiterating Jeannette's observation that women should have the right to vote to determine whether men go to war. The rally otherwise was uneventful, however, indicating the opposition had faded from power and Montana was ready to accept women in a new status.

The issue went to the polls on Nov. 3 and Montana became the first state in America to approve suffrage on the first referendum. The tally said 41,302 men had voted for the amendment and 37,588 had voted to defeat it. The 3,714-vote majority made Montana the 10th state to grant suffrage.

The vote highlighted Montana politics, giving the West a solid block of enfranchised states to pressure Congress more intensely for a federal suffrage amendment.

Many social reforms were adopted. Among the laws passed by 1917 that directly affected women and children were the eight-hour day for women; the Mother's Pension Law, boasted the best in the nation when it was drafted; the Lazy Husband Act, which made neglecting a wife or child a misdemeanor; the Abandonment Law, which made abandoning a child a felony, and a worker's compensation act.

Jeannette had foreseen such changes and persevered with the preliminary work, hoping the women would take their cue.

Laws such as financial aid for dependent orphans, and a retirement fund for public school teachers were enacted on the strength of women voters, and enjoyed by everyone.

As many other Montanans instrumental in reform, Jeannette had shared in the advent of a new era, where women who had worked beside men in the building of a new frontier now could work beside them in the governing of the state. Yet Anna Howard Shaw wrote in her autobiography — years after the suffrage campaign — that Jeannette deserved credit for the victory.

While most of the women who had participated in the campaign faded quietly from the streets to their kitchens to be mothers and wives once again, Montana had produced in Jeannette Rankin a leader, and she was feeling impulses to challenge the male world of politics. Momentarily, however, she focused on suffrage, traveling to Nashville to partake of the national convention and dutifully assisting as a Congressional lobbyist in Washington, D.C.

Jeannette finally acknowledged the exhaustion stalking her and in June 1915 boarded a ship at Seattle for New Zealand.

Characteristically, she turned a restful vacation into a learning experience. In Auckland only a few days, she became curious how New Zealand women used their ballot. To pay for rent and food, she contracted her skills as a seamstress. Ignoring the standard seamstress wage of five shillings a day, she hired out for 12 shillings and got all the work she could handle. "I had very little money," she wrote to Harriet Laidlaw, "and when I found what a delightful, restful country it is, I wanted to stay, so I went out sewing by the day. It was such a splendid way to learn of the living conditions of the people."

The Montana suffragist went into women's homes a seamstress and came out a crusader. Everywhere she worked, she talked of the power of the vote and inquired about wages and the influence of labor unions. While boarding at a cooperative home called The Girl's Friendly, she encouraged her roommates to seek increased pay and to organize.

Jeannette returned to America in the spring of 1916. As the ship sliced through the expansive ocean, her thoughts turned to the political helter-skelter atmosphere of a nation grappling with social change. She remembered she was campaigning for suffrage in a small Montana town when she heard war had broken out in Europe. She thought she was the only person who hadn't realized war was imminent. "If they are going to have a war, they ought to take the old men and leave the young men to propagate the race," she had blurted out.

President Woodrow Wilson was arming the military, although he had publicly denounced war. Congress, with Wilson's approval, in May 1916 doubled the regular army and gave the War Department more authority. Another bill was signed to accelerate the building of a stronger navy.

To Jeannette Rankin, war was a frightening prospect.

Her humanitarian mind shuddered at stories about heads blown away and entrails littering the ground, about homes burned and blasted and countryside laid barren. And yet how could Jeannette know — how could anyone know — that the most terrible war of all was just beginning in the fragrant French orchards and the quiet Polish woods?

Jeannette felt remorse and helplessness at the thought of war. Little did she know that she would have something to say about this new social horror, and millions of people would hear her words.

"If the hogs of the nation are 10 times more important than the children, it is high time that women should make their influence felt."

(Jeannette Rankin campaigning for Congress, 1916)

A MILESTONE FOR WOMEN
Chapter 4

The power of the vote made Montana women a new and vital political force by the summer of 1915, when Jeannette Rankin contemplated campaigning for Congress. She remained their visible leader, reminding them that with citizenship came the duty to investigate political, industrial and social conditions, and to become educated voters. Jeannette had led the women in achieving independence; now she was suggesting what they should do with it.

After she left Montana for her national suffrage commitments, her ideas prospered in the activities of her lieutenants.

At Jeannette's suggestion, the victorious suffragists reassembled into Good Government clubs, organized into a state central committee identical to the old suffrage structure, and represented more than a challenge to the industry-dominated politics in Montana. By this time, Jeannette was no greenhorn in politics and she knew active political machinery could be turned to other uses, to support other causes and possibly to elect a woman to Congress.

In her Progressive mind, a Congressional seat seemed logical for a woman seeking a federal suffrage amendment and the subsequent social reforms. Since Montana had no restrictive Congressional districts where candidates could keep a tight grip on smaller electorates, Jeannette thought she could nudge into the field on the strength of her reputation, her experience and her grassroots support.

Friends laughed.

They told her a suffrage victory in Montana was no reason to think she could be elected to Congress. Some women insisted that until America adopted a federal suffrage amendment, a woman could not win a Congressional seat. The women stopped laughing when Jeannette stared back silently with thoughtful dark eyes, for they knew she would campaign.

Jeannette waited a year to commit herself, however, believing Montana women should have an opportunity to demonstrate with their wisdom of the vote how they could make convincing changes in the state political system.

In early July 1916, she polled her colleagues again. Representatives of some Good Government clubs encouraged her to try for a lesser office, such as the state legislature. They feared she would fail miserably in her quest for Congress, humiliating women and destroying the reforms for which they were working. Their lack of faith angered Jeannette, and she turned to her brother Wellington for advice. Wellington was four years Jeannette's junior and already a stalwart in Montana political circles. He had built a thriving criminal law practice and would become Montana's attorney general in 1919.

"Well, now, you're going to run for Congress and I'm not very much interested in whether these women go along with you or not," he told Jeannette. "I'll manage your campaign and you'll be elected."

Jeannette announced her candidacy in a Butte restaurant on July 11, 1916. "The possibility of my being nominated," she told a friend a week later, "seems very good." Her platform contained planks for an eight-hour day for women, prohibition, revision of the tariff, child welfare, more efficient publicity on the business of congressmen and how they stand on issues, and most importantly, suffrage by federal amendment.

She was the lone woman in a field of eight. "Although it is a case of seven men against one woman, still I am entering the political fight unafraid," Jeannette promised. "The primal motive for my seeking a seat in the national congress is to further the suffrage work and to aid in every possible way the movement for nationwide suffrage, which will not cease until it is won."

Jeannette filed on the Republican ticket, a dubious move considering her strong Progressive leanings and her incessant references to democratic government. She was firmly opposed to war and echoed the peace rhetoric of Woodrow Wilson, yet she ran as a Republican knowing her attempt to unseat Democratic incumbent John B. Evans, trying for his third term, would prompt an immediate and bitter battle between an upstart female social reformer and a traditional old guard of politics.

As a Republican, she competed with a field of largely inexperienced candidates, most of whom had only fragmented support, and she was better able to express her prominence in a party yearning for a leader.

Jeannette, however, rejected the conservative pro-business philosophy of the Republicans. Predictably, her platform was radically nonpartisan, provoking jokes among newspaper editors that she desired the Democrats to forget she was a Republican.

Once Jeannette announced her candidacy, the uncertainty among Montana's women's rights leaders evaporated. Except for an inner circle of friends in Missoula, most had been skeptical. War in Europe had distracted from the fervor of the suffrage campaign of 1914, and many of the women believed momentum had been lost. But when they saw Jeannette's zeal, they united behind her. Wellington was unsettled, however. "I am shocked," he wrote his sister, "at the prejudice that exists against a woman going to Congress."

With less than two months before the primary election, Jeannette's campaign came alive.

'Generalissmo' Belle Fligelman — "80 pounds is really more than she weighs without overshoes, and she's a hair over five feet tall, in high-heeled shoes," giggled the *Montana Record-Herald* — quit her job as editor and manager of the *Montana Progressive*, opened campaign headquarters in Wellington's office in Helena, and began redirecting the organization that had won suffrage for Montana.

Having presided over the Helena Men's League for Woman Suffrage, Wellington was readily familiar with his sister's campaign abilities and he drew her campaign plans. He thought Jeannette could win extra votes in the eastern half of the state if she was especially vocal on prohibition and a wool tariff. He proposed that a Jeannette Rankin for Congress club be established immediately, and candidates for other offices should be encouraged to endorse her openly. Furthermore, Jeannette incorporated the entire program of the Good Government clubs into her platform.

By early August — only three weeks after Jeannette had announced her candidacy — her campaign had gained considerable momentum.

At tiny Fort Benton, where Jeannette's father had bought oxen and set off to build a new life in Montana Territory 47 years earlier, she was met by a brass band.

Harriet Laidlaw and another New Yorker, Rosalie Jones, were widely quoted in newspapers. "We are watching your political fight with great interest and your New York friends believe that a better Congressman could not be found and a victory for you will mean a victory for suffrage throughout the country," wrote the enterprising and beautiful Jones, a flamboyant demonstrator who later walked from New York to Washington, D.C., to promote equal suffrage.

The shrewd *Montana Progressive*, finding Jeannette an advocate for its editorial beliefs, predicted her nomination would advertise Montana from coast to coast and her election would aid in bringing progressive legislation into law. Jeannette's candidacy, the *Progressive* shouted, was significant because Jeannette could be the first woman to sit in Congress, but more importantly, because her candidacy implied a new idea of democracy.

Riding the crest of suffrage, Jeannette was greeted with an unprecedented clamor to integrate Congress.

She handled hecklers well, giving them no opportunity to capitalize on her femininity as a liability to being a member of Congress. Unabashed by the rough talk of men, she confronted smelter workers at East Helena, Great Falls and Anaconda, and prowled the railroad yards of Deer Lodge, Havre and Livingston. "Her finesse in rough-and-ready places was as expert as in any Washington drawing room," commented a political reporter.

Wellington made frequent appraisals of the huge election map on his office wall and directed Jeannette's stumping with observations of his own. Belle Fligelman flooded releases to the press. As in the suffrage days, Jeannette mingled with the voters, stressing the practical benefits of electing a woman to Congress and emphasizing the specific issues of mining, agriculture and labor.

Women mailed penny postcards by the thousands and conducted a telephone campaign on election day with the greeting: "Good morning. Have you voted for Jeannette Rankin?"

The strategy worked. Jeannette swept the field of Republican candidates in the primary, and only Democratic incumbent Evans had a greater margin of votes. Other candidates were befuddled at the outcome but Jeannette explained they had been afraid to meet the voters. "My opponents had too much dignity," she said.

Jeannette prepared for the general election in November, opposing two Democrats, one Republican and two Socialists. Anticipating her victory in the general election, other Republican candidates pounced on her coattails. "For the proper recognition of women in politics, every woman in Montana should support Miss Rankin for Congress," said Nathan Godfrey, a candidate for railroad commissioner.

They did. Jeannette got the support of the prohibitionists who, concerned with their own cause, had not contributed to the suffrage campaign in 1914. Also backing her were many of the anti-suffragists, enchanted by the momentum of her campaign.

Such conscientious support defied inadequate press coverage. Since the Anaconda Copper Mining Company owned most of Montana's newspapers — large and small — and simply figured her bid for Congress was a wild woman's dream, they ignored her campaign. The company correctly suspected that if Jeannette was elected, she would introduce legislation that might endanger its corporate standing in Montana.

Critics of Jeannette's candidacy implied she only was joining a trend that had generated female candidacies for Congress in Washington, Colorado and California. But if anything, they underestimated the hard-hitting intricacies of Jeannette's campaign structure, and her feeling for drama.

She angrily accused a male-oriented federal government inclined toward business of failing to protect the rights of children by appropriating $300,000 to study fodder for hogs, while setting aside only $30,000 to study the needs of children. "If the hogs of the nation are 10 times more important than the children, it is high time that women should make their influence felt," Jeannette admonished. "There are hundreds of men to care for the nation's tariff and foriegn policy and irrigation projects. But there isn't a single woman to look after the nation's greatest asset: its children."

Similarly helpful to her campaign was the powerful backing of her family. Years and miles had pushed the Rankins apart geographically, each intent on his or her own ventures, but letters and love had kept them together.

One of Jeannette's sisters had been married just two months, yet she kissed her husband goodbye and with a bundle of campaign pamphlets under her arm, spread the word; another had a child only two years old, but she traded diapers for doorsteps; a third sister also left school to campaign and sister Edna, a student in law school, abandoned the lecture hall for the political stump. Olive Rankin, now a gray-haired homemaker, was bewildered by this swift onrush of new ideas, but laid aside her knitting to offer motherish reasons for sending her daughter to Congress.

Jeannette delivered her final speech of the campaign on Nov. 6, 1916, in Missoula, after the Republican politician pretending to introduce her spoke for 90 minutes, until the angry crowd chanted, "Rankin! Rankin! Rankin!" and drove him from the podium. Jeannette observed, in the 11th hour, "I need only every other vote and then one to make a majority."

As election day lapsed into darkness, Jeannette picked up the receiver of the heavy black telephone in her home and asked 'central' for the local newspaper. Frigid gusts of November wind slapped the windows of the city room of the *Daily Missoulian* in downtown Missoula where an irritated newsman picked up the phone. He had been pestered all evening by curious voters, and the staff was having trouble compiling the vote stories anyway.

"How did [Woodrow] Wilson come out?" Jeannette asked, too nervous to reveal her identity. She inquired about a few other candidates before asking whether Jeannette Rankin had been elected to Congress. With a deadline bearing down and the confusion of incomplete voting returns littering his desk, the newsman was brief: "Oh, she lost."

Dejected, Jeannette went to bed and slept fitfully. The newsman probably had no idea of the elective status of Jeannette Rankin, but he figured she lost — a woman never had been elected to Congress. He went back to work, not knowing he had just rebuffed the first Congresswoman in the history of the United States.

Jeannette, however, was slow in realizing victory. The morning headlines of Nov. 8, 1916, were dismal, with reports that her Republican opponent, George Farr, had won the race. In those days of media innocence, waiting for election returns was a tedious and mostly agonizing predicament. Radio broadcasting hadn't been developed, and television was unknown. Ballots were counted by hand and often manipulated in precincts where the Anaconda Company had control of the vote. Tabulation was slow and results dribbled into newspaper city rooms. Jeannette was convinced she had fallen short of victory, and she was ready to concede the election to Farr.

Wellington, who had campaigned for Congress on the Progressive ticket in 1914, telephoned from Helena later that day with heartening news.

He had been surveying Montana voting patterns for five months, and in looking over partial returns, he saw that much of the Farr plurality was reported in the more urbanized western half of the state. The tabulation of votes in the far-flung prairies of eastern Montana had been slower, and Wellington predicted they would be the votes that would elect his sister to Congress.

He was right. Two days later, thanks to a coalition of women, laborers and farmers, Jeannette Rankin was the most talked about personality in America.

In the midst of more serious matters, the nation went head-over-heels with delight. War was looming on the foreign front and military preparedness was a volatile issue, but for a few raucous, carefree days, the nation turned its curious eyes to Jeannette Rankin.

Although panting from its coverage of the shocking expenditure of flesh and money in Europe, the press gaily recorded this progressive happening. Reporters and photographers thronged to the Rankin's Madison Street house, and the mailman was weary from the loads of letters and telegrams, many of which carried foreign stamps. Suffragists bridged the rifts fragmenting the movement, and beamed their approval. Montana had elected a woman to Congress, while in most states women still were denied the right to vote.

"Breathes there a man with heart so brave that he would want to become one of a deliberate body made up of 434 women and himself?" speculated the *Kentucky Courier-Journal*.

After 140 years, women and children now had an elected representative. Jeannette had proven to Americans that women could crash sex barriers and make themselves heard. Although many battles were yet to be fought, American women rejoiced at her election, for the work of more than a century had culminated in a voice for women in federal government.

"Why — Jeannette Rankin — you have given suffrage the

biggest push forward that could have possibly been given unless we could have elected a woman president," wrote 'General' Rosalie Jones from her apartment in New York City.

In a prepared statement to the press, Jeannette promised to represent not only the women of Montana, but all American women and children. Specifically, she would introduce legislation seeking an eight-hour work day for women, equal wages for equal work, and a federal suffrage amendment. Of interest to Montanans, she promised support for settlers' patents, reclamation projects and land laws.

Jeannette attributed her election to the equalitarianism of the pioneer days, when men thought of women as they thought of themselves. This feeling of equality was undiscovered in many other states, making Jeannette a unique candidate in a unique era, elected on a wave of a fresh awareness in politics. The new Congresswoman prepared for Washington's sacrosant male political world with a plethora of indistinct social philosophies on women and social reform. Her opponents shuddered at this advance to left-wing politics, while entrepreneurs tried to use her election to their advantage.

Letters contained proposals of marriage and requests for her photograph. An automobile business tried to capitalize on her election with an offer of a free automobile if her ownership could be exploited for advertising purposes. A toothpaste firm sought a bite of the action with a promise of $5,000 for a photograph of her teeth. And Comic Christopher Morley wrote in the *New York Times Magazine:*

> *We'll hear no more of shabbiness*
> *Among our legislators.*
> *She'll make them formal in their dress;*
> *They'll wear boiled shirts and gaiters.*

Jeannette was troubled by such publicity.

Only when America rose to its feet to gander at the "Lady from Montana" did Jeannette realize her election had won more than a vote for women. She suffered great shock in being exposed to such publicity, and could not comprehend she would be in the

public eye from that moment. To protect herself, Jeannette refused to leave her house until the photographers and reporters
who waited on the street had left.

The gesture was regrettable, although Jeannette gave it no
further thought. Had she met the curious media with enthusiasm
and weathered the initial weeks of gaudy misinterpretation and
sensationalism, she could have learned tactics and gained friends,
helping make her Congressional work more acceptable to the
public.

But Jeannette had a strange and unsettling fear of the press
that lasted throughout her life. Montana Republicans had no
special affinity for Jeannette anyway, but they accepted the responsibility for the news blackout, fearing the publicity might
class her as a freak and taint the party's image.

True blame for the blackout rested with Jeannette, however,
who was considerably more flamboyant than the timid Republican Party leaders, but overwhelmed with the attention the nation
had focused on her. Thoughtful and provocative articles filtered
through the screen of yellow journalism. Louis Levine, a professor of economics at the University of Montana, reviewed in the
New York Times a factual and fitting account of the background
and aspirations of the first Congresswoman.

"It would be premature to expect Miss Rankin to give a definite
answer to the many concrete questions which the acutely curious
or the insensitively studious like to ask," Levine wrote. "She will
have plenty of time between now and her first appearance in
Congress to think many things over and to form opinions on a
number of vital issues." Levine was, like Jeannette, an outspoken
dissenter who thrived on social causes and the scholarly investigation into change. He was a renowned teacher with doctoral de-
grees in economics and sociology and, despite being suspended
for conduct prejudicial to the university's welfare, he remained a
man of integrity.

His unerring studies of civilization were as reliable as his candid
observations about people, and with a great degree of emotion
and reverence, Levine wrote of Jeannette:

There is a great surprise in store for the members of the new Congress when they convene in Washington next year and meet their first woman colleague, 'The Lady from Montana.' They will have to throw overboard a lot of mental baggage which they may have valued very highly for many years. They will find in their midst not that impulsive, irrational, sentimental capriciously thinking and obstinately feeling being which many imagine woman to be, but a strong and well-balanced personality, scientifically trained, accustomed to strict reasoning, well versed in the art of politics, inspired by high social ideals, tempered by wide experience.

That Jeannette had a considerably less lofty opinion of herself was demonstrated in her first public statement, which she gave at a reception at the state university — her alma mater — the day after she drove the newsmen away from her house. "I am deeply conscious of the responsibility resting upon me," she told students crowded into an auditorium. "I earnestly hope that I may be of some substantial service, however slight, to the men and women of Montana, my native state, and of the nation."

Frightened and apprehensive, Jeannette was taking her step into the national spotlight with great care. Her work before had been as a volunteer, not as an elected representative. With a respect and awe of her future that afflicts many freshman Congressmen, Jeannette hoped to ease into her new role with dignity and a sense of duty.

No longer Jeannette Rankin of Missoula, but the first American Congresswoman, Jeannette had to act deliberately, presenting her developed, progressive ideas in a vigorous, but orderly manner. With the sensationalism stripped away, few people doubted that Jeannette's election to Congress was an outstanding milestone in the young century. Whatever she said would not be the opinion of an individual, but words of the American woman.

Wellington contracted with the Lee Keedick Speaking Bureau of New York City for Jeannette to present a series of speeches at $500 each, but he overlooked in a strangely unprofessional gesture a clause stating the contract would be cancelled if the war issue came up in Congress and Jeannette voted against it.

War was close, forcing news editors to give the encroaching issue more space and greater 'play' each week. Quietly at first, and then more overtly, the increasingly hostile situation among belligerent nations in Europe played on America's conscience. President Wilson tried vainly to demonstrate his moralist and progressive principles in diplomatic talks with the Germans, who thought they were too powerful to bow to cloaked threats of war. On Feb. 25, 1917, Wilson learned Germany was plotting against America.

British intelligence forces had intercepted secret orders from German foreign minister Arthur Zimmerman to the German ambassador to Mexico, telling him that in the event of war with America, an invitation should be extended to Mexico and Japan to join the Central Powers. The British leaked the order to Wilson, who was becoming increasingly distressed that his 1916 campaign slogan, "He kept us out of war," had been too premature.

On March 1, the President released the message to the press, and despite an isolationist national temperament, the revelation shocked America.

Wilson wanted to reinforce his proposal to Congress for armed merchant vessels to be protected against German submarines, and he thought public opinion would strengthen his hand. He was right. But a 'little group of willful men' in the House of Representatives and the Senate talked his bills to death, and the President armed the vessels anyway, fearing attacks. His efforts were in vain. German U-boats promptly sank three ships only two weeks after Wilson's second inauguration.

Caught in the confusion of the war issue, with stories about rumor, hate and bigotry punctuating the headlines of the daily press, Jeannette tried to maintain her posture as an elected representative of women and children.

That became difficult with the release of the Zimmerman note, as Jeannette was besieged with questions about how she would vote if the issue was decided in Congress. With this pressure, her life underwent a new twist. While she had been speaking in general terms of American defense policy, advocating only a coastal defense to discourage invasion, her principles had gone untested. She was surprised that war developed into a major issue so soon.

The politics of military preparedness threatened to relegate progressive legislation to a lesser role. Jeannette viewed the national sentiment and Wilson's moralist predicament with sarcasm. She figured Wilson's campaign slogan was a superficiality that didn't commit him to anything, yet suggested he wanted to keep America out of war. Jeannette gave her first press conference in the home of the Laidlaws in New York City, reiterating her concerns for a federal suffrage amendment and a federal Children's Bureau. But she was evasive about the war issue, leading a *Washington Post* newsman to blandly report that she would not state whether she was pacifist.

Former President Teddy Roosevelt, in a subtle attempt to influence her thinking before she went to Congress, invited Jeannette and Wellington to dine at his Oyster Bay home.

By 1917, Roosevelt had become a warmonger of extremist proportions. Although his hard-line dealings on American military policy turned many people against him, he was more adept in his political critique that most people thought. Surely his invitation to Jeannette was no casual affair, for throughout dinner he talked incessantly about American defense. Surprisingly, however, the opinionated ex-President didn't ask Jeannette how she would vote if Congress was asked to approve a war declaration. She reflected: "He realized that I was a symbol of democracy and he didn't want that symbol destroyed. He was a friend of my brother's."

After the initial agitation of the Zimmerman note, pressure from friends, suffrage colleagues and especially Wellington to make a stand on the possibility of an upcoming war vote continued to mount. The 65th Congress had been scheduled to begin Dec. 3, 1917, more than a year after Jeannette's election. But President Wilson called an emergency session to begin April 2, and although Jeannette's speaking tour was interrupted prematurely, she hurried to Washington.

Early on the morning of April 2, a reporter from the *Washington Times* appeared at Jeannette's apartment at 2030 California Street to interview her. He asked her what significance she intended to bestow upon her term in office. Flustered at having been called to Washington unexpectedly and not having time to prepare, she explained that...

> *You know, I am in a pretty predicament. I had no idea Congress was going to open so soon. At least, I didn't realize it and I made engagements to speak which kept me from getting here until today.... I have so much to learn that I don't know what to say and what not to say. So I have just decided not to say anything at all, for the present at least.*

Part of Jeannette's hesitation in commenting was due to pressure by aggressionist factions, which wanted her to commit herself in support of American intervention in the war in Europe.

She also was worried about the reaction of Capitol Hill's cigar-chomping, desk-pounding conservatives. Jeannette knew that in this early climate of change, a show of ignorance about the transaction of business in Congress could play into the hands of her critics. Because she was the first Congresswoman, inevitably she would become an easy target for people intent on upholding the female stereotype of obedience in the kitchen and docility in bed.

For this, Jeannette had good reason to be careful. Already she had been subjected to frightfully inaccurate articles meant to convey that she was a misplaced housewife who only would contribute comic relief to the intensity of America's serious political matters.

One account called her "a slip of a girl," while others commented salaciously on her red hair and delicious green or blue eyes. She was accused of being a suffragist right out of cattle country, who packed a .44-caliber six-shooter and trimmed her skirts with chaps fur. Her physical appearance was emphasized so extensively that America could have concluded Jeannette was a painted young hussy of the Calamity Jane variety.

Luckily for Jeannette, more accurate comments from responsible people balanced the picture.

Zoe Beckley satirized in the *Evening Mail* that he was "glad, glad, glad even to pollyannaism that Jeannette is not 'freakish' or 'mannish' or 'stand offish' or 'shrewish' or of any type likely to antagonize the company of gentlemen whose realm had hitherto been invaded by petticoats." Said a Montana rancher in an interview with the *Chicago Sunday-Herald*: "Jeannette will make 'em sit up and take notice. She comes from fighting stock and carries a kick in her arguments." Said Wellington of his sister: "Her life is devoted to the cause of mankind and government, first, last and always."

Despite all the ballyhoo, Jeannette remained typically feminine from the mass of brown hair streaked with gray to the tops of her less fashionable, but more practical, 'ground grippers.' She wore her hair *a la* Pompadour, emphasizing its abundance and presumably to draw attention away from her nose, which she thought was too large. Her slender figure was dressed in well-fitted and expensive New York-made garments.

Jeannette opened the doors of Congress to women, but the softer, symbolic ripeness of her power was evident in a face comfortable with the seriousness of her purpose.

Some women crusading for suffrage filled people with a desire to oppose them, because of their crass approach and their inexcusable rudeness. Jeannette was one of the few nationally prominent women who filled people with the instinctive desire to serve her by any means in their power.

The significance of Jeannette's presence in Washington didn't escape the women, either. In a symbolic thank you for her energetic determination, national suffragists representing all factions gave an honor breakfast for Jeannette at the Shoreham Hotel in Washington on the morning of Wilson's scheduled war message.

"The day of our deliverance is at hand," Carrie Chapman Catt told 150 women. "And I know, as we all know, that this deliverance is to be at the hand of a woman." Said Julia Lathrop, a national children's advocate: "Now that we have a pull in Congress, there is no telling what we will accomplish." Harriet Laidlaw rose to "shout hurrah for Jeannette Rankin."

Food went uneaten as women diverse in opinion as National Woman's Party leader Alice Paul, suffrage lobbyist Maud Wood Park and writer Katherine Anthony basked in the reverence of unity. Ten women spoke of the "sterling worth of the feminine legislator," their hearts light with the joy that culminated years of hard work and frustration.

With the weight of the testimonials sending a sudden surge of apprehension through her, Jeannette rose to speak. Spontaneously, the women pushed back their chairs and stood for an ovation, and Jeannette, clad in a black sailor hat and a dark chiffon gown over white silk, stood in embarrassment beside a bank of bright spring flowers. She waited for the clapping to stop, and with eyes sparkling from tears, bravely began her prepared text. In a moderately low-pitched voice, easily heard in the dead silence of the room, she outlined her ideals and intentions, but her speech was shortlived. She sank into her chair, biting her lip.

Jeannette was terrified looking at those women, who were bestowing their ultimate confidence that she could liberate them.

The breakfast had been a forum for strong, confident words from many mouths, but with a theme: Jeannette Rankin. Only 30 years earlier she had been racing through the range grass surrounding her rustic farmhouse. Now she was the hope of millions and intended to represent them the best she could. Her constituents sensed she would listen to their needs and demands, and Jeannette was tugged mercilessly to represent them.

Her suffrage sisters expected her main mission to be suffrage by federal amendment. To her Montana constituents, she had promised a revision of the tariff to protect farmers from Eastern agents who bought grain at second-grade prices and sold it at first-grade prices. Julia Lathrop depended on Jeannette to give a needed boost to the Children's Bureau in Congressional circles. Wellington, her brother, campaign manager, political advisor and confidante, wanted her to avoid controversial issues — especially a conspicuous vote against war — to preserve her re-election chances in Montana. Alice Paul wanted Jeannette to represent pacifists. Carrie Chapman Catt discouraged a pacifist stand, saying it would imply women were hysterical and ill-suited for Congressional duty.

The many faces at breakfast that morning reminded Jeannette of the immense task awaiting her. But more troubling were the many white armbands in the room, flashing like beacons in the night. They signalled open and heated discontent between pacifist Alice Paul and war advocate Carrie Chapman Catt, although a truce had been called to recognize this unprecedented and strategic advance for womanhood. Ironically, Paul sat at Jeannette's left and Catt to Jeannette's right, and each envisioned an opposite role the new Congresswoman must play in legitimizing the political realities of their sex.

If a war declaration came to a vote in Congress, Jeannette would have the uneasy task of deciding which suffrage faction she should represent. Considering that her immediate intention was to unite all American women, this was a tragic turn for the suffrage movement.

From the Shoreham Hotel, Jeannette was driven to national suffrage headquarters on Rhode Island Avenue, where she gave a short speech from the balcony to a crowd on the street. Then the big moment came for her to make her debut in Congress, and she climbed into the back seat of a shiny, open touring car and waved to onlookers while the gloved, capped chauffeur eased the automobile into a procession that included suffragists from nearly all the 48 states.

The flag-draped automobiles swept down Pennsylvania Avenue, and crowds of people hurrying toward the Capitol cheered as they recognized the 'Lady from Montana.' Jeannette was bemused at this attention, and when the procession stopped momentarily near the south steps of the Capitol, photographers rushed to her car, pushing and shoving for a clear portrait of the new Congresswoman.

Jeannette scampered to the House Office Building and rode Elevator No. 7 to the third floor, where she walked down the high-ceilinged white corridor to room No. 332, rumored to be across the hall from the office of the House's most confirmed bachelor. Before she could take off her gloves, she was surrounded by delegations of shouting school girls, pacifists, anti-pacifists and others, all anxious to shake hands. And before Jeannette could leave her office to go to the Capitol, she was besieged by people wanting her to sign autograph books or to carry part of her bouquet as she was sworn in.

Jeannette tried to please them all.

Clutching a bouquet of purple and yellow flowers, she entered the House chambers at 11:55 a.m., gripping the arm of John Evans, her elderly Montana colleague. The clothes she wore had been tailored by a New York dressmaker, who had exchanged his services for legal consultation with Wellington.

The special session of the House of Representatives was scheduled to convene at noon, and already about 100 Congressmen were in the room. They rose and applauded as Jeannette nervously strode down the aisle, refusing to look right or left until she reached her seat far back on the Republican side. Before she could sit, she was besieged by men jostling to shake her hand, and she returned the courtesies with a frank feminine smile. She was a sensible young woman going about her business. When her name was bellowed during roll call, the House cheered and stood, and Jeannette rose and bowed twice, first to the Republican side, then to the Democratic side.

The *New York Sun* cast a curious premonition of Jeannette's symbolism when it predicted the first time she arose to make a speech she would create a greater stir than the day Buck Kilgour kicked in the door of the House of Representatives.

Seating the first woman in Congress was a comforting distraction to the President's forthcoming war message, which he was to deliver to a joint session at 8 p.m. By late afternoon, the plaza outside the Capitol was seething with sightseers, police, pacifists, suffragists and reporters. The confusion worsened when a troop of cavalry arrived to guard the President.

Wilson grieved at what he was about to ask America to do. He spoke of "the spirit of ruthless brutality" that war would bring, yet he was convinced that Germany's reckless aggression would continue unless America threw her military might behind the Allies. The President condemned actions by the Germans as nothing less than war against America. He asked Congress to make the world safe for democracy, and after leaving the Capitol at 9:11 p.m. to be driven to the White House, he confided to his secretary: "Think what it was they were applauding. My message today was a message of death for our young men. How strange it seems to applaud that."

Congresswoman Rankin would have agreed.

She clearly was repulsed at the thought, having spoken of war as brutal and useless, and of American foreign policy as primitive. From the time Jeannette was a child, she had felt strong humanitarian tendencies, and she was bewildered and frightened at the prospect of being swept into the cry for blood. Moments after the joint session ended, she was cornered by electrifying war lobbyists. Sadly, the most vocal among them was her brother Wellington, and suffrage sisters with whom Jeannette had shared many battles.

While pro-war lobbyists peddled their spiels on Capitol Hill, Jeannette was driven home. A day that began in glory had ended in sorrow.

The possibility of America's intervention in international violence offered new implications and complexities to Jeannette's life, for the crisis facing her and the democratic world was a harrowing one.

People spoke blissfully of giving their lives for democracy and freedom, crazed to arms by this sudden surge of national jingoism. Selective Service offices filled and troop trains with their human cargoes chugged east to waiting ships. Spanking new flags were unfurled and the orthodox press mounted a vitriolic attack on the 'Huns' and the pacifists, accused of being German sympathizers. As if the obscene lessons of the Civil War and the Spanish-American War were not enough, young men playfully pitted their lives against the threat of the Grim Reaper as veterans slapped their backs and tousled their hair.

They were going to *WAR*, by damn!

Forgotten were the sea merchants who bolstered their profits by increased trading with the protection of a wartime American military. Forgotten was the steel industry, which built instruments of death, such as artillery and ammunition, and pocketed the millions of profits.

Forgotten were the enthusiastic blanket manufacturers, horse trainers and clothing designers. Forgotten were the thousands of destitute young men who rushed to the military recruiting depots to get the food, clothing and shelter they had not been able to find in their city ghettos.

Jeannette was more analytical. She foresaw the grief and despair war would bring.

Against the horror and destruction of war, Jeannette concluded, was balanced the love for humanity and peace. She toyed with the philosophical considerations, wondering if America could practically, logically or morally wage war for peace; to use the instrument of violence for humanitarian ends.

Could Jeannette justify killing for love? With a vote only a few days away, she struggled to make her decision.

*"Thereupon in that gray tense dawn, there arose in
the cold Congressional halls a strange sound. It was
a newborn sound. It was like the sob of a mother's
heart! By virtue of this heroic stand of Jeannette
Rankin, I hereby voice our appreciation, our deepest
gratitude and our loyalty to her."*

(Mrs. J.E. Erickson toasts Jeannette Rankin)

ONE WOMAN AND WAR
Chapter 5

White doves were seen circling the lighted dome of the United
States Capitol as Jeannette Rankin prepared to leave her office
for the House chambers. It was past midnight, and she was weary
from the many hours of debate with pro-war lobbyists. Vindic-
tively they had contested her reasons for believing in peace. War,
they told her, was inevitable. Why not acquiesce?

Jeannette and her brother Wellington joined a long procession
of people who filed sadly into the Capitol. The doves sweeping
graciously in the air above them carried no olive branches in their
beaks, but to the pacifists they signaled a final plea for peace. To
Jeannette, they symbolized the possibility that heartfelt debate by
self-collected men had reversed the trend toward war.

Still unsure how she would cast her vote, Jeannette took her
regular seat toward the back of the great hall. Her eyelids
drooped with fatigue and her mind churned with confusion. The
debate wore on monotonously as one Congressman after another
arose to enunciate fiery diatribes in favor of war. Jeannette remained silent as she fought to decide how she would vote when

the debate came to an end, and glanced frequently at the big clock beneath the press gallery. Its hands crept tediously around the dial.

She was not oblivious to the somber chatter in the galleries above her, where behind fluttering handkerchiefs and crumpled evening editions of the *Times* were the dark faces of men and women who wondered how the first Congresswoman would vote on the resolution.

Jeannette wanted to vote for peace. The threat of war essentially destroyed her optimistic vision of a better life for women and children, a threat to which she reacted in anger.

But Wellington argued that she was on trial before America and must convey a sense of patriotic duty, imploring her to vote 'a man's vote.' Quietly, Jeannette suffered. She had been absent from the House chambers for most of the debate, instead confronting her family, friends and colleagues in her office.

They had accosted her with vicious denouncements of her stand against war. Carrie Chapman Catt, fearing a negative vote would do irreconcilable damage to a federal suffrage amendment, hurried from New York to lobby with Jeannette. Harriet Laidlaw, whose money had supported Jeannette since the early days of suffrage, and whose bank account had diminished with her Congressional campaign, urged Jeannette to vote for war. She believed Jeannette should remain as inconspicuous as possible on the war issue to add impetus and credibility to suffrage, and feared a negative vote would imply women were neither courageous nor competent to hold office.

Jeannette was bothered that these women sought the freedom of the vote, yet they feared angering men by confrontation.

But the most crushing hurt in her desire to vote for peace was inflicted by Wellington, who promised to join the Tank Corps to demonstrate his support for the war. Wellington had been described as "young, vulnerable, controversial, aggressive, vigorous," by the *Montana Progressive*. He had been a godsend in Jeannette's election to Congress, for without his political intuition and astute engineering she probably would not have won. But he was proving to be a veritable nuisance with his prediction that if Jeannette voted for peace, she would destroy the expectation of a woman in public office.

Wellington argued that she could go on record against war by speaking of its futility on the House floor, but stressed she must cast an 'aye' vote. She resisted his pleas, and after concluding she would prefer to be burned at the stake or be imprisoned for her ideal, he conceded Jeannette should vote her conscience.

Arguments raged in her office for several hours. Wellington sent Jeannette's secretary and long-time ally, Belle Fligelman, to the Capitol to check the progress of the debate. Secretly, he rejoiced that he had succeeded in eliminating Jeannette's faithful friend from the argument. As the combatants became frustrated, their tempers flared. Jeannette's friends deplored her contempt of compromise. "So what if you vote for war," she was told. "You have many other battles to fight."

At the Capitol, messengers and soldiers rushed in confusion. Hard-boiled Congressmen listened solemnly to eager lobbyists, and appeared to be persuaded by their arguments. Jeannette observed several of the lawmakers were inspired and ready to act on the referendum, nearly shouting cadence from the rows of mahogany chairs.

As Jeannette sat in the House chambers among arguing, cajoling lawmakers, some of whom wept, she tried to shut from her mind the horrible banter of war debate.

Peace never seemed so lonely, unpopular and untried. Jeannette wanted to cry, but she was jolted from her thoughts by the silence settling over the House chamber. The debate was nearly finished and soon she would be required to cast her vote. The Senate two days earlier had voted for a war declaration by a vote of 82 to six, and a nation seething with vengeance pressed the House to make war a reality.

Men sobbed at what they were about to do. North Carolina's Claude Kitchen, the majority leader, climbed solemnly to the podium and with reason sweet to Jeannette's ears, reminded:

In view of the many assumptions of loyalty and patriotism on

the part of some of those who favor the resolution, and insinu-
ations of cowardice and disloyalty on the part of those who
oppose it...let me at once remind the House that it takes neither
moral nor physical courage to declare a war for others to fight.

Congressman Fred Britten of Illinois, a proponent of the resolution, preceptively asked the House if it would return the declaration to the Committee of Foreign Affairs for an amendment
stating no American would be sent to Europe, Africa or Asia
without the consent of Congress.

Members killed the motion, believing soldiers would not
be sent overseas anyway. Freshman Congressman Fiorella La-
Guardia, who was to become one of Jeannette's closest friends,
later wrote in his autobiography that "at least 60 to 65 per cent of
the members who voted for war, did so in the firm belief that no
United States soldier would be sent overseas."

The Senate earlier had voted with only eight abstentions, and a
similar desire to be on the record was evident in the House. The
American people had been stirred by inflammatory speeches
about patriotism and by volatile newspaper accounts of how the
country was arming itself.

Woodrow Wilson, in his haste to equip a huge American army
had, before Congress even decided the war resolution, commissioned the military to purchase miles of cloth, hundreds of
thousands of shirts, leggings, shoes and hats, buttons, shoelaces,
underwear, insignia, tent cloth and neckties.

The War Department had prepared reports indicating how
many safety pins a volunteer army of two million men required.
Manufacturers hustled with bids for tent poles, rifles, batteries,
butchers' knives, saddles, horse brushes and telescopes.

"The vast expenditures of the Allies in this country have
perfected American manufacturers in producing shrapnel and
explosive shells," the *San Francisco Examiner* had reported on
April 1, 1917. "Rifle manufacturing is by far the most difficult of
all munitions business, there being over 2,000 operations in the
manufacturing of a single rifle."

Secretary of the Navy Joseph Daniels and Secretary of War

Newton D. Baker appealed to the nation's young men to join the military. And the American mood rapidly was accommodating their pleas. Telegrams poured into the Oval Office, beseeching President Wilson to clothe his notions of mercy and humanity in a doughboy's uniform to intimidate warring nations and bring quick relief to misguided and suffering people.

This was the pressure with which Jeannette had to contend. She had campaigned for Congress on the promise she never would vote to send Montana boys to war, and she now knew she could not break that promise.

The resolution finally came to a vote at 3 a.m. on Good Friday, April 6, 1917. Reporters watched the only Congresswoman agonize her predicament from their lair in the press gallery.

They saw a woman who was 36 years old, her blue dress a pleasant contrast to the stark background of pressed black suits and starched white collars. She frequently lifted her anguished face to look at the high ceiling, while nervously clasping her hands to her throat. Her abundant chestnut hair was tied in a knot at the top of her head, yet it was loose and tousled. Jeannette religiously wore a colorful, flowery hat, believing it detracted attention from a long surgical scar on her neck, yet tonight she was without a hat.

Racing through her mind in those final moments before the roll call were the many arguments of the past three days. Everyone except the pacifists had been urging her to vote for war. She could not forget the pleas of her many suffrage sisters. They had begged her not to jeopardize the chances of a federal suffrage amendment with an unpopular vote on the issue.

Conversely, Jeannette was bothered that war seemed to be the antithesis of the welfare of women and children. She knew Congress was being asked to vote for a commercial war — that none of the idealistic hopes would be carried out — and she was aware of the falseness of much of the propaganda.

The rhetoric of the militarists was easy to dispute, but to oppose well-meaning friends and relatives pained her. In trying to be fair, she said she would listen only to those people who favored war, and would not vote until the final opportunity.

The reading clerk began the roll call.

As he progressed toward the 'R's,' Jeannette felt her stomach tighten. "Rankin?" the clerk asked loudly. Jeannette didn't answer. "Rankin?" he asked once more. Still Jeannette failed to respond and stared at the ceiling, her face ashen with despair. The clerk resumed his roll call, and the galleries hummed with conversation. The 'Lady from Montana' apparently was going to wait for the second roll call to cast her vote, although that procedure was reserved for Congressmen not seated for the first. Jeannette's fellow lawmakers turned in their chairs and stared at her, mystified.

Rep. 'Uncle Joe' Cannon of Illinois entered the floor after the roll call and, after being told Jeannette had not cast a vote, he went to her. Thinking she was unfamiliar with the House voting rules, he was reported to have said to her:

> *Little woman, you cannot afford not to vote. You represent the womanhood of the country in the American Congress. I shall not advise you how to vote, but you should vote one way or the other, as your conscience dictates.*

The reading clerk began the second roll call, this time getting to "Rankin" much faster. Jeannette sat solemnly in a moment of breathless silence. Then she rose and gripped the chair in front of her. Tears wandered down her cheeks. Other Congressmen wept openly and unashamed as they watched. Finally, lifting her eyes to the front of the chambers, she said softly:

"I want to stand by my country, but I cannot vote for war. I vote no."

A hush followed applause by a smattering of pacifists in the gallery. Jeannette had broken a 140-year precedent that no comments be made during roll call, a privilege reserved for senators. The reading clerk, too shocked to hear Jeannette cast her negative vote, turned to House Speaker Champ Clark for instructions. "Continue the call," Clark said, and Jeannette was recorded in the negative.

She slumped in her chair until the roll call was finished. In precisely 12 minutes America decided to go to war with Germany.

Jeannette arose and hurried out of the House. At that moment she was not consoled to think the first vote cast by a woman in Congress was a vote for peace.

Jeannette joined Wellington in the hallway and together they left the Capitol and strolled in the cool night air. Wellington was perturbed and he found his sister unusually subdued. "You know you're not going to be re-elected. You know there will be a lot of feeling," he warned her.

"I'm not interested in that," she replied. "All I'm interested in is what they will say 50 years from now."

Wellington escorted his sister home. Belle Fligelman slept in a bedroom adjoining the living room of the apartment, but awoke when she heard the apartment door close softly. Jeannette and Wellington were arguing. From the tone of Wellington's voice, Belle knew Jeannette had voted for peace. "Think what you've done," Wellington insisted. "Think what you've done."

Jeannette did not go to the House Office Building that day. Overwrought by conflicting emotions and a reportedly fragile mental state, she stayed at home, unwilling to face the friends she had disappointed.

Suffrage leaders — with the exception of pacifist Alice Paul, who was delighted — reacted in horror at the vote and spoke funereally about the chance of the federal suffrage amendment. Although Jeannette was one of 56 members of Congress voting against American entry into war with Germany, she had provided the ammunition her male critics needed to discredit the ability of a woman to hold high public office.

"You should have a picture of yourself as people really see you," advised Edwin J. Heath of Washington, D.C. "You are just a cheap little actress, putting on a sob act to land publicity to help sell tickets for your lecture bureau...."

And conservative suffrage coalitions used Jeannette's negative vote to disassociate themselves from a woman they believed was becoming too radical to represent their cause.

Most of the backlash was from conservatives shocked that this new creature in Congress — the American woman — should make such a bold and dramatic entrance into the annals of American statesmanship. "It is possible that no more dramatic scene has been staged in the House of Representatives than when Miss Rankin, casting her initial vote in the lower body, interrupted the roll call to say, in thirteen words, that she could not vote for war," reported the *New York Times*.

The wave of public sentiment that followed her vote was partly a reflection of the bigotry and fear that had welled within the nation's conscience since the advent of the Progressive Era, when reform had become a popular issue.

Jeannette was singled out for abuse by the hysterical and unwitting because she depicted a move to the left of the American political spectrum. Women were flooding into jobs as traffic cops, streetcar conductors and auto mechanics, toting ice and joining the Navy, yet society condoned those radical social advances. A woman who dared to confront male macho society's sacred institution of war, however, got no such tolerance. How dare Jeannette Rankin fashion a new image of the American woman in 13 simple words!

The meaning of those words was analyzed and debated emphatically by people demanding to know why she had not at least bled profusions of patriotism and allegiance.

Somber editorial writers, thumbing through reference books in their city rooms, debated the implications of her statement. Did Jeannette mean to say she could not stand by her country if it was to vote for war? Or did she mean to say that, "I want to stand by my country, therefore, I cannot vote for war?"

For months after her vote, theorists and academicians struggled with interpretations. In their haste to pin a badge of treason on the 'Lady from Montana,' they failed to understand that she saw the decline of women and children in the enthusiasm for war, and she was rejecting America's chauvinism as being unrepresentative of its people. Jeannette thought her vote a greater patriotism than the nebulous concept the war hawks advocated.

Jeannette suspected an international plot to lead America into war — if not by research, by instinct — and particularly was

suspicious of the Lusitania incident, when the Germans tor-
pedoed and sank a British ocean liner, with 128 Americans
among the passengers. Rumors that the passenger ship was
loaded with explosives as a decoy to entice the Germans into battle
— and subsequently, the Americans into war — abounded freely
after the powerful ship perished in a fiery death. But if Jeannette
feared a conspiracy she made no mention of the matter on the
House floor.

Her silence angered the war hawks, who sought to regain their
segregated Congress. They watched Jeannette shrewdly during
the days after the vote, but she considered herself mostly ignorant
about House rules and cautiously avoided debate.

Her dramatic outburst of peace philosophy as she cast her vote
startled men favoring war, however, and given no more substantial basis to judge her character, her silence made her the target of
ridicule and scorn. "The statement she made on the floor of
Congress is equal to saying, 'I know what my duty is, but being a
woman, I can't do it,' " concluded Guy Norman, a Rhode Island
state senator.

Most of the criticism focused on Jeannette's gentle weeping
which, as her tiny handbag, was pinned on her as the emblem of
her sex. The daily press — including her hometown newspaper
— reported in heavy-face headlines that Jeannette had sobbed
when she voted, sensationalizing the incident to the extent that
reporters who had not seen the drama were writing stories about
it.

Jeannette considered the weeping stories the only effective
weapon the militarists could use. But they did it effectively, and
she was subjected to this type of hyperbole until she was cast
tragically as a woman who had exceeded her capabilities.

The Capitol Hill mail service toted at least two large blue canvas
mail bags to her office each day, containing hundreds of letters of
approval or criticism, enabling Jeannette to judge that Americans
were embroiled in debate about whether a woman should make a
'man's' judgment about war.

The hysterical sobbing scene attributed to Jeannette was conceived spontaneously by news correspondents to add color and melodrama to the quiet scene that had unfolded before them. Some people who had been in the House chambers at the time of Jeannette's vote questioned the importance of making an issue of whether Jeannette wept.

Ellen Maury Slayden, a gossip of the Washington social set and wife of a Congressman from Texas, observed in a published journal of memories that "Miss Rankin's weeping and hysterics when she cast her vote are almost entirely apocryphal." Maud Wood Park, a Capitol Hill suffrage lobbyist who had been sitting in the gallery, remembered Jeannette was well composed. People asked Rep. Fiorella LaGuardia whether he had seen Jeannette weep. "I do not know, for I could not see because of the tears in my own eyes," he told them.

But a pioneer woman weeping before the public was not in vogue, and in this inference the press convinced the American people that Jeannette was a blubbering, incompetent fool. An incident of a few second's duration was transformed into a major news event, and people easily were led to believe it.

Among the more objective students of Jeannette's performance was a rabbi who questioned why critics were capitalizing on a weeping argument to deny women the ballot. "I have more respect for a woman who cries before she votes upon whether or not we shall have war than for the man who goes to a saloon and takes three highballs in a similar situation," he said.

Wrote Vachel Lindsey to Jane Addams at Hull House: "I hate a hyphenated American. If I had been in Congress I would have voted with Miss Rankin and would have considered it a sufficient reason to say, 'I will not vote for war till she does.'"

Some of the best observations of the significance of Jeannette's vote came from the 'Tattler,' a columnist for *The Nation* magazine:

> *Whether she was visibly and audibly overcome by her emotions*
> *— a question on which much stress is laid in certain quarters*
> *— we may leave the historians to decide among themselves.*
> *Male lawmakers have occasionally exhibited emotional weakness under equally trying conditions, without provoking in-*

vidious comments on the capacity of their sex as a whole. Miss Rankin having happened to be the first and only woman in Congress when the war crisis arose, it is far too soon to draw sweeping conclusions on the wisdom of our latest suffrage experiment.

The Tattler speculated Jeannette had killed her chances for political prestige. He predicted her attitude on the war issue never could be erased from the record, however earnestly she might devote her energies elsewhere.

Jeannette immediately experienced the lasting impact of her vote. Other suffragists believed they had lost everything by Jeannette's vote for peace in the darkening climate of war, having a short-sighted view of the extent to which she could further the role of women. The hawkish Carrie Chapman Catt remarked bitterly to a friend that Jeannette was a 'joker,' who cost the suffrage movement a million votes each time she answered a roll call.

Publicly Catt was more benign. "Miss Rankin has done nothing to be ashamed of, far from it, and she can be counted upon to do nothing that she need be ashamed of," she said. "She did her duty as her duty appeared to her. It was not for anyone else to make her decision for her."

Harriet Laidlaw had been in the House gallery when the war vote was taken and had returned to New York City immediately afterward. Laidlaw saw Jeannette as a tragic figure in one of the most terrible mental debates any woman ever had. She told the *New York Times:*

> *It is not true that Miss Rankin wept, fainted, or had to be carried from her seat. She was perfectly composed. She had been asked by so many of her friends to vote for the resolution; at the same time, she was gripped by a desire to express a woman's horror of war and her principles against it. When she finally voted, she voted with intense sincerity, knowing that she was not doing the popular thing, but refusing the allow herself to be governed by motives of expediency. She just couldn't vote for war.*

Some critics were unable to accept the innovation of a woman voting on serious political matters in Congress. Robert Watson, a Scotch Presbyterian minister, complained to his congregation that if Jeannette Rankin was not willing to stand by her country in that "terrible and trying" hour, she should resign at once.

In Montana, Jeannette's predominantly rural constituency relied on her to introduce legislation that would enhance their farming and mining interests, but they did not expect her to become the precursor of the peace movement in America. Her hometown newspaper, *The Missoulian*, had been a blushing supporter during her Congressional campaign, despite being an Anaconda Company mouthpiece. But its editorial mood became ugly after Jeannette spoke for peace, and she was crucified in a front-page political cartoon depicting a beautiful, busty girl in a white robe presenting Uncle Sam with a lengthy scroll of war pledges. The caption, blossoming from Uncle Sam's mouth, said: "Any gift from the city that gave us Congressman Rankin will be doubly accepted."

The unanswered question, however, was why Jeannette should receive more negative attention for her vote than any of the 55 men who joined her in protest, or the men who abstained to avoid controversy with their constituencies.

Courtesy and justice, her sympathizers pointed out, demanded she should receive no more critical attention for her actions and votes from editors and correspondents than any man who could have been elected in her place, or any other new member of Congress. The symbolism of her presence took a new twist. How could one woman represent womanhood more than one man could represent manhood?

Yet as the first woman in Congress, Jeannette could not avoid that role. "I feel it is a source of satisfaction that you, representing in a way all the women of the country, took the stand you did," wrote an office secretary for the Woman's Peace Party, who thanked Jeannette for her "splendid" defiance of war. And the 'practical men' of the House believed Jeannette missed an opportunity to assist the advancement of women in federal government circles, although they generally regarded her vote as one dictated by the inherent abhorrence of women for war.

If anything saved Jeannette from the tiring, persevering reaction, it was the kind empathy of her more sensitive colleagues, who attended to her as a big family of boys with a little sister. She accepted their companionship with dignified composure. While fellow Congressmen overwhelmed her with attention, however, the news media continued to rave about her unsuitability for office. A reporter who cornered her to ask if she had found any boyfriends among the Congressmen was told abruptly, "I expect to put in my time here learning the ropes."

Adverse and sensational news coverage of Jeannette's first vote in Congress spelled the end of the giddy celebration of her election.

The possibility that she would be anything but a surrogate representative of women generally was inconceivable to the national media, and while newspapers had bequeathed carefree observation to the novelty of her first few days in Congress, they had cancelled that gift at the first few days of betrayal.

Unwilling to explain this conspicuous behavior of the first Congresswoman, the news media sensationalized the trivia of her presence, reminding Jeannette that yellow journalism had not died in America. That she could have been portrayed as intense, challenging and formidable in the business of the House would have given a boost to the image of women, but the penalty for trifling with the male business of war was ridicule.

The daily press of 1917 was unlike the eager social revolutionary of the late Sixties and the Seventies that awoke to the role of women in American progress. Rather, the press was sexist and myopic, preserving tradition and reinforcing the goals of the business world.

Beginning to understand that war could be women's greatest enemy, Jeannette nonetheless was mystified by the chilly reaction to what she believed was an act of honor. The pernicious response educated her that people could not accept peace when the government glorified war.

"Vote for war," the Congressional orators had bellowed, "and not an American boy will have to set foot on foreign soil. Our very declaration of war will stop Germany." While before the declaration Americans had been singing the pacifist song, "I Didn't Raise My Boy To Be A Soldier," now they were singing rousing Army tunes about war abroad.

Jeannette was mysteriously defiant of public opinion. "I'm sorry I had to disappoint you," she wrote her brother a week after the vote. "I still feel that this was the only way I could go."

"Small use will it be to save democracy for the race if we cannot at the same time save the race for democracy."

(Jeannette Rankin evaluates World War I)

POLITICKING FOR LIBERATION
Chapter 6

Although only a few weeks had passed since Jeannette Rankin entered Congress, her conscience already had proved to be her major political weakness.

The press had given her a stiff strapping for her indiscretions. The *New York Times*, for example, had printed the names of the 50 members of the House of Representatives voting in the negative, in a prominent box at the top of the front page, as if to persecute them for their stand. But of the 50, only Jeannette had to endure the humiliation of her vote being panned in the lead story. She was furious with the convoluted editorial policies, and refused to politick with news reporters.

Late in April 1917, as Congress was embroiled in debate on conscription, an Associated Press reporter stopped at her office for her comments on the draft bills. Jeannette was seated at her desk behind a partition, and when secretary Belle Fligelman told her why the reporter wanted to see her, stressful Jeannette yelled, "Tell him to go to hell!" The reporter wheeled and strode from the room, and her newspaper publicity suffered an alarming decline.

Blind to the obvious, Jeannette continued to evade public opinion. She clung to her political ideals, although she had been wrenched from her pedestal by people who thought she had been too flippant with sacred traditions. For the first time in her public service career, Jeannette Rankin had suffered a major defeat. She was insecure, thinking her symbolism had shattered, and afraid her future was in shambles.

Yet Jeannette refused to be intimidated. She fought to satisfy the goals of her Congressional work, knowing the blood of the Rankin family flowed like steel when confronted by the fight.

Her determination had its rewards. A legend had been born, and visitors to the House of Representatives asked tour guides to show them Jeannette before they saw luminaries such as Speaker Champ Clark or 'Uncle Joe' Cannon. If the tourists expected an Amazon freak — as Jeannette was popularly portrayed by some magazines — they were surprised by the feminine woman whose motions were lithe and her manner vivaciously serious. She was neither beautiful nor pretty, yet an attractive charisma suggested a powerful personality.

Jeannette was not the hard-visaged feminist exploited in political cartoons. She rarely was without the companionship of a colleague when she was on the House floor, falling into whispered conversation about proposed amendments and jotting down suggested changes with pad and pencil. To the careful observer, she was rather conservative, preferring to be a student of the affairs of the House.

Her more reactionary constituents in Montana hesitated to appreciate these cautious attributes of their unique representative, however. The war hysteria spread rapidly throughout Montana, with the vitriolic and disoriented Will Campbell, an Anaconda Company newspaper editor, at its forefront. Campbell and his cronies remembered Jeannette's vote for peace and built a case against her presence in Congress, padding cryptic statements about her integrity as a citizen with didactic tales of German outposts hidden in the prairies of north-central Montana.

Jeannette undertook the sale of liberty bonds, partly to ease misgivings among her constituency, and to expedite the war.

She traveled to Deer Lodge — a small Montana agricultural community — to speak on behalf of the bonds, and found the doors of the hall locked. In another town, Montanans were so bitter about her vote they forced her to speak in a park during a snowstorm, where she held onto a fence so she wouldn't be blown to the ground.

This was a tragic ordeal for a woman who had risen to national fame with such pomp and flair. That she begged to sell liberty bonds in Montana while movie idol Douglas Fairbanks had the attention of hundreds of thousands at the New York Public Library with his plan to deck the Kaiser, showed how she strove to help her constituents forget the politics of her vote to gain their full support for social legislation.

Jeannette was depressed by the fuss toward her stand on peace, as she confided to friends, yet she felt deep satisfaction in knowing she had made her debut in the world of politics and survived.

"Miss Rankin has a hard job," observed writer Gilson Gardner. "If she pleases half the suffragists she will be pretty sure to offend the other half. If she pleases one political party she will offend the other. And every girl in her state and district who wants a job and can't get it will be quite sure that woman suffrage is a failure."

Constituents and friends inquired whether her vote meant she was a failure in Congress, and Jeannette in private letters replied that in her campaign she had judged the sentiment of Montana to be overwhelmingly against war. She had detected a shift in public sentiment immediately before the resolution, yet letters and telegrams from Montana had been 16 to one against the war. "I tried to let Montana people know that whenever a question arose on which I had received no definite instructions from them I would vote in accordance with my highest ideals," she wrote.

This highest ideal — daring to raise a voice for women in an atmosphere of war — marked Jeannette's commitment to pacifism as a means of pursuing the liberation of American women

But her awareness of war and peace was raw and untried.

During the suffrage campaigns, she had been influenced by Katherine Devereux Blake, a New York principal, who argued peace was a natural extension of suffrage. Blake impressively had gathered 355,000 signatures of schoolchildren protesting the possibility of America entering the European conflict, which suggested to Jeannette that war might have been a learned habit, rather than an instinct. "One of the first things we had talked about in woman suffrage [was] that it was a woman's job to get rid of war," she had reflected.

As World War I brought the Progressive Era to a crashing halt, Jeannette perceived more clearly the relationship between war and social legislation. War, to Jeannette, was a method of destroying civilization, while social legislation was a method of offering the best to humankind.

She remained more of a reformer who disdained the oppression of war than a pacifist, objecting to war on moral and spiritual grounds. Rarely did her religious attitudes surface, although she plainly thought organized religion had contributed to war and social disease. The many priests and ministers who condemned her vote reinforced that belief.

Jeannette's subsequent wholesale commitment to peace, and associations with the teachings of Indian pacifist Mohandas K. Gandhi and the writings of philosopher Henry David Thoreau and British sociologist Benjamin Kidd made her, anachronistically, the veritable pacifist Americans thought she was.

But from the moment she cast her vote for peace in the shadow of World War I, she was an enduring feminist, deciding war was a theatrical display of force serving no useful purpose.

"The feeling aroused in Congress over the war was something of an achievement," the *Des Moines Register* of Iowa said of Jeannette's performance, "and will go much further to fortify women in politics than any goals she could have made with friends of the war measure."

Jeannette never quit being a social reformer.

At the instant she defied the warnings and pleadings of friends and relatives to stand in the House and vote a conspicuous 'no' against war, she had made a subtle statement that peace was woman's work. But she worked less for the inner contentment of peace than for the greater good of women, again bringing to light her peculiar — and curiously unfounded — will to martyr her personal happiness to sustain her idealism.

As the first American caissons rolled into battle in France, Jeannette schemed a new direction in the liberation of women, obsessed with the desire that women should use the power of the ballot to end war.

Had she been a true pacifist, she would not have voted in late 1917 for a war declaration against Austria-Hungary.

Members of the House of Representatives expected another anti-war outburst when debate began on the declaration, but Jeannette was carefully attentive.

Toward the end of the debate she spoke:

> *I still believe war is a stupid and futile way of attempting to settle international difficulties. I believe war can be avoided and will be avoided when the people, the men and women in America, as well as in Germany, have the controlling voice in their government. Today special interests are controlling the world.*

The speech reflected the ideals of a pacifist, yet Jeannette voted 'yea' on the declaration. "This is a vote on a mere technicality in the prosecution of a war already declared," she told the House. "I shall vote for this as I voted for money and men." The *New York Times* immediately recognized the conflict between this vote and that against Germany, smirking that "it is better to be right part of the time than wrong all the time."

In voting for a declaration of war against Austria-Hungary, however, she missed a generous opportunity as a woman to cast another shadow of doubt over the American role in World War I. Her chances of re-election had been destroyed by her first vote. Yet she voted for legislation that would pump millions of dollars into factories to build weapons and ammunition and to enable the military to transport more men to the battlefield.

Jeannette argued that because war was reality, only an increased expenditure of money would expedite the inevitable killing and hurry the warring nations to the conference table. She supported the Wilson Administration in its subsequent war politics, except for the Espionage Act of 1917.

If history was to judge that single inconsistency in Jeannette's determined opposition to war, her vote in favor of battle with Austria-Hungary belied her love of peace and justice to save herself from the perils of a society mad with the fever of war. She commented sarcastically: "Small use will it be to save democracy for the race if we cannot at the same time save the race for democracy."

Jeannette plunged into the war activity, making every attempt to hasten an end to the conflict. She was a guardian to Montana boys heading to combat in Europe and to American women and children who became victims of the madcap domestic confusion.

Utilizing a year's contract with the *Chicago Sunday-Herald*, stories appeared under Jeannette's byline discussing topics such as wage problems of women working in defense plants, the protection of women in the crisis of war, and toil-worn child workers on the farm. "Women must not only prepare themselves...for thrifty administration in their kitchen, but also for professional and paid work," she warned. The $100 weekly columns were ghost-written by Belle Fligelman, but Jeannette provided many of the ideas and approved most of the final drafts before they were sent to Chicago.

She hosted regular Sunday evening dinners at her apartment for Montana boys who sat stiffly in woolen khaki and asked timid questions about life in Washington and reports of fighting in Europe. The menu never differed, but for some, the prospect of returning for another of Jeannette's Montana-style meals would end quietly in the muddy, bloody trenches of the Meuse-Argonne or Belleau Wood.

Jeannette had prefaced her entry into Congress with plans for legislation to benefit women and children, but she managed only occasionally to get Congress to listen to her proposals.

Congress looked to the foreign front with all its energy, relieved at gaining an opportunity to ignore the pressing business
of social change at home.

Jeannette believed America courted death by maintaining the
'war habit.' Wars ended in armed truce with neither country
having gained an understanding of the other's problems. Millions
of people died. The spirit of one country was crushed while the
military might of the other triumphed.

A common theme in Jeannette's arguments for peace was that
men were stampeded to arms by 'superpatriots' and militarists
who thundered that war was glorious and honorable.

She was fond of relating the story of six Congressmen who told
her after the declaration of war against Germany: "If I had
known you were going to vote against it, I might have done it
myself." She was convinced a secret vote would have defeated the
resolution.

Jeannette's new image as a maverick attracted constituents
convinced she had the courage to circumvent the bureaucracy
and provide answers to their long-sought questions. Three
hundred letters were carried to her office each day. While most
members of Congress employed only one secretary, she needed
three. Louise Puffer of Washington, D.C., joined Belle Fligelman
and Florence Leach, who had helped Jeannette in the Montana
suffrage campaign. Jeannette's younger sister, Harriet — affec-
tionately called Hattie — joined the staff later that year as office
manager.

Every letter got a reply.

They contained proposals of marriage, included requests for
research on legislation, and asked Jeannette to seek pardons for
friends in penitentiaries. They demanded action on homestead
entries, and complained about her vote for peace.

The Rankin-Sheppard Bill was introduced to retain the citizenship status of American women who married foreign men.
Jeannette wrote the bill after a plea from Crystal Eastman, sister
of Max Eastman, editor of the Socialist weekly, *The Masses*. Miss
Eastman wanted to marry an Englishman but did not want to lose
her citizenship in exchange for an act of love.

And Jeannette embarrassed prudent politicians by joining with Julia Lathrop of the Children's Bureau to push the first bill on instruction in female hygiene, maternity and infant care. Known as the Rankin-Robertson Bill, the measure was designed to educate women about venereal disease and birth control. But America was not ready for Jeannette's frank look at women's bodies, and unfortunately, her bill gained nearly as many adversaries among women as among men.

Jeannette bitterly blamed the pervasive war mentality for the bill's defeat under her sponsorship, for the measure had been supported by millions of people. But Congress gave it little attention. Such legislation had been pushed for years by the Children's Bureau and the American Public Health Association, and Jeannette's representation was the only hope they had.

She viewed social legislation as something that aspired to a 'higher good,' a moral responsibility of government that required it to feed, clothe and protect the American people. Fighting wars was to her far more than a social impracticality, it was a moral crime, requiring lying, stealing, killing and hate to survive. This moral fiber was a principle to which Jeannette clung firmly.

Incidents such as the Federal Bureau of Printing and Engraving scandal of 1917 supported Jeannette in her opinion that war steered government away from the miseries of its own domain, offering a slick alternative to domestic pressures. If the scandal proved anything, it proved morality was absent in times of war production.

Jeannette was at work in the House Office Building one day when the sister of a Montana constituent visited with a tale of woe about working conditions in the bureau, which in the prosperity of war was printing currency and Liberty Bonds faster than ever. The woman whispered to Jeannette that employees were forced to work as long as 14 hours a day while being paid only 35 cents an hour. Women workers were threatened with sexual assault. Requests to transfer to other agencies were said to be denied by Director Joseph Ralph.

Instead of confronting the director with the allegations, Jeannette decided to visit the bureau as a sleuth to examine the complaints personally.

Purporting to be another Congressman's constituent, she toured the plant. She found pleasant physical conditions, but women were required to stand for 10 to 12 hours at counting machines to inspect bills and bonds for errors. Jeannette found the bureau to be in obvious violation of the federal eight-hour wage law. She returned to her office and wired Elizabeth Watson, a New York private investigator who once had disguised herself as a convict at Auburn Prison to gather information for the New York Prison Commission. Watson joined Jeannette's secretarial staff and gathered affadavits documenting the bureau's working conditions.

A few days later, Jeannette met Director Ralph in his office and showed him the evidence. Ralph yawned and said he would talk with Treasury Secretary William McAdoo about her demand that he restore an eight-hour day. He said his workers preferred longer days for fatter paychecks and argued he was short of laborers to meet the demands for the production of currency. Jeannette reminded him the Civil Service list bore the names of 500 people seeking employment.

She was not convinced Ralph would act on her complaints. Earlier protests by the National Consumer's League, the National American Woman Suffrage Association, and the National Women's Trade Union League had left Ralph unimpressed. Jeannette decided to gather more evidence. Secretly, she invited workers to meet at her apartment. She recorded their complaints in a card index — a tactic she had learned in the suffrage movement — and then visited Secretary McAdoo, threatening Congressional investigation if he failed to act.

On July 9, 1917, the Treasury Department conducted a special hearing. Two hundred women arrived to testify, and in six hours, 46 of them told the investigating committee that overtime was compulsory and sick leave, rest periods and vacations had been eliminated on the excuse that a nation at war must maintain production.

McAdoo ordered an eight-hour day and restored privileges. Any employee wanting a transfer could apply. Upset at this challenge to his authority, Ralph resigned to become president of a banknote company.

In exposing the bureau scandal, Jeannette was introduced publicly as a friend of labor. Considering her early love for Progressivism, her involvement was not surprising, however. The scandal was a clear case of the government abusing the people it allegedly represented, and to Jeannette, overlooking a scandal was hypocritical and immoral.

This philosophy led her into a deep entanglement with striking miners in Butte, Montana, in the late summer of 1917. On June 8, 1917, a fire raged through the Speculator mine, killing 162 men. Three days later, workers formed the Metal Mine Workers Union and demanded that the mammoth Anaconda Copper Mining Company, which owned more than 25 percent of the world's copper production, recognize the union and make much-needed labor reform.

The company refused. By July 29, about 15,000 workers in Butte, Anaconda and Great Falls were on strike. Among their major protests was the company's use of the 'rustling card' system, which required workers to carry a card stating they had been loyal to company policies. Without the card, a miner was rejected when he applied for a job.

The Anaconda Company had clear control of the mines, and it wanted the miners to remember that. Production came to a stand-still, but the company refused to recognize the miners' demands, assailing them without mercy in the state's company-owned newspapers.

Jeannette anticipated violence, for the Industrial Workers of the World — known as the 'Wobblies' — had widespread influence with the workers in Montana. These garrulous Socialist laborers were encouraging miners to grab control of company property, and when Jeannette was asked by the Metal Mine Workers to find a federal investigator to visit Butte, she responded quickly.

Talking with Labor Secretary William B. Wilson proved futile. Jeannette contacted President Wilson and he only referred her back to the Labor Department.

Perhaps the men did not take Jeannette seriously because she was a freshman legislator and a woman. Their hesitation in investigating the strike, however, led to the death of Wobblies organizer Frank Little, who was wrestled violently from his Butte hotel room by six masked men, dragged screaming behind an automobile until his kneecaps were scraped off, and then hanged from a railroad trestle. His brutal murder exemplified the tense labor situation.

Jeannette's pipeline of information from Butte was her aging suffrage ally, Mary O'Neill, who complained that the entire western mining world was throttled by industrial bickering in Butte, not by agitators as management claimed. "You know this I.W.W. howl is only a poisonous cloud sent out to discolor clear sightedness into real conditions," she said in accusing the company of perpetuating labor unrest.

Jeannette's concern for the welfare of the workers and her belief that government should regulate industry caused her to consider intervening in the Butte strike personally.

O'Neill thought Jeannette's visit would be a political masterstroke, and Wellington suggested she hint to Cornelius Kelly, vice president of operations in Butte, that she had been invited by labor to act as a mediator in the strike. But her request before Congress on Aug. 7, 1917, to empower the President to nationalize mines essential to the war effort infuriated the company. This was a dangerous blow to corporate politics, since the bill would allow federal troops to control the mines if an unresolved dispute let to violence, a drop in production or interfered with America's defense. Jeannette had argued on the House floor:

> *In a crisis of this kind, coming as it does in time of war, when all our national attention should be centered upon the enemy and not on local difficulties, there should be some effective means by which the Government would be able to protect itself against a decrease in necessary productiveness, and by which*

> *the people of each State would be guaranteed the protection*
> *provided by the Constitution of the United States.*

Jeannette's speech was a thinly veiled attempt to subdue the belligerent corporation, and Kelly fired a telegram to her: "The unwarranted attack made by you without an investigation upon the Anaconda Company and its officials precludes your being accepted as mediator or my conferring with you relative to existing labor troubles." Jeannette went to Butte anyway, refusing to hide her misgivings about the company and her backing of labor. This only reaffirmed the company's opinion that she had lost objectivity and would make a poor mediator.

When she stepped onto the train platform in Butte, she was met by thousands of cheering miners, but six burly police officers whisked her to the security of a hotel. The police department feared her presence would incite more violence. Only a few days earlier, she had crucified the company in an interview with the *Washington Times*. She knew the company would react with malice to the comments she made in Congress and she told a reporter:

> *They'll try to do to me just what they have done to everyone who*
> *ever tried to oppose them.... They own the State. They own the*
> *Government. They own the press.... First I'll be roasted from*
> *one end of the State to the other. Every newspaper will print*
> *my shortcomings, real or fancied, in the largest type. They*
> *probably won't assassinate me. They use more subtle methods*
> *now.... If the Anaconda Company prevents my ever returning*
> *to Congress, I'll at least have the satisfaction of having done*
> *what I could for my constituency while I was here.*

Jeannette in her first few days in Butte conferred with union representatives and local public officials. Kelly tucked himself away on the sixth floor of the company's Hennessy Building and refused to talk with her.

On Aug. 18, Jeannette spoke to 15,000 miners and their families, who packed the Columbia Gardens ballpark to the outfield fence. She told them misguided patriotism allowed the government to ignore industrial conditions during war. She sympathized with their demands, although refusing to condone the violence advocated by the Wobblie sect, and she promised to strive for a peaceful end to labor troubles. "It doesn't matter from the government's point of view what these miners belong to, or whether they're in the union or not in the union," she told them. "What we need are laws that will protect anybody that's working." Applause reportedly lasted 15 minutes.

After returning to Washington, Jeannette worked harder to take the Butte labor issue to President Wilson. They met personally and she tried to use the crisis of war to her advantage, explaining the spirit of patriotism fails when workers feel nonproductive in their jobs and in their lives. She was embarrassed to learn the strike had been settled secretly a few days before her final appeal to the President.

Jeannette thought if industry could control people through labor, it also could control people through government. She was naturally inclined to hate corporate electioneering. She had seen plenty of proof in Montana that corporations elected candidates and then pressured them to perform like puppets for selected financial interests.

Her solid support for farmers demonstrated her tendency to fight for the little person. Angered that greedy capitalists were uncaring that farmers fed America with their labor, Jeannette complained on the House floor in 1918 about inequities in government farm loans. She asked for an amendment to contract with farmers for the growing of wheat through advances and loans, tried to cut costs of production and transportation, and supported bills for tariffs on foreign farm products.

Summarily she urged the passage of legislation to cut Montana farmers free from the strings of state political control, a slap aimed at the Anaconda Company.

With such blatant defiance of private business, however, Jeannette seemed close to an abrupt end of her Congressional career. She became more vulnerable when she introduced her resolution to grant American recognition of the independence of Ireland, which proposed America count Ireland among the countries for whose freedom and democracy it was fighting.

The resolution angered conservatives who interpreted it as a tool of the Sinn Feiners, an anti-British, Irish nationalist group. Jeannette had enabled the war hawks to link her to pro-German sympathies, altogether a bold conclusion for so flimsy a premise. Irish-Americans in Montana — congregated mostly in the labor centers of Butte and Anaconda — were delighted with their Congresswoman's actions.

But pro-war newspapers grabbed the opportunity to continue their lectures on Jeannette's unsuitability for office.

"Her action will give rise in some quarters to the suspicion that her vote against war was not prompted by feminine repugnance to violence of all kinds, but by a disloyal dislike of violence employed against the enemies of her country," droned the *Toronto Mail and Empire*. Jeannette was labeled "the female LaFollette" by the *Adrian Telegram* of Michigan. The *Helena Independent* of Montana spoke of "our busy war obstructionist," whose bill "has for its purpose the stirring up of trouble in the United States and thus complicates the work of the nation in fighting Germany."

Meanwhile, Montana's political obstructionists were busy stirring up trouble. Industrial lobbyists in the legislature succeeded in dividing the Congressman-at-large district into eastern and western districts. Jeannette was gerrymandered to the western district, effectively isolated from the rural support of the eastern plains.

She had barely any support from Montana newspapers, and furthermore, the war fervor was at its height. As early as February 1918, she realized as Wellington had predicted that she had no chance for re-election.

She telegrammed half-heartedly: "I do not want my family and friends to make the necessary sacrifices unless they feel that there is a chance for success."

Congresswoman Rankin got a weak reply of support and chose a bolder alternative. On July 16, 1918, she announced plans to campaign for the Senate, with the slogan, "Win the War First." If nominated and elected she promised to urge President Wilson to bring war to a victorious conclusion and to vote for every measure he recommended to more efficiently prosecute the war.

Some constituents questioned her intentions.

Wrote Annabel Rooney to one of the Democratic contenders: "It is hard to know her personally and not feel a very small affection for her, but since she has entered politics, we feel that she had been the narrowest of politicians and as a Congressman a colossal failure."

Jeannette's opponent was Oscar M. Lanstrum, publisher of the *Montana Record-Herald*. She lost the Republican primary to the former Progressive by less than five percent of the votes: 18,805 to 17,091. The showing was remarkable for a candidate who received only adverse newspaper coverage and who had been so controversial in Congress.

Jeannette consulted Wellington about running in the general election on a third party ticket, and he agreed she should try. Her Democratic opponent was Thomas Walsh, a senior senator destined to win fame when he uncovered the Teapot Dome scandal in the Twenties. Walsh was a flamboyant, cold-eyed statesman, held in high esteem by his constituents, and after Jeannette's defeat in the primary, he was confident he would be re-elected. His left-wing support gave him the edge over Lanstrum. He had a good record in the Senate and beamed the appearance of a man of impeccable integrity.

By September 1918, Walsh heard rumors that Jeannette was campaigning on the Nationalist Party ticket. The rumor proved true, for Jeannette was a certified Nationalist Party candidate, and had negotiated for organized support from the Montana branch of the Non-Partisan League. The Nationalist Party had been founded by Socialist John Spargo, the author of *The Bitter Cry of the Children*, a provocative book about life in the slums. Although the party was a coalition of pro-war Socialists, anti-war Progressives and prohibitionists, all of whom embodied in some fashion Jeannette's attitudes, she recognized it more as a vehicle for her candidacy than as a representation of her political beliefs.

The Non-Partisan League comprised disgruntled farmers and independent politicians who preferred to work outside the two-party system.

"There are a great many farmers who have strong radical ideas and who are very much opposed to the war, a good many having the idea that Wall Street and the munitions manufacturers of the east have done a great deal to bring it on," an associate wrote Walsh.

Walsh became worried. Jeannette's popularity among liberals and radicals threatened to drain his support. "Every influence possible should be brought on Wellington not to have her run," wrote C.B. Nolan to Walsh, his former law partner. Wellington was asked to convince Jeannette that Walsh could get her an overseas appointment, the purpose of which would be to retire her from politics gracefully. But Wellington and Jeannette heard rumors she had been bribed, and she continued to campaign to prove she hadn't accepted money or political favors.

Walsh tried another tactic. He had been urged by R.R. Purcell, the mayor of Helena, "to arrange with John D. Ryan [president of the Anaconda Company] to have the company quietly get in line because you have a hard fight on your hands with Jeannette Rankin in the field." Walsh sought support of the Anaconda Company by asking for the resignation of U.S. District Attorney Burton K. Wheeler, his friend and appointee. Wheeler had been an enemy of the company and was accused of sympathies toward the Germans and the International Workers of the World, a radical labor organization. Wheeler's resignation enabled the company and conservative voters to support Walsh.

Montana newspapers generally regarded Walsh and Lanstrum as major contenders, except for the labor-controlled *Butte Daily Bulletin*, which said of Jeannette in an editorial:

> *With a steadfast courage...she has spoken for the lowly and the oppressed with no possibility of reward.... She is stronger than the servile Lanstrum...and brave enough to risk her political fortunes for what she believes is right.*

Suffragist Carrie Chapman Catt, continuing to crucify Jeannette for failing to comply with her wish to vote for war with Germany, endorsed Walsh for his "continued and invaluable aid for federal suffrage," while Jeannette got the support of Frances

Willard, national president of the Women's Christian Temperance Union.

Jeannette ran a distant third in the general election, garnering 26,013 votes to Walsh's 46,160 and Lanstrum's 40,229. She had not expected to win the election, and grieved that a simple expression of peace — her vote against a declaration of war with Germany — had killed her politically. Wellington, although ashamed he had tried to persuade her vote, had been accurate in his prediction: too many Montanans thought Jeannette in her conspicuous stand against war had gone too far.

Among her most aching regrets was that the equal suffrage lobby had been unable to obtain the vote by federal amendment, and when victory finally was to be enjoyed, she would not be in Congress to celebrate it.

Her foray into the issue as the nation's first Congresswoman had been impressive. In an address to the House of Representatives in January 1918, only a few weeks after the signing of the Prohibition amendment into law, Jeannette asked why men who had spent their lives thinking in terms of commercial profit found difficulty in adjusting to human needs.

With the abundance of coal, and with great stretches of idle, fertile land, Jeannette pointed out, babies continued to die from hunger and cold, and soldiers died from lack of a woolen shirt. Might not women provide the resources of human needs? She asked of her colleagues:

> *Can we afford to allow these men and women to doubt for a single instant the sincerity of our protestations of democracy? How shall we answer their challenge, gentlemen; how shall we explain to them the meaning of democracy if the same Congress that voted for war to make the world safe for democracy refuses to give this small measure of democracy to the women of our country?*

Congress needed time to contemplate the question. Not until 1919 did the lawmakers approve a federal suffrage amendment, and by August 1920 the states ratified it.

The Twenties offered a golden age for peacemakers. Looking

back on the carnage of the great World War, Americans sought to explore alternatives to such human wreckage.

One of those Americans was Jeannette Rankin, embittered that war had been an affront to the welfare of women and children. On a little plot of land in Georgia she set out to prove to the world that peace was more than a dream.

The Rankin family, about 1895. From left in back are John, Jeannette, Harriet, Wellington and Olive. Sitting in front are Mary, Edna and Grace. The photo portrait shows Philena, Jeannette's deceased sister.

PHOTO ALBUM

Jeannette Rankin poses for a formal portrait by Harris and Ewing Photographers of Washington, D.C., in 1917, before she entered Congress. The business-like mood created by her uplifted chin and the periodical contrasted sharply with the popular image of women.

Moments before departing for her first day in Congress on April 6, 1917, Jeannette Rankin speaks to women from the balcony of the National American Woman Suffrage Association headquarters in Washington, D.C. Behind her is Carrie Chapman Catt, president of the Association.

Meeting for a reunion and dinner party on April 6, 1937, in Washington, D.C., were 11 persons who had voted against American entry into war with Germany in 1917. Seated from left are Sen. Ernest Lundeen of Minnesota, Rep. Harold Knutson of Minnesota, former Rep. Jeannette Rankin of Montana, Sen. George W. Norris of Nebraska and former Rep. Royal C. Johnson of South Dakota. Standing, from left, are former Rep. Harry E. Hull of Iowa, former Rep. Edward Keating of Colorado, former Rep. C.C. Dill of Washington, former Rep. Fred Britten of Illinois, former Rep. James A. Frear of Wisconsin and former Rep. Edward E. Browne of Wisconsin.

Jeannette Rankin stands beside her Bogart, Ga., home, which she purchased in 1925. She considered her farm a 'center of infection' from which a peace epidemic could spread, and although the Twenties and Thirties were ripe for pacificists, Jeannette found that superpatriots were popular in Georgia.

Although a former member of Congress, Jeannette Rankin was active on Capitol Hill during the Twenties and Thirties as a lobbyist. Here she testifies before the House Naval Affairs Committee on Feb. 9, 1938. As a legislative secretary of the National Council for Prevention of War, she opposed Navy building programs.

Jeannette Rankin retreated to a telephone booth in the House of Representatives cloakroom after having cast a 'no' vote against American entry into war with Japan on Dec. 8, 1941. Fearing physical injury, she held the door closed and dialed Capitol police to escort her to her office.

The Jeannette Rankin Brigade, named in honor of the first female member of Congress, was the first large group of women to protest the Vietnam War. Jeannette Rankin is in the center (wearing glasses) as the women begin their march from Union Station to the U.S. Capitol on Jan. 15, 1968, the opening day of the 90th Congress.

Jeannette Rankin as she appeared in 1963 during a visit to Helena, Montana, where her brother, Wellington, owned a prosperous law practice.

*"Atlanta Post No. 1 does not want the school of
thought propagated by Miss Rankin to take root in
the south or anywhere else. We will use our best
efforts to counteract the influence...."*
(American Legion Commander Kenneth Murrell in a letter to the president of Georgia's Brenau College)

THE GEORGIA EXPERIMENT
Chapter 7

A blue Japanese lantern cast soft azure light on Jeannette's
graying hair and her light summer dress as the little barefoot boys
knelt around her. Some of the faces were white; some were black.
The boys listened motionlessly to her fascinating tales, so trans-
fixed by visions of Gandhi and the Congress that the watermelons
hanging to cool in the well were forgotten.

Softly, Jeannette sketched pictures of intrigue in the humid
Georgia air, while a chorus of crickets hummed harmony in the
pool of black beyond the white gauze screen protecting her from
the insects.

The little boys spent many steamy nights at Jeannette's house,
captivated by the learning she offered them. They had unkempt
mops of hair and ragged trousers, but they always wore clean
shirts when they came to visit her. They asked few questions
about her stories because she anticipated what they wanted to
hear, and as they listened in the soft light they found magic in her
words. Their minds wandered dreamily when she spoke of fara-
way places.

Life in Georgia seemed to be less complex than the world of which Jeannette spoke. This was rural America, comfortably detached from the high living of the prosperous urban centers.

A bucket was made do for a sink. Pecan and fruit trees provided the shade for the house and larder for the pantry. Breathing old Southern tunes on a jew's harp was the heart of family entertainment. In the morning, when the bright sun burned the dew off the ground and sticky perspiration drove them to the swimming hole, life in Georgia would be the same for the little boys. But in the encroaching darkness of the summer evening, Jeannette brought the world to them.

Caught in the web of her smooth persuasiveness, the boys did not bother to wonder what had brought her to Georgia. Yet the story affecting Jeannette Rankin the most is a story she did not tell them.

Her strong constituency had been bashed apart by the temperament of the changing times. Suddenly the crowds were gone, the cheering was muffled. Jeannette was left to lick her wounds, and the very real danger existed that her political future was yet another casualty of the war. Facing the post-war years actually was a greater challenge for Jeannette than having won a seat in Congress, for now she stood alone. She had gambled that America was ready for the voice of women in federal government and lost; now she must pick up the pieces of her career and start anew.

In Georgia, Jeannette began the first psychologically trying test of her professional career. She was greatly humbled, having been deprived of her forum for social change. Now she had no platform, no constituency and no title. She was unemployed and convinced she had bled her final political fortunes from Montana.

But most heinous of all the calamaties that had befallen Jeannette was that war had emerged the victor during the potent years of her life when she emulated love. Politically she had seen war as a complicated set of circumstances arranged by special interest groups for profit. Personally she saw war as a pestilent single entity to be battled for the sake of survival. Although temporarily browbeaten, she quietly pledged lifelong opposition to this political disease, and revamped her personal style to meet the challenge.

While in Congress she had become enchanted with the mystique of the South, detecting a stronger current of anti-war feeling that she attributed to memories of the Civil War. She had observed from talking with Southern Congressmen:

> *The attitude of the South is toward peace, for another war would not necessarily mean more production, higher prices, and more grain. It is easier to talk to a people who are interested in humanity more than in cold dollars.*

With her philosophy of women and peace, Jeannette sought an environment in which her ideas could prosper, a place where she could build a constituency that would grow and influence peace campaigns in other states. She found in the South a fertile field of politics, pregnant with possibilities for a peace movement, for Southern Congressmen and the Southern press had led in criticizing American entry into war with Germany.

Among the notables were Claude Kitchen of North Carolina, who had struck the poignant scene in the House of Representatives about the moral atrocities of war, and editor Clark Howell of Georgia's *Atlanta Constitution*, who promised "tears will some day move all the women of the world to be consulted before the 'War Lords' tear their sons from their bosoms." And Jeannette, although remembering that Southerners vigorously had opposed suffrage, nonetheless praised them for conscionably questioning the morality of war.

The issue of war and peace was close to the maternal heart of Southern motherhood, and for that, Jeannette was fortunate. "What could I say to my son if war comes, if I take a stand against war?" asked a Southern mother.

"Surely," Jeannette replied, "you don't want to say to him, 'I haven't turned my hand to stop this war.'"

The woman thought a moment. "No, I don't. I'm with you."

But in her idealism Jeannette unsuspectingly was stumbling

into a hotbed of militarism. Even the chronic conflict she endured with her brother about peace ideas would not prove as formidable as the clash brewing in gentle Georgia.

Jeannette chose Georgia on the advice of friends, who suggested she settle near Athens where she could have the benefit of country living and still be near the state university. During the Christmas season of 1924 she paid $500 for a 64-acre farm near Bogart, 10 miles south of Athens.

It was an unlikely home for an emerging pacifist, miles away from the world of politics. The ground was a paradise of tangled honeysuckle and grapevines and wild plums and wild cherry, beckoning Jeannette to drop her load of worry and enter into its Garden of Eden. The fragrance of the flowers, the melody of the birds and the vivid reds and yellows and greens made the farm a deceptive place; a lulling world where war did not exist.

Yet, Jeannette had a plan. She promised to maintain a simple existence in Georgia when she needed a rest from her national politicking, but hidden in this simplicity was a purpose of extravagant proportions. Replete with a penniless lifestyle and a wealthy personal philosophy, Jeannette Rankin intended to convince the world that peace could succeed with a little feminine coaxing.

Georgia was to become her laboratory for an experiment, a 'center of infection,' from where a peace epidemic could spread.

"Aspasia is a pioneer," observed writer Katharine Anthony, who thought her good friend resembled in vision and intellect the Greek goddess of that name, who had led the women of Athens to revolt. "She would never buy a farm which others had cultivated. She likes to blaze trails for others to follow and plough new lands for others to cultivate. The edge of cultivation has no terrors for Aspasia. She would always go beyond the edge and set her plow in virgin soil."

At age 44, Jeannette had created a fourth base of political contact. The first was the frontier equalitarianism of the West. The second was the status quo Eastern Establishment. The third was the political heartbeat on Capitol Hill.

This new and quiet scheme to liberate women was innocent enough.

The farm had only acres of neglected land and a small cotton crib, standing like a silent sentinel as a testimonial to the challenge awaiting Jeannette. With no running water, no electricity and no toilet, the homestead was lost in the quiet of rural Georgia. Predictably, Jeannette bought it for these reasons.

Her first mission was to rebuild the farm into a prototype of self-sufficiency. With the help of two black sharecroppers who did the sawing and the nailing, Jeannette designed and constructed a functional one-room house intended to demonstrate a new lifestyle. Life in Georgia in the Twenties was mostly provincial, with poor sharecroppers struggling to rise out of the agrarian depression that had gripped them since the Civil War. To gain the confidence of the people with whom she would agitate for peace, Jeannette believed she could not display a facade of comparative wealth.

Jeannette hadn't lost her inherent will to be resourceful and frugal. With $75 a month from her father's estate, she found no difficulty in adjusting to poverty, neurotically finding indecency in displaying wealth.

Flamboyance and the waste of money were not hallmarks of her personality. Her growing hatred of the role of the dollar in the war profit system also contributed to the swiftness in which she adapted to the change.

The house was a unique expression of Jeannette's newfound ideology. Having no kitchen facilities in the main building, she extended a plank of wood to the rustic cotton crib, which became her cookhouse. She had no sink, so she drained water through a gasoline funnel sunk into the counter to the ground outside.

Although most homes in rural America had outhouses a breathless few hundred feet from the house, Jeannette rejected the notion and built her toilet inside a small closet in the cookhouse. The convenience of having the toilet handy to the house was negated by the bother of having to empty the apple box commode, which Jeannette pulled through a small trapdoor on the side of the cookhouse. Frequently she found herself taking a quick jaunt down the lane with commode in hand, watching nervously for unexpected visitors.

Jeannette drew her water from a well with a rope and a bucket. Light came from lanterns and candles. Heat was supplied by steam from a car radiator, which Jeannette had improvised along one wall. Water pipes ran from the radiator to the fireplace, where the water was heated.

The plain, whitewashed house — which ceremoniously she named the White House — hardly was fitting for an ex-Congresswoman, especially the *first* ex-Congresswoman. But Jeannette enjoyed the trivialities that made her a rebel among her contemporaries, as a modern-day hippie gone back to the land. She slept in the screened porch until the water froze in her glass on the night stand. Reluctantly, as if disturbed by autumn's calling, she moved her bed inside her house for colder weather.

Although this spartan existence seemingly conflicted with Jeannette's opinion that women should have the power to better conditions in the home, she was at ease. By the time she moved to Georgia, she casually had dispensed with social convention.

She had been booed, ostracized, insulted and spat upon. Of what consequence was it to her that traditionalists condemned her for stirring up trouble in politics instead of being home with a husband, caring for children, and planning a card party for the second Thursday of the month?

She was not a woman to exhibit frills and false impressions. Her stubborn insistence to forge ahead without patronizing the expectations of society had not been without its frustrations, however, since at middle age she found herself single and often lonely, married only to the cause of reform.

Even as a girl, Jeannette had behaved as a serious young woman ignored by adolescence. Her practicality would not allow her to be giddy, selfish or frivolous. Her young sister Harriet was carefree and lively with the boys, who came merrily to the Rankin home to date her, and more than once Jeannette had watched from dark corners with a tinge of jealousy. Jeannette had wanted to have boyfriends, but she lacked the patience for what she saw as the silly details and formalities that accompanied such relationships.

As a grown woman, she looked back on a few romantic interests, but none of the men she had known had inspired her to marriage; clearly she avoided it as a threat to her independence.

She was fond of joking about marriage, partly from the pleasure of seeing men subdued by women, partly from the fear of being subdued herself. She was asked by a Boston woman about the possibility of a woman president, and replied: "Why, certainly. It is inevitable, and more important, even desirable. That time is not very distant — probably 50 years, possibly sooner."

"Will the men *want* a woman president?" she was asked.

"They'll be delighted," she said. "A man inherently likes to be governed by a woman. Matrimony proves that."

Marriage in the pre-World War II years demanded that women discard their opinions and assume those of the family leader — invariably the husband — with convention and grace. Jeannette, conversely, refused to be a chattel for a man, for she was motivated by an urge to be a leader of social causes. Such an autonomous personality precluded the gaiety and irrelevancies of being a 45-year-old single woman in the Jazz Age.

"My family always have [sic] been alarmed at the inclination I have to select unpopular causes, but at the present time I see no more urgent cause for women to back than...outlawing war," she told a Cleveland, Ohio, audience shortly after moving to Georgia.

Few people who knew Jeannette well believed Georgia was a retreat for relaxation between speeches and lobbying on Capitol Hill. Her mind always was active, even when she tilled the rich black soil in her garden. Behind every innocent appearance — including relieving oneself — was a purpose for living and learning. "I remember the outhouse in Bogart," said Dorothy McKinnon Brown, a niece. "I felt very sorry for myself, since we had *The Nation* and *The New Republic* for toilet paper, and very rough paper it was, while all our neighbors wiped on catalogues with slick paper."

Jeannette's aggressive, serious attitude toward life was exiled in Georgia, where she had the freedom to enjoy the contrast of blue-collar labor and white-collar intellectualism. The hot sun burned her skin a deep red, and she struck the pose of a struggling dirt farmer, an earthy woman gone back to the land. She could tease her supper from the garden one week and lecture intelligently and forcefully before the staid faces of a Congressional committee the next week.

She wore ragged clothes when she was at the farm, much to the dismay of her mother, who since her early years of marriage had bathed every afternoon and donned a fresh dress before her husband returned home from work. When Olive Rankin visited the farm, she habitually scolded Jeannette for not having changed out of her bathrobe for days.

Mrs. Rankin demanded to know how Jeannette could be serious about this business of lobbying for peace while so flippant with her appearance. Jeannette's opinion of clothes was simple. Why throw out a new pair of stockings if one had a flaw? Certainly one run did not make a stocking colder. She was not interested in wasting valuable time changing clothes when she could read a book or write a letter. In public, however, she always wore jewelry and pretty dresses, for she possessed a startling ability to make a plain dress look good by employing imaginative manuevers of needle and thread.

Although Jeannette left her farmhouse in early 1925 to accept a job as field secretary of the American Section of the Women's International League for Peace and Freedom, she returned during vacations.

She regularly invited people to stay for a few days, and added four bedrooms to accommodate guests. Inevitably dinner conversations turned to war and peace, and Jeannette became ecstatic, her eyes wandering among her guests with great excitement. If anyone said, "Oh, but you can't stop war," she threw up her hands in dismay and laughingly exclaimed, "Why do you say that? They said you couldn't stop cholera and you couldn't stop small pox, and women could never vote. I hate these nevers."

Her existence was not without its hypocrisy.

In a single-minded sense, she accepted money from her brother Wellington — a fervent believer of the patriotic implications of war — to help stock her cupboards and buy her gasoline so she could wage her private peace campaign. Wellington had ascended to the top of Montana politics. His quick mind served him well in the courtroom. He was shrewd like his father and steadily built his bank account, generously offering Jeannette money when she was in need: brotherly love simply was stronger than his distaste for her intensive peace activities.

In the seven years since leaving Congress, Jeannette had argued many of the ideas about women that had characterized her suffrage years. But as women won the right to vote in 1920 with the ratification of the federal amendment by Tennessee, she was envisioning that the ultimate reform — peace — was a woman's job. While Americans were singing, "Yes, We Have No Bananas," Jeannette was teaching Americans that the peace movement could bear fruit.

"The work of educating the world to peace is the woman's job, because men have a natural fear of being classed as cowards if they oppose war," serious-minded Jeannette told a Cleveland audience amid an era of short skirts and real estate booms.

Jeannette seemed eternally committed to the solemn side of life. Before coming to Georgia, she had matured from student to teacher, lobbying for the National Consumer's League and the International League for Peace and Freedom (WIL), the offspring of the Woman's Peace Party. Jeannette had helped found the League in Zurich, Switzerland, with Jane Addams and other American pacifists and feminists. In January 1920, the WIL had sent Jeannette as its delegate to Washington, D.C., to encourage the State Department to seek the early release of all prisoners of war and to suggest the release of political offenders.

In November 1920 she became field secretary for the National Consumer's League under the guidance of general secretary Florence Kelley of Pennsylvania, and her first assignment was to push for passage of the Sheppard-Towner Bill, the maternity measure she had introduced in the previous Congress as the Rankin-Robertson Bill.

For the next four years she lobbied primarily for state and federal legislation affecting women and children, struggling to make 'live issues' out of reform legislation. For a woman shy and timid when a college student, she was articulate and persuasive before college audiences, and spoke at universities in Iowa, Nebraska, Illinois, Kentucky, Ohio and Missouri. Aside from her salaried job with the National Consumer's League, she remained active in the WIL, and addressed its Fourth Congress in Washington, D.C., with the words:

> *The human spirit...must be won by a positive vision of a world at peace, a world in which life and not death is honored, humanity and not wealth is valued, love and not hate is practiced. A nation must see that war is a crime before there can be a spiritual awakening...to find another way out.*

Jeannette took a leave of absence in the spring of 1924 to return to Montana to assist Wellington in his senatorial campaign, and after his narrow defeat she quit the National Consumer's League to begin her Georgia experiment.

She confronted neighboring shopkeepers, newspaper editors, farmers and housewives with her ideas, and gradually expanded her influence to university intellectuals in Athens. By 1928 she had a circle of acquaintances with a common goal, and one evening they met in the one-room studio apartment of Lucy Stanton, a prominent Georgia painter, to form the Georgia Peace Society.

Jeannette was elected secretary, but retained control with a clause stating she had the power to call the meetings. The group comprised locally prominent women and men whose purpose was to study American foreign policy to encourage the settlement of international disputes by arbitration. Jeannette instigated most of the activities, and the society usually convened only when she was in Athens.

She was an unlikely companion to her colleagues, who had the impressive diplomas and the formal social status to back their convictions. They had wealth, education and prominence. She was a gadfly from the uncultured mountain folk of western Montana, possessing an ill-fitting college education and a rebel image.

They were consumers who talked of the effect of war on international trade over drinks at cocktail parties, while Jeannette lured dinner guests to her modest farmhouse and talked of the causes of war and how they could be eradicated. She granted less importance to the role of America in international consumerism than to discussions of war as a toxic substance that had infected the American political system.

Yet intellectually Jeannette was a leader among her university friends, for she better understood the plight of the working class American. In her deliberate pursuit of freedom she was a voice for the poor, the helpless, the radical and the minority, although she did not share their simple material-oriented views of happiness. She wanted to work for them but she was not one of them, for she envisioned a higher level of freedom than they sought for themselves.

While some members of the Georgia Peace Society scoffed that the masses were incapable of changing their destinies, Jeannette clung to her belief that the exchange of free ideas — particularly knowledge about the cause and antecedents of war — would generate social change among them.

Sometimes she scorned this vast majority, however, angry that her peace ideas did not seem to influence their thinking. Blaming this poor response on the lack of stimulation, she said because they suffered the repression of ideas they would not be intelligent enough to shake the misery of economic slavery. As early as 1917, for example, when Columbia University trustees dismissed two pacifists, she warned:

> As soon as suppression is applied...ideas which would normally find their way toward expression are forced back to smoulder in the mind.... From such suppression come [sic] our dullards and our so-called 'industrial fanatics.' From such suppression comes a sharper and sharper cleavage between social factions.... The danger lies in forcing advanced ideas

*upon the minds of those untrained, unintelligent masses to
whom revolution means only sabotage.*

Jeannette remained persistently optimistic that the working
class — particularly the unliberated woman — could see the value
of working for peace. But her involvement with the Athens college crowd demonstrated her Progressive belief that social
change must be taught by intellectual activists such as herself,
before it could be spontaneous among the masses, sick of being
oppressed; a change precipitated only by people willing to work
for it.

By the Thirties, American pacifists sensed fresh threats of war.
Japan in 1931 had invaded and was occupying Manchuria in
defiance of the Kellogg-Briand Peace Pact.

"Do you want to help China?" she was asked by a militarist.

"Of course I want to help China," she replied, "but I am not
going to throw myself out of a 17th story window to help China."

American sentiment against war had cooled during the 'Flap-
per Era,' and pacifists sensed a new urgency in their work.
Jeannette Rankin was sufficiently disappointed that women were
not using the power of the ballot to prevent war.

She had quit the International League for Peace and Freedom,
and after a stint with the Women's Peace Union, she wrote
Frederick Libby, executive director of the National Council for
Prevention of War (NCPW), who had suggested she direct a
proposed NCPW regional office in Atlanta for expenses only.
Then Libby postponed the project — the first of many disappointments Jeannette would face in her 10-year stint with the
NCPW — and she wrote him angrily: "Nobody wants me. I hate
day-to-day jobs and have had them all my life." Finally she was
employed as a salaried field secretary, but because her paychecks
were small and irregular, the work mostly was honorary.

That was the price of her cause, however, and Jeannette was
prepared to meet the commitment with her self-induced poverty.
While the Georgia Peace Society, and other Rankin ventures,
such as the Georgia Conference on the Cause and Cure of War,
had succeeded in creating an awareness, Jeannette had been
unable to satisfy the intent of the Georgia experiment.

She found an opportunity to awake the state's support when, under the auspices of the NCPW, she started a debate with Carl Vinson, a prominent war hawk from the Sixth Congressional District.

In 1931, Jeannette conducted a referendum poll in Georgia to oppose a $616-million naval building bill. Vinson had introduced the bill into Congress after he was named chairman of the House Naval Affairs Committee. Jeannette viewed the bill as an insult to the taxpayer, and Vinson's home newspaper, *The Macon Telegraph*, agreed. "It is absurd for a nation with a tremendous deficit to go spending money on 'shooting irons' when it will have to buy bread for a great many of its family," the newspaper said in an editorial.

To support her pro-peace stand, Jeannette received 159 postcards from 62 towns protesting the bill and she presented them to Vinson during lunch one day. He accurately accused her of trying to build support to defeat the bill when it came to a vote in Congress.

Because of pressure from Jeannette and her satellite groups — the Georgia Peace Society and the Georgia Committee on Disarmament — the bill died in committee.

Much to her chagrin, the Vinson bill resurfaced in 1933 and passed the next year, and contrary to her predictions, Vinson was re-elected to Congress by a three-to-one margin over his opponent.

By 1934 Jeannette had built a reputation in Georgia as a woman forever doing things women weren't supposed to do, things not in vogue with the times. She continually was out of step with history, but her work was fashionable, as the era of anti-war specialty groups was in full swing. Lobbies such as the NCPW and the Georgia Peace Society flourished because workaholics such as Jeannette Rankin made them go. They were not the will of the people, however, as was the anti-war movement of the Vietnam War era.

Personalities built the anti-war groups of the Thirties, but they did not build public opinion. Struggling under the influence of the Depression, Americans were less interested in world war than being fed and clothed. In this climate, Jeannette was unequivocally branded a 'pacifist,' and although she never forgot she was working for the liberation of women, she adopted the label in reference to herself.

Her work had few rewards. If she gave a speech and received promises in return, she knew she had done her job well; if she was given money, she had gained a convert; if she won a volunteer, she had lessened the forces of war by one. The psychology of dissent was not for gentle minds, for Jeannette endured a vicious daily routine that exhausted most enthusiasts, and she struggled for nine years to build an awareness in Georgia.

Sometimes in her tortured dedication she behaved as a woman crazed by the fear of failure and driven by the lust for success. She enjoyed vacations in Montana and projected moments of leisure to casual observers, yet within her mind was a cancerous infatuation with her work. The securing of peace appeared to be Jeannette's single chosen destiny; alternately she would be forced to consider herself a failure. In 1933, complaining to Libby about a speaking tour she would begin, she wrote:

> *I don't know how I could possibly spend three months travel-ing and survive. It is going to be very difficult for me to keep going for the three months of the Western trip. It is quite necessary for me to be at home to relax and secure courage to go out and face the cold, stupid world again.... To put it mildly, making people listen to me is part of the work that appeals to me very little.*

But Jeannette persevered, sensing the approach of war. She was in no danger of being aloof and misguided, as *Public Opinion Quarterly* forecast a shadow of war crossing the face of the earth. Her battle was one against the world, for she spoke of foreign powers as if they were little children. In a mood of futility and anger, she again wrote to Libby:

> *I am feeling very much let down, after making twenty-two speeches and driving the car over a thousand miles, getting more than sixty resolutions with every congressional district in*

*Georgia represented, and spending one whole night catching
a train, then to have England and France acting like stupid
children.... Roosevelt decides to build tanks and airplanes
while the Disarmament Conference is still struggling.*

Yet Jeannette's compelling love for peace supplanted all other
concerns. She challenged public opinion, militarism and even
Franklin D. Roosevelt. Hours were spent in sorrow at her losses,
but she always fought again.

Her careening Georgia escapades nearly ended in a crash,
however, when she was weakened and embittered by a flagrant
attack on her personal integrity that caused her more consternation than withstanding the anger of the entire nation to her vote
for peace in 1917.

One of the darkest times in her life came in 1934, when she was
swept into a bitter feud with the American Legion. This symbolized Jeannette's drift away from the prevailing conservative
mood depicted in Upton Sinclair's *Main Street,* and exemplified
the growing struggle between pacifists and militarists, and
Jeannette's mistaken assumption that Georgia would offer little
resistance to her peace epidemic.

If she had considered the impact of the squabble on public
opinion — most Georgia newspapers actively endorsed her de-
fensively and her cause received immense publicity — she would
have been grateful she had gained a measure of renown in exchange for a little bad press.

Yet beneath Jeannette's tough exterior was a fear of personal
attacks, and she soon became encumbered with a nebulous controversy. Her personality underwent a startling change. Suddenly, this fighter for peace, a leader of women and an aggressor
for human rights, found herself retreating from militarists for
more than two years.

The controversy had started with a commendation from the
Georgia Peace Society for her work in Georgia. Rabbi Abraham
Shusterman of the Athens Synagogue had said of Jeannette, on
behalf of the Society:

She had induced us with the conviction that the individual effort is meaningful and efficacious.... She has brought us the enthusiasm to make ours a truly moral nation.... Finally, Miss Rankin has brought us a new vision of the meaning of democracy.

Jeannette's prominence earned her a contract for a series of lectures at Brenau College, a female liberal arts institution in Gainesville, 60 miles from Atlanta in the Blue Ridge Mountains. She arrived for the first lecture on Oct. 25, 1934. Vice President H.J. Pearce Jr., administering the college in the absence of his father, introduced Jeannette to journalism and political science students as a likely candidate for a 'Chair of Peace' that Brenau College trustees were thinking about establishing. An overzealous news reporter jotted down her notes and raced from the room. The next day, the *Atlanta Constitution* reported Brenau College already had established a Chair of Peace and Jeannette Rankin had been hired as the first 'Professor of Peace.'

The story stirred to action the American Legion's Atlanta Post No. 1, which had seethed with rage for many years over Jeannette's influence of "the young womanhood of the South" and her pointed remarks concerning American military expenditures.

This was the first indication that Georgia had been simmering with discontent about Jeannette's peace antics, and the Legion wanted to drag her into a perilous controversy to force her to stop teaching 'communistic' principles.

Kenneth Murrell, commander of the Atlanta post, promised that the American Legion would resist stubbornly any efforts by Brenau College to teach pacifism to its students. He talked of a spirit of unrest and uneasiness throughout the world, and warned that to create an interest in any 'ism' other than Americanism among youth was branded by his organization as 'un-Americanism.'

Pearce reacted angrily that the nature of the proposed chair was misunderstood by the Legion, suggesting an inquiry before action would have prevented confusion.

The fight had begun. Jeannette faded temporarily from the scene, as the Legion focused its initial assault on Brenau. The college and the American Legion traded jabs until Pearce, speaking for his father, Brenau President H.J. Pearce Sr., told an Atlanta newspaper he could not accept such righteous statements as the true sentiment of the American Legion. Cleverly, he suggested Murrell must have been misquoted, saying neither Washington, Jefferson, Lincoln, President Wilson, Jesus nor the Apostle Paul would be acceptable as Americans under the restrictions to which he was credited.

The Legion left the Brenau administration smarting from the hurt and focused on Jeannette, who had described war as "a mad dog that should be locked up." She had spent long hours staring across the Georgia countryside with the unsettling controversy fresh in mind, and was thankful the Pearces had come to her defense, yet saddened that much of their interest was inspired by the publicity being enjoyed by the college.

"Atlanta Post No. 1 does not want the school of thought propagated by Miss Rankin to take root in the south or anywhere else," Murrell wrote in a letter to the Brenau vice president. "We will use our efforts to counteract the influence which Brenau will exert with Jeanette [sic] Rankin as a member of its faculty."

The Legionnaires received little sympathy in their plight to save Georgia from Jeannette Rankin.

"Why is it that supposedly responsible Georgians are so fond of making themselves ludicrous?" asked the Richmond *News Leader* of Virginia. "Is there something in the atmosphere down there which is conducive to such antics?" The Memphis *Commerical-Appeal* of Tennessee said the Legionnaires were being hypocritical in assailing a college and a woman dedicated to the understanding of war and peace. "It seems rather ridiculous, therefore, that there should be raised a great outcry against the appointment of Miss Jeanette [sic] Rankin," the newspaper said.

Chortled the *Gainesville Eagle* of Georgia:

> *As we see it, the Legionaires [sic] of Atlanta went off half-cocked, are most unwise in their choice of words, and are making accusations unfounded by the facts. The only way their act would be justifiable, as we see it, would be for Miss*

Rankin to be a rabid pacifist, unwilling to protect her nation's honor and integrity at any cost and preferring, instead, to turn the country to an invader rather than fight. Knowing Miss Rankin, we know this to be untrue.

Although the Great Depression threatened any chance of money for a Chair of Peace anyway, the arguments continued. As if begging for an opportunity to decide the question of the right to agitate for peace, college professors, students, national news magazines and friends sided with Jeannette.

"We say welcome to Miss Rankin," said the Brenau student newspaper in an editorial. "Welcome to all those whose desire it is to build of America a more wonderful nation. We are not Hottentots, not Communists, nor radically free thinkers. We are Americans interested in the affairs of our country." Editorialized *The New Republic*, a national news opinion magazine: "If the American Legionaires [sic] thought they could turn Miss Rankin from her purposes, they were naive. Having braved the ill wind of a whole nation, it is not likely she will be disturbed by empty flag waving and a few harsh words."

But she was. In a two-page typed letter to the president of Brenau, Jeannette felt compelled to defend herself.

"The sum of my reputed radicalism seems to be my opposition to war, to competitive armaments and to predatory interests," she wrote the elder Pearce. "I have no quarrel with the American Legion. I grant them the same American and constitutional freedom of conscience and freedom of speech which I claim for myself."

H.J. Pearce Sr. accused the Legion of throttling freedom of speech by attempting to dictate what subjects should be taught at the college. He invited Murrell and 11 Legionnaires to dine in the college dormitory one Sunday afternoon and listen to Jeannette speak in the college auditorium that evening. Murrell refused, objecting to Jeannette's renowned pacifism.

The upheaval was calmed only temporarily when Pearce met with a committee of Legionnaires in his office, who agreed to speak on peace from their point of view. The first lecturer was

Capt. A.L. Hensen, director of the Veteran Service Bureau in Atlanta, who argued that the draft was a peace measure.

Meanwhile, the Brenau board of trustees was collecting money for the Chair of Peace. Fifty thousand dollars would be devoted to the salary of the professor and $100,000 would be used to establish a Department of Peace, hardly a modest sum while many Americans starved. Faculty members generally assumed the college president would recommend Jeannette as the first occupant of the new chair.

Brenau hoped the disciplines of economics, politics, international law, diplomacy, international finance and history could shed light on the causes and costs of war. Despite the wide scope of the intended Chair of Peace, the Brenau faculty did not balk at the inadequacy of Jeannette's formal education, which included none of the subjects they wished her to teach. Decades of self study had erased concern for her early background but had not minimized the impact of her poor spelling and her distaste for writing.

The Brenau controversy came amid post-Depression rebuilding and the dream of a peace professorship died for a lack of hard cash.

Resentment toward Jeannette's presence continued, however. Macon had changed to a hotbed of conservatism since the *Evening News* had lauded Jeannette's efforts with the Georgia Peace Society six years earlier.

W.T. Anderson, who edited the *Evening News* and the *Macon Telegraph*, characterized Jeannette in an editorial as a moral loser whose friends were pacifists, defeatists and communists. He accused her of trying to undermine the manhood and patriotism of America, and complained that her vote against American entry into war in 1917 had helped give the Germans the impression America would not fight, therefore prolonging the war. "All this pacifism just invites war, and the more encouragement given to the people of the Rankin type, the more certain is disaster," he wrote.

The Macon critics quieted their attacks for several months, but when Jeannette returned to the area in October 1935 to build public sentiment for the Kellogg-Briand Peace Pact, she was libeled viciously as a woman "fired from the faculty of one of the South's finest schools."

An innocuous Legionnaire named Bill Janes wrote in an *Evening News* column headed "Up Pops the Devil" that Jeannette was branded a rank communist in Atlanta district court and was accused of belonging to several communist organizations. Janes claimed Georgia newspapers had commended the American Legion for exposing Jeannette and said she was preaching doctrines that were unAmerican and not needed in Georgia.

Jeannette returned to her boarding house at Sandersville that evening to find a copy of the *Evening News* on the porch. She was shocked by the allegations and showed the column to her landlady. "Look what they said in the paper," Jeannette groaned, slapping the newspaper. The woman looked puzzled. "Isn't it true?" she asked.

Jeannette believed the column and the ensuing publicity threatened to destroy her peace work in Georgia, and privately, she appealed for support from Roger Baldwin of the American Civil Liberties Union, Frederick Libby of the National Council for Prevention of War, and Fiorella LaGuardia, an old friend from Congress who had been elected mayor of New York City. "Their continuous stories that I am a communist are getting quite unbearable," she wrote LaGuardia, hoping he would assure her not to worry. "If I sue, I may need your deposition that I am not a Communist. It seems silly to worry about it, but they have some queer laws in Georgia and the people take them rather seriously."

Jeannette asked the American Civil Liberties Union to provide evidence she was not a communist. Baldwin advised her to reconsider suing the *Evening News,* suggesting newspapers band together when in trouble. Earlier, however, he had expressed his private concern for her predicament. "What a tough bunch you ran into," he wrote in a pencilled scrawl at the bottom of an official letter.

After Jeannette decided to sue Bill Janes and the *Evening News* for libel, Libby responded to her plea for help. The executive board of the National Council for Prevention of War voted to give her $500 to decrease the legal fees, stipulating somewhat condescendingly that she hire a competent lawyer. She employed Walter G. Cornett, an Athens attorney, who promptly filed a $50,000 libel suit, believing any three statements made by Janes were sufficient to win the case. Cornett wrote Harry F. Ward, chairman of the American Civil Liberties Union, that Jeannette...

> *will stand or fall in the State by the results of this case and, of course, if she is driven out of Georgia she will be followed elsewhere by the same forces. We Georgians have prejudices deep rooted in our back-ground [sic].*

Although depressed and disgusted by the growing reaction in Georgia toward peace in general and herself in particular, Jeannette hoped the libel suit would vindicate her from the barrage of rightist propaganda, and would encourage more responsible newspaper reporting of the pacifist cause. Experience had taught her that newspapers often made misrepresentations and failed to correct them. She believed the only alternative was to bring suit and have the facts established in court.

H.J. Pearce Sr. supported Jeannette, writing in a letter to the editor of the *Evening News* that he was in thorough sympathy with those people who were trying to establish Americanism, but greatly saddened by the rabid attacks on 'good Americans' such as Jeannette Rankin. Editor Anderson felt the pressure, but not until more than a year after the libel occurred did *The Macon News Printing Company* offer to settle out of court for $1,000 and a published retraction.

Jeannette accepted reluctantly. She was fatigued by two years of vicious criticism and hateful deceit, and she wanted to forget the matter. She did so with regret, having hoped the publicity of a jury trial would have forced a fresh look at peace and exposed the people who had contrived the attacks. "They gave me $1,000 and said I was a nice lady," she said of the experience.

Anderson printed a front-page retraction. "She is held in the highest esteem for the sincerity of her efforts," he observed. "She has an international reputation as a pacifist. This newspaper disagreed with her only in the matter of disarmament."

Most of the ammunition used to make war on Georgia's leading peace advocate apparently had been lifted from an outrageous, self-published book entitled *The Red Network*, which listed Jeannette among 1,300 Americans accused of belonging to communist, socialist, radical, anarchist and International Workers of the World-controlled organizations. The book was written by Elizabeth Dilling, a woman convinced she must expose "the truth about the Communist-Socialist world conspiracy."

Dilling ambitiously listed the names of the suspected organizations and the people affiliated with them, and the American Legion, believing the book to be a bible for its cause, bought copies and sold them in Georgia for $1 each to document its allegations about Jeannette.

The settled court case marked the end of one of the most tortured times in Jeannette Rankin's life. Had she not experienced such image roasting before, the American Legion might have driven her from Georgia. Instead she turned on the militarists in defiance — although she cherished scarcely half a victory for two years of agony — and with 14 volunteers at her command, campaigned intensely to defeat Carl Vinson for re-election. His district included Macon and Sandersville, where she found little support.

Nobody stepped forward to campaign against Vinson, Jeannette ran short of money, and he was re-elected by such a large majority that she believed she had guaranteed his victory by her mere presence in his district. "I am very tired," she confided to Libby after Vinson had been renominated. "If we would only make peace a hot issue."

Jeannette's supposition that Georgia was an ideal anti-war state had been shadowed by the Bureau incident and the Janes libel suit, accentuating her portentous confidence in social change. Being eternally optimistic in the will of the people to better their destinies, she sometimes overlooked the evils lurking below the surface of humanity. Would not the same state that allowed the

Ku Klux Klan to prosper try to obstruct a woman dedicated to civil rights among nations?

As one woman wrote in 1930, Georgia unquestionably was the stronghold of "militarism, professional patriots and rotten politicians." Jeannette's Georgia experiment was a personal failure, for while grassroots stumping had proved useful during the fight for suffrage, American society had evolved into an era of big business where dollars for war dwarfed pennies for peace.

Jeannette in 1933 had complained in frustration that "we are walking in the direction of war and we can get a war anytime the munitions makers and profit makers demand it." Money, she argued, was the motive for war, and she told a Congressional committee:

> *You should pay $30 or whatever the soldier's wage is, to everyone, and let everyone have a tin cup and bread card and subsist on the same food that the soldier does, beginning with the President. For members of Congress who have voted for war, not only the $30 a month but also the honor of carrying the flag in battle, so that they would feel that they are doing their bit.*

Angered that American mothers' sons had died on foreign battlefields to support profiteers in their luxury living, she sensed she must contrast human needs with the dollar to demonstrate war was not patriotic.

At the 20th anniversary of American entry into World War I, Jeannette emerged a leader once again, using ploys such as banner-carrying children — "War Will Make Us Lame, Blind, Orphans, Armless, and Humpbacked" — to demonstrate war was a dead issue without the power of the dollar.

"If we do not crystalize public opinion we are going directly to war because the munitions makers...must use up their stockpiles."

(Jeannette Rankin quoted in a Michigan newspaper in 1934)

LOBBYING FOR PEACE
Chapter 8

The year was 1937. With the advent of swing and the big band craze of Benny Goodman, Tommy Dorsey and Glenn Miller, sentimental movies such as "The Wizard of Oz," and radio that had a mood and taste for everyone, the financial and social consequences of the Great Depression seemed to evaporate in a riotous celebration. Even the ominous cold winds of recession that blew into America in the autumn didn't shake the confidence of people wanting more of life than dread and discord.

Jeannette Rankin shunned the jubilee of arts, music, sports, literature and drama, and foreboded tragedy.

America was alive with ways to spend money, enjoying movies, automobiles, books, magazines, phonograph records and legal drinking with the repeal of Prohibition, and Jeannette, too, emerged from the somber isolationism of the early Thirties enjoying a fresh role in life. She was a leader among the pacifists, predicting the onslaught of war and trying to stop it.

A large majority of Americans polled believed the nation should have avoided involvement in World War I, and

Jeannette's ideas were popular again. She was telling Americans the greatest abuse of their money defied the happiness of their national rebirth, fearing that unless the profit was taken out of war, the 'flaming youth' of the Twenties would become quite literal.

From the Congressional office of the National Council for Prevention of War in downtown Washington, D.C., she gazed across bustling Northwest 17th Street to the State Department, a symbol of authority on which she affixed a stare of apprehension and distrust. Jeannette urged Americans never to forget the horrors of World War I.

"Be not satisfied with a reprint...about profiteers in Europe, but insist upon having information regarding our own American patriots who are willing to give the life of your son for their profit," she insisted. And in the midst of economic greed she wondered what had happened to the "traditional responsibility from time immemorial to care for the children, to nurse the sick, to feed the hungry, and to protect the old."

Any reader of current affairs could learn of the atrocities behind the scenes. Page after page told of the sanctimonious profiteering by corporate racketeers, and Jeannette feared that unless public opinion was crystalized in favor of peace, the munitions makers would force a war to deplete their stockpiles.

The Senate's Special Munitions Investigating Committee — more commonly known as the Nye Committee — in 1935 had paraded before its benches tales of outrage about the corporate encouragement or war. Charging that armament firms bribed government officials, disregarded national policies, sold weapons to enemy countries, lobbied for military appropriations and thrived on excess profit, the committee accused the 'Big Three' — Bethlehem Steel, Newport News and New York Shipbuilding — of collusive bidding on naval expenditures in 1933 to drive up profits and minimize competition.

Assistant Secretary of the Navy Henry L. Roosevelt and Navy Admirals Land and Robinson, asked to explain why they had failed to defend the nation's pocketbook, testified they were ignorant of the cost of shipbuilding, and were unaware whether the corporations had conspired to raise prices. Investigator Steven Raushenbush was astonished. He demanded to know why the naval administration was not suspicious of Bethlehem's $3,542,000 increase in bidding within seven months on identical ships. Sen. Arthur Vandenburg was shocked that the Navy, in its ignorance, appeared to be linked to the conspiracy.

Jeannette Rankin, however, was not surprised. She believed the entire military system was structured to encourage collusion with enterprising corporations. "Is the Navy for the defense of our shores? Or to protect American private property on other continents?" she wondered aloud many times.

Even as early as 1933 she had argued before Congress that war was fought for economic profit. In testimony on the exporting of arms and munitions, she had debated with Melvin Maas of the House Foreign Affairs Committee:

Maas: "Do you believe that traffic in munitions is in itself a cause of war?"

Rankin: "Yes, I believe that wars in the past have been started that way."

Maas: "It appears that the real causes of war are economic."

Rankin: "Yes...under the economic system war eventually comes, but in the meantime we can get rid of this habit. If we develop the habit of peace and think in terms of peace, we could cease to operate under the militaristic system."

Maas: "I still contend that to solve the problems of war you have to solve economic problems and not militaristic problems. The militaristic follows as an incident of the economic...."

Rankin: "The militaristic system forces an economic problem upon us...."

During the Depression when luck was laid low, Americans were not interested when Jeannette spoke of the threats to their pocketbooks. Now, with glaring facts of profit flaunting, Jeannette spoke with authority.

A $1,300,000 bonus had been awarded to Eugene Grace, president of the Bethlehem Steel Corporation, for the production of ships and steel in 1917. A World War I profit for the United States Steel Corporation exceeded one billion dollars, equal to the pay of two million American soldiers in the trenches and fields of France. A $32 million profit — a 200 percent increase — was enjoyed by the Utah Copper Company in 1917. The meat packers — Armour, Swift, Morris, Cudahy — had tripled their profits in 1917. The flour mills, the button makers, the shirt manufacturers with their 'educational orders' for war....

Jeannette explained to the House of Representatives committee on military affairs that anti-profit legislation only blinded Americans into thinking war could be fought without profit. Conscription had to be enacted during World War I, she argued, because otherwise the poor man was unwilling to fight a rich man's war.

One of the anti-profit bills she criticized most intently was the McSwain resolution, which put a ceiling on industrial profiteering. She called the bill a hoax and a sham because it promised to lull Americans into a false sense of security.

By early 1935, she already had heard numerous bills presented to take the profit out of war, all of which seemed to elude the target she wanted perforated: the people who made money from the deaths of American soldiers, sailors, marines and pilots. "It is perfectly possible to take the profit out of war," she testified. "But it is not possible by any of the schemes rich men suggest, and you haven't had any proposals for taking the profit out of war from the poor man."

She was asked: "So you think we made a mistake in going to war with Germany?"

"I made no mistake, I am sure of that. I voted against it," she replied.

"Who won?" asked another committee member.

"We all lost," a colleague answered.

"Who won the San Francisco earthquake?" asked another.

"You can no more win a war than you can win an earthquake," Jeannette observed.

She loved to fight, but she had particular distaste for battlefields and killing.

And Jeannette cried from podium and panel that the greed of these war producers was leading America into another world conflict. Her exasperated attacks on the merchants of death who testified ignorance before Congressional committees made her a leader among people feeling a moral duty in exposing the corruption.

Who was responsible for this subtle, but tragic, aggression? Jeannette blamed the munitions makers, who built the actual implements and materials of war — cannon, guns, ammunition, tanks, military aircraft and naval vessels — and the allied banking, industrial and commercial firms that profited by war. She fumed that the greatest threat to peace was the barrage of rightist propaganda portraying war as decent, honorable and patriotic.

Jeannette thought the issue of military preparedness, for example, which justified the expenditure of billions of dollars for the sake of national 'defense,' was a misnomer.

She contended the military was being armed not for defense of American shores, but for the possibility of foreign invasion to protect American financial investments in foreign countries. "The word 'preparedness,' according to its most frequent present use, comes under the title, 'deception as a fine art,' " Jeannette had quoted Charles A. Lindbergh Sr. in one of her radio speeches. "It was seized on by the war-munition lords as a substitute for 'armament,' because armament would suggest what was really meant."

In the 20 years since Jeannette's dramatic vote against war with Germany, her hair had gone white and her face was fuller. She had lost the youthful innocence marking her introduction to Congress in 1917.

During the succeeding two decades, she frequently visited Congress as a lobbyist, giving thousands of words of testimony to committees on disarmament, profiteering and military appropriations. Despite her apparent fanaticism with peace, her relentless attacks on war propagandists earned her the reputation of an elder stateswoman and inspired one expert to conclude she was the best lobbyist Capitol Hill had seen.

Such deliberate suspicion of the insurmountable powers of government and the corporations that pushed it to the brink of war found unabashed admiration in the eyes of many people, including Gaylord Douglass, a faculty member of the Wellesley Institute in Boston and like Jeannette, an associate secretary of the National Council for Prevention of War. He wrote Frederick Libby concerning Jeannette: "Politically and personally, she is incomparable." A friend to Douglass had said succinctly: "She brings the most challenging message we have ever had. If there was a Jeannette Rankin in every state our country would never go to war."

Libby, as Jeannette, was a long-time peace agitator who once again enjoyed the thrill that his ideas were in vogue, and he capitalized on her leadership qualities. In a letter to Management Ernest Briggs Inc., a New York speaking bureau, he explained that Jeannette...

> is one of the most attractive women speakers in the public eye today. Her vote against the World War when it meant political suicide was just like her. She has convictions for which she is willing to die any time but fortunately lives to give brilliant expression to them with a force and sincerity that carry conviction.

Having worked for the National Council for Prevention of War for eight years, Jeannette was tired and wanted to go to her Georgia farm for a rest. The Congressional work had been unusually demanding, with Libby pushing her for more results.

He had circulated a prospectus promoting the reputation of the NCPW via the public distinction of Jeannette Rankin.

She was only one of 18 associate secretaries with the NCPW, but Libby's bold gesture in trying to cast the weight of its convictions on her slender shoulders did not surprise her. She had been using the reputation of the NCPW for years, to the same advantage. She didn't mind shouldering the load, but she barely had money to cover her expenses and soon became downright adamant that Libby fill his letters with cash instead of apologies.

The NCPW publicly promoted Jeannette to lunch-counter

Rotary Clubs and cautious school superintendents as a stirring, majestic, intellectual speaker, and privately heralded her as a smooth and seductive persuader with a talent to cajole and convince.

"The most startling and truthful of statements uttered by John Doe is *not* news but a far less interesting statement by Jeanette [sic] Rankin...*is* decidedly news," the prospectus said.

Nationwide lobbying by peace advocates such as the National Council for Prevention of War and peace advocates like Jeannette Rankin had become so intense by 1937 that it culminated in a battle with pro-war advocates to win the confidence of the American on the street.

Public Opinion Quarterly estimated the presence of 50 national 'patriotic' organizations, 27 national peace organizations, and 43 national organizations whose activities enhanced international understanding. High school students assembled to hear a pacifist speak on one day, and heard pro-war comments from the Veterans of Foreign Wars the next day.

Among other organizations representing the militarists' point of view were the American Legion, the Daughters of the American Revolution, the United Spanish War Veterans, and the Navy League of the United States. Resisting the militarists' arguments and generating propaganda of their own were groups such as the NCPW, the Fellowship of Reconciliation, the War Resisters League and the League for Industrial Democracy. The noncommitted American was caught in a vicious swirl of propaganda.

The tool of mass education succeeded in deluging school and home mailboxes with instructions explaining how to join any particular movement. Full-page advertisements graphically portraying the horror of war competed with full-page advertisements boasting the glory and honor of military preparedness.

One of Jeannette's favorite tools for peace propaganda was George Gershwin's Broadway musical, "Strike Up The Band," and she particularly liked one verse: "We're in a bigger, better war for your patriotic past-time. We don't know what we're fighting for, but we didn't know the last time."

Hard-hitting books like Engelbrecht and Hanighen's *Merchants of Death*, Charles Beard's *The Devil Theory of War*, and Walter Millis' *The Road to War* contained painstaking documentation of careful plans by profiteers to enhance business by supplying belligerent nations — including Germany — with food, clothing and munitions for their armies. The books were released at the zenith of the munitions issue in 1934 and offered considerable support to war critics who howled that economic collusion in years preceding 1917 would happen again.

While the Nye Committee was uncovering economic motives for war, a lengthy article in *Fortune* magazine entitled "Arms and the Men" revealed Germany was arming, with the help of her fearful European neighbors and American profiteers. The National Council for Prevention of War circulated 100,000 reprints.

Jeannette used these revelations to her advantage. She argued repeatedly that American public opinion was being manipulated in an elaborate scheme to promote war in the interest of dollars. She blamed financial pressure by controlling corporations for America's entry into World War I, and believed the jingoistic press had facilitated corporate domination of public opinion with lavish editorials on the merits of 'patriotism,' and the unquestioning publication of news dispatches from war zones.

Admirals of the United States Navy shuddered when Jeannette borrowed their testimony to document her contentions that munitions makers, shipbuilders and others were spending two million dollars a day for propaganda to support war. Jeannette, in an appearance before the Senate Committee on Naval Affairs in 1934, had fumed bluntly that the scheme of the militarists should be apparent to anyone who had wanted to see the truth.

To Jeannette, construction of a new fleet of ships would serve two purposes only: armed transportation or security for commerce ships to expedite profiteering, or transportation of military forces overseas.

Liberally quoting a popular national news article written by Wayne Francis Palmer, a former naval officer, Jeannette described how a fleet of ships was obsolete in the days of bombing planes. She said ships could operate only if the enemy overlooked the potential of smoke screens and scrambled wire communications, which as Palmer had written, would make ships "deaf and dumb."

The economic term 'patriotism' particularly incensed Jeannette, for she believed it had been fabricated by the corporate world to insinuate that anyone failing to support America in its war activities was a traitor. She pointed in vain to the General Pact for the Renunciation of War, instigated by America and signed by 63 nations. She knew America faced difficulty in conforming to the rules of the pact because propaganda from the profiteers was overwhelming. War always had been legal, honorable, justifiable and 'patriotic' — the history books were quick to find romance even in the tragic Civil War — and a paper agreement to stop war was an exercise in futility.

Jeannette had lectured audiences in 1936 that America already was spending one billion dollars a year to violate the treaty, and the waste of money was obvious in appropriations for polo ponies for Army brass and hundreds of thousands of Jeep motors, kept in warehouses where they became obsolete before they were used. The Army was being trained to fight in foreign countries. The Navy was being trained to fight in foreign seas. Neither were being trained to defend American soil. The military still maintained a cavalry, which could be decimated by the hellish fire from fighter planes. Jeannette never tired of putting these facts before the public. "It will take...action on our part to sober the war-mad rulers," she told one audience. "It is the American people who decide whether or not they want to prevent war."

She was full of simple anecdotes about America's preparation for war.

A country that arms itself seeks trouble to play with its new toy, Jeannette believed: "When countries are armed they are like the little boy who received the gun and the diary for Christmas. The next day he wrote in his diary: 'Snowing, can't go hunting.' The third day he wrote: 'Snowing yet, can't go hunting.' The fourth day he wrote: 'Snowing still, shot grandma.'

She remembered a story told by a Sunday school teacher, who asked a group of little boys to share with the class good deeds they had performed that week. As the bigger boys were reciting their good deeds, the eyes of the smallest boy were sparkling as he made up his story. When his turn came he said: "I saw a big boy jumping on a little boy and I took an axe and cut his head open." To Jeannette, that story exemplified the difference between aggression and defense: the punishment inflicted was much worse than the crime committed.

She found little wonder that the military was prepared to fight in foreign wars and had no intention of training for coastal defense. Calling President Roosevelt a dictator, she demanded he define American defense boundaries instead of preparing people for war.

Roosevelt in an Oct. 5, 1937, speech in Chicago warned American peace might be challenged by aggressor nations:

> *There is a solidarity and interdependence about the modern world both technically and morally, which makes it impossible for any nation to isolate itself from economic and political upheavals in the rest of the world, especially when such upheavals appear to be spreading and not declining.*

Jeannette's interpretation of this statement was that Roosevelt had abandoned neutrality and was anxious to get America into war, a complaint she explored widely in the 149 speeches she made in the subsequent eight months. She reasoned that with the friendly nations of Canada on the north and Mexico on the south, and expansive oceans to the east and west, America was the best-equipped nation in the world to repel invasion. Why did the military persist in training men and buying munitions?

"Anyone with common sense knows that a lot of little boys lying on their stomachs shooting popguns is no defense in a period devoted to poison gas and bombing planes," she epostulated in one of her many fact sheets on military training.

"Preparation for war leads to war," she had said in a 1934 speech. "If we are to have peace, we must achieve peace by preparing for it. Some government must take the lead, but it can only be taken when there is an enlightened public opinion demanding intelligent action." Jeannette blamed propaganda for creating a syndrome of ignorance she labeled "the fear psychosis." And she argued Americans were paralyzed by insinuations of corporate America that they would be subject to the ruthless and gruesome horrors of invasion if wars were not fought.

Jeannette feared the clutter of propaganda would perpetuate a distaste toward peace and serve to calm people in their criticism of profiteering. She was quoted in the *World Outlook:*

> *We Americans must be aware of 'holy wars.' Ask the American people to give their lives in a foreign war for the expressed purpose of turning attention from the economic and social problems at home, or to solve unemployment by making munitions, or to protect their homes by fighting in a country thousands of miles away, to believe that we can profit in other people's wars without being drawn into them, and their scornful laughter would ring around the world. But ask them to fight for a lofty ideal or even to protect their homes without mentioning the attacking country which high-pressure propaganda can make appear reasonable, and that is quite a different story.*

On Dec. 29, 1937, Jeannette entered the studio of the Inter-City Network radio station shortly after 8 p.m., clutching her typed speech tightly in one hand and nervously awaiting her turn at the microphone. She had spoken on a national radio network before — including the previous April on the day of her 20th anniversary of her vote against war — but the battle was becoming more intense. She struggled to find fresh arguments because everybody was spending money for propaganda. Jeannette planned to tell her audience to disregard the war propaganda and listen to her peace propaganda, and she knew she must leave a lasting impression.

At 8:45 p.m., Jeannette was sitting before the bulky microphone, prepared to give her speech. She thanked the station for the opportunity to talk on the air. "Nineteen thirty-seven is ending with everyone hearing a great deal about war," she said. "There is propaganda everywhere, propaganda for war and propaganda against war. You who are listening are in a tight place. It is hard for you to know how to weigh all sides and come to a sane conclusion."

Jeannette told of an experience in Missouri. She had met a man reprimanded by his wife for not believing stories about war atrocities. The man could neither read nor write, and his wife told him, "If you could read, you would know these stories are true." The man replied, "If you could not read, you would know they are not true."

People huddling around the crackling radio sets in their living rooms were told the propaganda Jeannette despised the most was what she called the "It can't be done" propaganda by people who said, "Well, we've always had war and always will." She asked her audience:

> Where would we be today if the leaders of humanity had listened to 'It can't be done' — Columbus, Washington, Susan B. Anthony, Pasteur, Edison, the Wright brothers? What if we have had war in the past? The men and women living in homes, loving their children, don't want war. Why should they let it come?

Jeannette knew the answer.

Decades of media influence had taught Americans that war was essential to American freedom, liberty and the pursuit of happiness. In the public glorification of war, statues made heroes of soldiers, memorials enshrined the dead, movies dignified killing and hymns brimmed with emotion.

Jeannette wanted to break this habit, which she found ingrained in her own personality. Decades of imbalanced folk tales had taken their toll on her. She admitted during hearings on amending the Constitution to outlaw war that "we cannot get away from our tradition.... I still hate England, but I know I should not."

Liberty bonds — floated by the federal government to help finance the shipments of munitions, food, clothing and other supplies to allies during war — exemplified the subconscious belief among Americans that they must support war. In a sense, each person who bought a bond was a shareholder in the macabre, for profiteers cleverly had assimilated the people into their plot.

How ironic that Jeannette should participate in such a plan during World War I, yet 20 years later dedicate every waking moment to the abolition of it. Not until one night at her Georgia farm did she understand her own fears and misconceptions about breaking the war habit:

> *When I first came to Georgia, I would lock the door, and then*
> *at night I would hear every pine cone that fell. One night I*
> *forgot to lock the door and I didn't hear the pine cones.*
> *Locking the door was what frightened me.*

Jeannette thought life in America was much the same, believing the power of propaganda taught people to be afraid. She was convinced that in eliminating war propaganda, Americans could end the habit of jumping into war to settle international disputes. To do that, however, women needed a voice in government.

Equal suffrage taught her that serious social problems arose when only a fraction of the American population was represented in federal government. She had favored a grassroots approach to social change, hoping to influence public opinion rather than to beg corrupt or conservative politicians to parcel out human rights.

She detested suit-coat politicians and patronizing lobbyists afraid of entering the sanctums of rural America to seek change. She hated government leaders who found time for cocktail parties in Washington's opulent Georgetown suburbia but professed ignorance of the concerns of their constituents. She became most wildly upset that politicians and corporate directors bickered the affairs of government in plush, walnut-paneled offices, shunning the working class as a fatal disease. Jeannette, although a rare intuitive thinker, was impatient that other brilliant minds ignored the value of a grassroots democracy.

Repeatedly, in speeches over the airwaves of radio, in speeches on Capitol Hill, and in speeches to students and civic groups she touched a common theme:

> *The only safe way of preventing war and waste and confusion will be through broadening the base of political control.... Peace is coming not through political leaders but through the voter. The great value of political action lies in its power to educate the masses.*

Educate, she did. The National Council for Prevention of War kept her moving in a whistlestop campaign for peace across America, commonly scheduling her appearances in such rapid-fire sequence that often she was left stranded on railway platforms and in dingy hotel rooms, waiting for money, reservations and orders. In an ordeal reminiscent of her days with the Women's International League for Peace and Freedom, she had to cope with hasty, sketchy schedules, sophomoric calculations by headquarters staff about the political makeup of her audiences, and tea parties hosted by banal, conformist matrons.

Yet Jeannette survived, managing to chop a path of awareness through the rough timber of American public opinion. Tempered by years of thankless suffrage work, she only could ignore the predictable frustrations and focus her goals on the spirit of peace.

She spoke to a Rotary Club in Flagstaff, Ariz., visited a NCPW chapter in Eugene, Ore., and met with the congregation of a Methodist church in Fulton, Mo. She mesmerized her audiences with her ability to make war look silly and vapid, and with her styled delivery. And women and children added their support to Jeannette's efforts. Commented a West Coast member of the NCPW:

> *With all of her public work and experience she remains delightfully feminine, and her sense of humor is a saving grace and a refreshing oasis in [a] desert of bitter problems. We can scarcely praise Miss Rankin too highly for her clear insight into the whole question of war and peace, her keen analysis of the problem, her practical plans for attacking it, and the enthusiasm she inspires by showing her audience how*

> *the ordinary citizen may actually accomplish much toward the*
> *establishment of permanent peace.*

Speculated a Roosevelt High School student in Washington, D.C.: "I think Miss Rankin is right. It would be better to think about whether we should fight, rather than how we should fight." And First Lady Eleanor Roosevelt agreed in a personal letter to Jeannette that if the will for peace could grow in the hearts of women everywhere they may be able to calm the tense situation in Europe.

American women failed to meet those expectations, yet Jeannette emerged a darkhorse of the peace movement. Her ideas were effective and convincing, although she did not build a loud defiance of war. She was a realist, preferring hard, revealing stumping to materialistic worshipping of flag and country. Her dynamic presentation of facts about war profiteering and propaganda earned her the attention of American audiences.

Jeannette aptly filled the void created by the death of peace matriarch Jane Addams, who had been determined to open America's eyes to the horrors of slum living, the cogent power of the 'weaker' sex, and the brutality of war. Jeannette had spent a few months at Hull House in Chicago after she left Congress in 1918, and joined with Addams in 1932 in Jeannette's "To Chicago" plan as women, children and college students converged on Republican and Democratic party conventions with anti-war sentiment. They became friends bound by their identical approach to securing the change needed to establish and maintain peace in America.

Jeannette Rankin and Jane Addams agreed peace should start with the teamster behind the plow, the preacher in the pulpit, the garment seamstress at the sewing machine, and the newspaper editor, the firefighter, the delicatessan proprietor, the woman with eight children howling for more food to eat, and the black man looking for his first job in a white city.

The transformation of life in the slum world surrounding Hull House demonstrated what Jane Addams believed the poor and the downtrodden could attain if they were given encouragement and conviction. A lively role for women was manifest in Jeannette Rankin's philosophy, for she believed that people — whatever color, whatever sex, whatever religion — were fools to wait for their government to give them privileges they deserved under the Constitution.

Unlike Frederick Libby, whose pacifism was inherent in his conversion to the Quaker religion, Jeannette felt a compelling responsibility to better what she believed were abuses of American civil rights.

By 1937, Jane Addams was dead, and Jeannette still was smarting from the rough treatment she received for her peace stand in 1917. She vigorously agitated for nonviolent revolution, convinced Americans must regain their government or they would be robbed freely of life and money by special interest racketeers depending on ignorance to sustain them.

Critics of Jeannette's work generally believed in the method of building public policy from the top of the power structure. Jeannette thought that plan was ridiculous. If the war mongers were in cahoots with the men in the executive, legislative or judicial branches, what could be gained by arguing with the politicians and lawmakers?

Jeannette believed convincing the nation's war lords to court peace was as futile as fighting a war to settle international disputes. "No one fears the results of the peace worker who made sentimental speeches at ladies' teas, but when pioneer work is done among responsible citizens, it is a different story," she wrote.

Jeannette said war was the greatest menace to society because it killed the finest men, had an aftermath of disease, caused a deterioration of the race and eventually would destroy it. She pointed to the catastrophic burden of the taxpayer who must pay for war debts, veterans, machinery and war's 'reconstruction.' In a moral tone, she questioned why innocent people were subjected to the indescribable devastation of bombing planes and chemical warfare, masterminded by people in safe places many miles away.

The Nye Committee had concluded in its investigation that

thwarting capitalist manufacturers would reduce or eliminate the incentive to become involved in foreign markets on the precipice of war. As Charles Beard pointed out in his book *The Devil Theory of War*, American business had invested seven billion dollars into World War I in the three years before American entry. Beard contended President Wilson was forced to commit America to war to prevent a domestic banking crash.

His small book, filled with secret cables between Wilson and Robert Lansing, who in 1914 was chief lawyer for the State Department, documented a growing financial commitment to the war efforts of foreign countries.

The resulting big prosperity became insecure by 1917, when American business, led by the J.P. Morgan Company of New York, feared financial collapse if the military did not move to protect American investments on foreign soil. Beard estimated that such greedy speculating cost America $100 billion, including outlays for pensions, bonuses and other war charges. The death and suffering could not be measured. Beard theorized that the stock market crash of 1929 was the direct result of war profiteering.

By 1939, Jeannette Rankin was breaking away from the less incisive National Council for Prevention of War. The NCPW had publicized her dramatically but used her badly for 10 years. The lack of money was an immediate problem. Fire burned her Georgia farm to the foundation in 1935. Unable to rebuild, for she had neither the time nor the money, she bought another farm at Watkinsville, 10 miles from Bogart. She paid only $300 for a cottage on 33 acres. It needed repairs and she found herself turning to Frederick Libby for help.

"Am living in true Georgia fashion," she wrote him. "No money. The stores are furnishing me with food and gas. They say, 'It's been so long since we've had any money we done got used to it.' Please don't think I can get used to it."

Libby had sympathy for Jeannette's impoverished lifestyle, but times were hard for the NCPW, too. He forwarded Jeannette a pittance of her pay only infrequently, forcing her to write him in

1938 that "I've no doubt money is slow in coming in, but if you can send me some or put me on a weekly payroll it will help a lot. It hurts my spirits so to be broke."

Because Libby had a devout Quaker allegiance to peace, he rationalized poverty of his field workers. Jeannette, having no such religious inclination, was experiencing a growing suspicion that Libby was exploiting her expertise.

As rumors spread, Jeannette understood why. Other NCPW workers were whispering among themselves that because Jeannette's brother had a prosperous law practice, her NCPW paycheck could be spent elsewhere within the organization. This infuriated Jeannette, and when Libby asked her to begin a peace society in rural Colorado, she flared at his insolence. "My day for doing the spade work as I did in Georgia is past," she quipped, positively hating his insensitivity to her needs.

Jeannette's financial feud with Libby and the NCPW involved more than her paycheck, however. She became increasingly concerned about the NCPW having to compete with other peace organizations for the dwindling reservoir of peace funds, and she was impatient with some of her colleagues, such as Education Secretary Florence Boeckel, who wanted to put more emphasis on Congressional work. Mostly, Jeannette was embarrassed that her unveiled dislike for Libby's inability to feed his workers was leading her to backwoods door-to-door work with little reward or recognition from him.

Mild disagreements grew into such a rift that Jeannette resigned, and she was excluded from the NCPW budget in December 1939. That she stuck with the organization for so long is surprising. Since her early days in the suffrage campaigns she had been a maverick, working loosely within the philosophies of established groups while following her intuitive moods. She hadn't changed. Even members of the Georgia Peace Society resented her independence, calling her a dictator in private, and accusing her of using the name and letterhead of the organization to her own end.

Having fought her own battles since the day she decided war was the major oppressor of women, Jeannette had little patience for compromise. Even as she had testified as an expert witness on munitions control before the Nye Committee, she had drifted from the precise lobbying techniques of the National Council for Prevention of War, casually tossing her personal ideas to the Congressmen on a whim. While Libby continually had cautioned her to avoid direct attacks on President Roosevelt, which he thought might lose public support for the NCPW, she relentlessly criticized the incestuous marriage of government and corporation.

And while the National Council for Prevention of War and many other pacifist groups were prepared to accept compromising anti-profit legislation as a better-than-nothing proposition, Jeannette independently introduced her own scheme to slash profits from war.

Her solution was to have the Secretary of the Treasury withdraw all money and credit at the first hint of a national emergency, and replace it with *fiat* bills equal in face value. This 'emergency currency' would be legal tender for the duration of the war.

When peace was restored, each person would have his frozen pre-war credit or peace dollars returned, at the value at which they had been exchanged. The *fiat* dollars then became worthless, allowing no one to make a profit from war.

The plan was not feasible to employ, considering the immense task to exchange money or credit in the midst of an emergency, and because American investments started long before the outbreak of war. Jeannette proved, however, that as a single citizen she had a plan to offer, although it was not well received by the Nye Committee. She complained miserably that her plan wasn't adopted because "you seldom meet those who want all the profits removed."

The Nye Committee never proposed a sensible plan to take the profits out of war, in Jeannette's opinion, but continuing investigations led to the Neutrality Act of 1935, which put a mandatory embargo on arms and munitions to belligerents, forbade American ships to transport munitions to countries at war, and later restricted loans to warring countries.

Jeannette found more support in her lobbying to outlaw war. Her scheme called for an International Court of Justice, a world peace court that would regulate governments of the world by the power of opinion. The world court would be comparable in status and operation to the United States Supreme Court, which Jeannette believed had functioned flawlessly with the tool of public opinion. She was a proponent of a world court because she thought the General Pact for the Renunciation of War—merely a condemnation — and the Kellogg-Briand Peace Pact, which outlawed war, would succeed only until economic disputes began.

She proved to be correct. The advent of a new world war over money and territorial boundaries meant hundreds of thousands of people would be killed and millions of square miles of land destroyed. Although Jeannette favored the peace pacts as positive acknowledgements by nations that war failed to solve conflicts, but made new ones, she wanted to cry out in protest of the terrible slaughter.

Jeannette got her chance. Millions of Americans listened, but this time she had a mission more well-defined — and more lonely — than any she had experienced.

> *"Dear Jenny — and you look it. You are an old fossil. Hitler aid — never should you have been an official of any kind — rather an undertaker's assistant for women only."*
>
> (Letter from A.R. McCullock of Jacksonville, Fla.)

THE LONELY DISSENTER
Chapter 9

While Adolf Hitler's Third Reich was crushing democratic Europe and the Americans were bickering frantically over the shipment of munitions and arms to belligerent countries, Jeannette Rankin was contemplating the prospect of campaigning for Congress on a peace platform. Public opinion had been trapped in a monumental tug-of-war between the pacifists and the militarists, starting with a gentle pull in the early Thirties and culminating in a frenzy in the early Forties.

Jeannette was among the pacifists who pulled the hardest.

Being a habitual wanderer, she had returned to Montana in the spring of 1940, and had driven through the state's western district to take a public opinion poll of her own. She was not pleased with what she learned. President Roosevelt had created suspicion of pacifists with his warnings about the military buildup in Europe, and Jeannette's consensus was that peaceful Montanans deploring war now feared they could not survive without it.

Infuriated, she fired a letter off to Frederick Libby. "Again we hear that the troubles of the world are caused by the 'damn pacifists,' " she raged.

Jeannette had been conspicuously distrustful that Americans would be committed to another world war by the surreptitious economic dealings of the United States. She was angered and depressed that two tumultuous decades of peace work should culminate in war. Using the popular forum of radio, she asked Montanans to beseech the government to avoid the use of violent Hitlerian methods to cool the war in Europe. Americans should have every means that money, ingenuity and science could devise to protect the United States from invasion, but they should not be inclined to intervene in century-old European problems on the basis of changing and unknown facts, she cautioned.

For a few months, Jeannette toyed with the idea of filing for Congress, uneasy that in her long absence from Montana she mostly had been forgotten and would face a new generation undecided and unprepared for war. She observed her 60th birthday amid the confusion, knowing if she decided to run, her campaign would be much tougher than that of 1916. The novelty of her election had faded, for other women sat in Congress, and the winds of war made peace a less popular belief.

Although her visits to Montana had been limited mostly to summer vacations, Jeannette had maintained her voting residence there. On June 5, 1940, one day before the deadline, she filed for the Congressional seat from the Western District. Nobody who knew Jeannette well was surprised, for the campaign was her final frantic attempt to avert America's participation in world war.

Her campaign platform, with the slogan, "Prepare to the limit for defense, keep our men out of Europe," was nailed solidly with pro-peace planks, and Jeannette rallied the cause of pacifism defiantly. She solicited criticism, for if Montanans did not want peace, she did not want to be their Congressional representative. She said in a campaign speech reported in the *Butte Daily Post*, an Anaconda Company newspaper:

> *We have a marvelous opportunity to build a race of human beings superior to anything we have produced because we*

> *have the traits, culture and experience of all the nations
> mingled in our blood. In the present crisis, the strength that is
> needed is the contribution of women in realizing that they must
> do something now if they are going to prevent this nation from
> becoming involved in the chaos of Europe. As women we will
> join together and say, 'we are going to protect our product, our
> young manhood.'*

Carefully she sampled the public mood. The St. Louis Button
Co. offered her 50,000 celluloid campaign buttons stating,
"Jeannette Rankin for Congress," for $440. Somewhat timidly,
she ordered only 10,000, waiting to see what support she would
garner.

While women, pacifists and disgruntled Socialist farmers predictably backed Jeannette, a genuine surprise came in the support of prominent American men — leaders of liberal political
thought — who long before 1940 had forgotten their concerns
about her membership in the 'weaker' sex and welcomed her into
their ranks as a fighter and a dissenter.

Liberal Congressman Harold Knutson of Minnesota wrote:
"Jeannette Rankin is one of the great humanitarians of the age.
Miss Rankin has labored ... for legislation that would help the lot
of the underprivileged, the friendless and the toiler."

Said Sen. Robert M. LaFollette Jr., whose father had been
among the leaders in the fight against the war declaration of
1917: "America needs leaders in Congress like Jeannette
Rankin."

Bruce Barton, a noted author and for many years one of the
most widely published writers in national periodicals, wired a
dispatch to Montana asking Jeannette if he could assist her
campaign.

Bennett Champ Clark, a Democratic senator from Missouri,
crossed party lines to endorse Jeannette's candidacy. "I had the
pleasure of knowing you and of observing your work in the very
trying position of being the first woman member of ... a war
congress," he wrote to her. "I admired your courage and ability."

Gerald P. Nye, a Congressman before whom Jeannette had

testified, noted that the primary purpose of every American should be to keep America out of war. "Jeannette Rankin has won so profound a place in the peace cause and work that her presence in Congress in these times would serve a most salutary purpose," he observed.

Among the best promotions came from her old friend Fiorella LaGuardia, who as mayor of New York City had won prominence fighting graft and corruption, and was a renowned voice for the oppressed and the poor.

Jeannette had met the 'Little Flower' when they had been freshman Congressmen in 1917, and although he left Congress in August 1917 to be commissioned a lieutenant in the U.S. Air Service, they had fallen into a warm relationship just short of love. LaGuardia was only 5'2", but although short on height, he was tall on dedication to the betterment of the masses, and in this egalitarian personality Jeannette found a man who appreciated her role in life.

The extent of their intimacy was unknown even by the people closest to Jeannette, for she did not talk of personal concerns. But she and LaGuardia were frequent dinner companions and he telephoned her whenever he was in Washington. Jeannette deplored 'kitchen gossip' and surrounded herself only with men who matched her intellectually. LaGuardia, who enjoyed her gift of dissent and political prowess, clearly was in favor with her.

Once he slid his arm around Jeannette and said to her youngest sister, Edna: "You don't know how hard I tried to get this gal to marry me." Jeannette's supreme independence, however, had defied marriage, and in 1929, LaGuardia had married Marie Fisher, his Washington secretary, and they adopted two children. In his autobiography, *The Making of an Insurgent,* he mentioned Jeannette only in reference to the War Congress of 1917, but after she filed for Congress in 1940 he jumped to her aid:

> *Jeannette Rankin has the training, experience and understanding to intelligently serve the people of Montana.... I know of no one who has kept in closer touch with economic, social and political conditions in this country.... This woman*

has more courage and packs a harder punch than a regiment of regular line politicians.

Jeannette printed most of the effusive campaign promotions such as LaGuardia's blurb in her campaign pamphlet, neutralizing contentions that she was a rebellious, radical nonconformist, out of touch with the American mood.

Curiously absent from the pamphlet was a letter from Norman Thomas, the Socialist candidate for president, who told Jeannette he would support her because she was unopposed by a Socialist candidate and because she strongly opposed totalitarianism, whether fascist or communist. Interestingly, Jeannette voted for Thomas each time he ran for the presidency.

With the primary election less than a month away, Jeannette employed many of the simple, but effective, campaign tactics she had used since the Montana suffrage campaign of 1914. Jeannette took her arguments to the people, refusing to rely on the forums of media and lecture hall. The only difference was that in 1916 she was explaining why women should have the right to vote; now she told women to use their vote to prevent going to war.

Believing world war was inevitable, Jeannette wanted to be sent to Washington by people who believed in peace. She got her mandate, winning a close primary victory over Republican incumbent Jacob Thorkelson in July and defeating Democrat Jerry O'Connell by a vote of 56,616 to 47,352 in the November election. Although national sentiment was shifting to the right of the political spectrum, Jeannette was elected as a peace candidate to the 77th Congress in an election year that won Franklin D. Roosevelt and the Democratic Party huge pluralities.

Again a member of Congress after a 22-year interlude, Jeannette immediately resisted subtle efforts by fellow Congressmen and President Roosevelt to slip America into war. Hundreds of women wrote letters investing their faith, and among them was Mrs. O.G. Marksen, who asked: "By doing all in your power toward keeping the United States out of this tragic threatening war, we citizens here will back you up 100%. You can depend on us — can we depend on you?"

In January 1941, the Roosevelt Administration began promoting a controversial piece of legislation known as the Lend-Lease Act, which would give the President power to commit American weapons to defend Britain or any other country. Congressional foes reacted bitterly, asking unbelievingly how America could presume to become the sole policeman of the world's armory.

Jeannette joined her Montana colleague, Sen. Burton K. Wheeler, in denouncing the bill. Wheeler roared in testimony that Lend-Lease would insure a grave for every fourth American boy, and Jeannette fumed more diplomatically that the measure would bring America one step closer to war. "Mothers alone can prevent our entering the war if they will express their opinions now," she said.

She introduced an amendment prohibiting President Roosevelt from committing any soldier, sailor, marine or aircraft pilot to war with another nation unless Congress gave its specific authorization. But Congress defeated her amendment, 137 to 82, before approving the bill.

For nine months preceding the Japanese attack on Pearl Harbor, Jeannette tried to subdue the momentum of military legislation by introducing peace legislation. She was unhappy about American diplomatic relations with Japan, and commented in Congress: "I commend patience to them. If their talks serve to put off or avert a war, I hope they go on tirelessly. Here is an occasion for the much-derided diplomatic tea sipping and cake pushing to vindicate itself."

She ridiculed the military Chiefs of Staff for what she called their "annual war scare for appropriations," and for the moment, Jeannette's portended belief that Americans would resist the opportunity to enter world war was correct.

Said Roosevelt in October 1940: "I have said this before, but I shall say it again and again and again: your boys are not going to be sent into any foreign wars."

While Americans hoped that prediction was correct, the isolationist mood of the Thirties began to change after Hitler invaded Poland, Denmark, Norway, Belgium, Luxembourg and the

Netherlands, crushed mighty France and gained Italy as an ally. CBS correspondent Edward R. Murrow shocked Americans nightly with his sonorous on-the-spot coverage of Germany's wholesale bombing of London. Pollster Elmo Roper reported Americans radically had reversed their stand on war and in less than six months, a majority favored American intervention to end German aggression.

Jeannette Rankin had vowed a negative vote if Congress considered a declaration of war. She was seemingly oblivious to the dramatic reversal of public opinion. In one of her rare departures from reality, she refused to believe Americans wanted war. She forged ahead recklessly to commit women to her peace ideal through her example, despite facts to the contrary.

She hurriedly pushed a resolution onto the House calendar in mid-November 1941 to poll the American people of their opinions toward war. But, the Dec. 7 attack on Pearl Harbor made the poll unnecessary. As news of the Japanese attack reached the mainland, people expressed disbelief.

A woman loitering at a newsstand at the corner of Michigan and Randolph streets in Chicago glanced at the headlines and asked, "What's this?"

The vendor replied in horror, "We're at war, lady, for crying out loud."

She replied: "Well, what do you know. Who with?"

As the initial confusion melted into deafening cries of outrage — much louder than the voices of the pacifists had been — America was ready for war. President Roosevelt called secretary Grace Tully into his study and dictated: "Yesterday comma December seven comma nineteen forty-one dash a date which will live in infamy dash."

Jeannette and her sister Edna were at home in Jeannette's apartment when they heard the news of the attack on a broadcast from a Washington radio station.

Jeannette refused to believe the tortured, sketchy news reports. She had maintained for 20 years that America would not be invaded unless the government courted another world war to protect the interests of speculators in foreign countries.

She simply could not fathom that such a tragic possibility could become reality.

In the midst of national confusion and uncertainty about what really had happened at Pearl Harbor, Jeannette defied the news as war propaganda and boarded a train for Detroit, where she had a speaking engagement. Lying in an upper berth, listening intently to a radio, she learned Roosevelt would address a joint session of Congress the next day to ask for a declaration of war. She left the train in Pittsburgh and caught another back to Washington.

The futile train trip was a typical Rankin tactic. Knowing her brother and other war lobbyists frantically were trying to contact her, Jeannette was gliding across the Pennsylvania countryside, staring out the window at peaceful meadows and forests. For the quiet hours she rode the rails, she was an anonymous, rambling vagabond, unworried of the somber and intrusive responsibilities of Capitol Hill. As a gladiator prepares for the last battle, Jeannette sat meditatively, preparing for the onerous rush of hysteria that would slap her in the face like a cold wind when she stepped off the train in Washington.

Jeannette returned home late on the day of the bombings. Already she saw evidence of a great military mobilization. People rushing about the station had feverish stares of anticipation in their eyes. She climbed into bed and fell asleep but was shocked rudely to consciousness by the loud jangling of her telephone. Her anxious brother muttered relief.

Wellington knew his sister well. If President Roosevelt proposed a declaration of war against Japan, she would vote against it. Still, he pleaded with her, begging that she vote for the resolution to protect herself. He suggested she could rationalize a 'yes' vote for the sake of self defense.

In 1917 Wellington had been a young, strutting military patriot, charged with traditional beliefs about the nation's honor and anxious to protect his law profession in Montana. Now he was much of a rebel himself, and although never convinced by Jeannette's arguments that America should stay out of war, family love permitted respect for her commitment to peace. However, he could better see the impact of a negative vote than his idealistic sister, who refused to compromise her stand.

Jeannette left her apartment early the next morning and nudged her automobile into heavy traffic. All morning she wandered alone in the city to avoid visitors or telephone calls. Frequently, the Capitol dome popped into view, reminding her she was about to endure an attack by the war hawks. Riding through Washington, waiting for her political execution, was one of the most terrible experiences of her life. Shortly before noon, Jeannette drove to her office. Her face was a mask of mental anguish, but she composed herself, giving Frances Elge, her personal secretary, the impression she was unruffled about the forthcoming confrontation.

In an uncanny repetition of her war vote 24 years earlier, Jeannette waited solemnly for the walk to the House chambers while friends whispered encouragement to her. Another of Jeannette's secretaries, Sigrid Scannell, was trying to console her when the session bell rang. Proudly, defiantly, Jeannette pushed herself away and trekked to the Capitol, where she nudged a path to her seat on the crowded House floor.

Aides and messengers rushed about excitedly. Unlike the war vote of 1917, when the judgment to send America into war with Germany had been remorseful and indecisive, faces now reflected purpose and duty. Grimly the Senators and Congressmen quieted while Roosevelt in a terse address asked that they recognize a state of war with Japan.

After the President had left, Congressmen in dramatic wild speeches called for a declaration of war. Congressman John Gibson of Georgia demanded that Americans unite in thought, purpose and determination to resurrect freedom that otherwise would perish "before the forces of cowards who do not feel the impulses of honor." Echoed Congressman Earl Wilson of Indiana: "We have done our best to avoid this war with Japan. ("We have?" Jeannette asked herself.) Now she has asked for it," Wilson argued. "The only thing we can do is let her have it. By that I mean complete destruction of her war machine. Let us hope and pray that a minimum of lives will be lost."

Bellowed Congressman Chauncey Reed of Illinois: "America aroused will hesitate not an instant and will never rest until the world is rid of the monsters who planned and executed yesterday's dastardly outrage. Japan will rue the day that the fury of peaceful, liberty-loving people was unleashed."

Congressman John McCormack of Massachusetts immediately asked for a vote on the resolution. Jeannette tried to delay the House from a vote without discussion.

"Mr. Speaker...," she began.

Sam Rayburn, caught by the intense fervor gripping the House, ignored the 'Lady from Montana.'

"The gentleman from Massachusetts demands the yeas and nays," Rayburn roared. "Those who favor taking this vote by the yeas and nays will rise and remain standing until counted."

Jeannette well remembered the travesty of failing to defend her first war vote on the House floor, and she didn't want the nation to go to war without an argument for peace. Shrilly she called for recognition a second time:

"Mr. Speaker, I would like to be heard!"

Aware that Jeannette only would try to obstruct the resolution if she was allowed to speak, Rayburn ignored her again.

"The yeas and nays have been ordered," he said. "The question is, will the House suspend the rules and pass the resolution?"

For a third time, Jeannette's shrill voice rose above the melee. This time she was heard clearly by radio newsmen who had mounted a microphone on the speaker's podium. Her pleading was broadcast into the packed antechambers surrounding the House floor. "Mr. Speaker, a point of order," she called.

"Sit down sister," someone shouted.

"A roll call may not be interrupted," Rayburn yelled in reply to Jeannette.

Quickly, as if the enthusiasm might fade, the roll call began. Allen, Andrews, Arnold, all yes. McLean, McMillan, Maciejewski, all yes....

Rankin: "As a woman, I can't go to war and I refuse to send anyone else."

Stratton, Sumner, Sweeney, yes....

As Jeannette recorded her vote, people from the floor and the gallery booed and glared with hate and distrust. This time she was allowed no sympathy or compassion. Gone was her youthful curiosity of 1917 that had graced the House floor and caused such unflagging interest. She was no longer an innovation; some Congressmen complained loathingly that she was an undesirable fixture that should be placed in storage.

From the moment the roll call ended, Jeannette was alone.

The war resolution had swept through the House without another dissenting vote. Other Congressmen who also might have voted in the negative abstained and withdrew from the chambers quietly, knowing their constituents would be less harsh with a neutral stand. Confused and humiliated that she was the only person in the entire House carrying the banner for peace, Jeannette stumbled through the crush of people to the cloakroom, where she learned the Senate had voted unanimously for a declaration of war. She met a shocked Sen. Everett Dirksen, who demanded an explanation for her vote. "I can't bear to be a worm," she informed him, using one of her favorite expressions.

The vote in Congress, as the nation's newspapers reported that evening, was 470 to one: 82 'yeas' in the Senate and 388 in the House. One small, lonely voice crying to be recognized. One black mark on the nation's conscience.

The cloakroom was choked with angry, unauthorized people, including Capitol police intoxicated with liquor and emotion. They swarmed Jeannette, grabbing and pushing at her and demanding she change her vote. Afraid she would get no help from the police and sure the situation was close to a riot, Jeannette escaped into a telephone booth and slammed the doors. A policeman pounded on the glass and Jeannette thought he wanted to escort her to safety. She opened the door, smelling alcohol on his breath as he muttered incoherently. "You're drunk," Jeannette told him, and he scurried for the hallway.

Jeannette dialed the Capitol switchboard for help. Flashbulbs popped, and despite the hysteria, she was shown in newspapers across the country the next day in a typically relaxed pose, cradling the telephone receiver conversationally.

Yet she was churning inside.

Sober Capitol police dutifully accompanied Jeannette to her office and stood guard outside while she sat at her desk and composed a letter of explanation to her constituents. She explained she did not know enough facts about the Japanese attack on Pearl Harbor to justify a hasty vote for war.

"While I believed that the stories were probably true," she penned, "still I believed that such a momentous vote, one which could mean peace or war for our country, should be based on more authentic evidence...." Reminding her constituents of her campaign pledges for peace, Jeannette said she had voted her convictions.

Then she telephoned Wellington in Montana and he snorted in disgust: "Montana is 110 percent against you." Later that night, Jeannette gestured despairingly. "I have nothing left now except my integrity," she mused to a friend.

Jeannette failed even to quiet angry rumblings among her constituents, and thousands of letters of condemnation flooded her office. "You made an ass out of yourself trying to be like a man. Now, come home like a lady," snarled the Young Republicans of Harlem, Mont. While her peace vote of 1917 had been chided as the weakness of a woman's heart, her latest was regarded by many people as treason. Even the pacifist Quakers, who had made a fuss on her behalf the first time, now were conspicuously silent. One comic laconically observed that Jeannette would make an ideal wife, for her pacifist qualities would prevent her from declaring war on her husband at home.

"What kind of a creature can you be?" demanded a California woman. "In 1917 American women by the thousands bowed their heads in shame because of you. Now every American mother must curse you for the shame you have brought upon our sex."

Jeannette maintained a cool exterior, appearing undaunted by the criticism. Inside she was bewildered that she should be accused of rendering havoc with the pride of women. While they complained Jeannette had brought shame to womanhood, she had been convinced she was guiding them to liberation. For more than 20 years peace had been her utopia in life, and she never wandered from her argument that women could be free if they would rise as a political bloc and wipe the war blemish from the face of the earth.

While Jeannette's vote against Germany in 1917 had been a footnote in history, she believed her lonely vote against war with Japan in 1941 had lost much of its impact because it was only a public display of more extensive, meaningful peace work.

She contended her vote had saved America from a totalitarian war regime, however, publicly acclaiming it as an example of democracy at work. The vote also proved to be nicely symbolic of the independence of womanhood, but Jeannette regretted having been on trial that way. She had vowed at least six years earlier that she would vote against war, "today — tomorrow — and forever —" and she was disappointed and dismayed that America suddenly should awaken to her actions and react with such hysteria. She wrote Frederick Libby:

> *What one decides to do in a crisis depends upon one's philosophy in life, and that philosophy cannot be changed by an accident. If one hasn't any philosophy, in crises others make the decision. The most disappointing feature of working for a cause is that so few people have a clear philosophy of life. We used to say, in the suffrage movement, that we could trust the woman who believed in suffrage, but we could never trust the woman who just wanted to vote.*

This frustration with women who regarded the vote as a novelty but not a means to liberation infuriated Jeannette. While fighting for the welfare of the masses, she was not one of them, and she sometimes complained acidly that they refused to follow the path lighted for them.

With the advent of World War II, Jeannette was enduring one of the cycles of hatred that plagued her work, reminding her that while she campaigned for what she believed to be a perfectly sensible cause — peace — she again was branded a radical as she had been in Georgia because national sentiment temporarily did not see merit in her cause.

The national mood was like a yo-yo, ricocheting from conservatism to tolerance to liberalism through the decades while Jeannette in her steady commitment to peace was thrown violently in and out of perspective. The public opinion makers, the historians, the preachers who spoke gloomily of the obligation of war as a Biblical tradition; Jeannette saw them as America's greatest enemies because they built and controlled a society based on war.

She was rejected and denigrated as Americans were panicked to their guns, and yet her message was always the same: war is the most evil of all oppressors.

Sometimes the master aggressor, the champion of women, the precursor of peace, momentarily Jeannette no longer was in vogue with much of America. Letters were proof of that cruel fact.

"Traitor Nazi.

"Jap.

"Skunk."

"Your half-baked idea is an insult to us," wrote a Montanan. "I was one of the fools who voted for you, but you may be sure of one thing, the people of this state will vote you out of office next fall so fast you will wonder what happened."

Wrote another: "I sincerely hope that your failure to stand by your people of Montana, and the United States, will cause you to send in your resignation immediately, and drop out of public life, where it is now apparent that you never belonged."

Yet another constituent wrote ironically: "Sentimentalism has no place in times of crisis when clear thinking is demanded."

The Cowpokes Union of Deer Lodge, Mont., telegraphed colorfully:

In view of the bad storms in the offing and the way you botched up the last branding we would like to have you saddle up your bronc, tie your bed roll on behind and just ride home. As we have decided it best to let the rest of our critters run as mavericks until we have a chance to send a new representative after the next election.

Jeannette's worth to America was compared with droughts, grasshoppers and dust storms. She was encouraged facetiously to wrap herself in a bedsheet so she could look the part of Mahatma Rankin (a jibe directed at the Indian pacifist Mohandas Gandhi). She was ordered to hang herself. Some outraged Americans merely questioned why Jeannette had voted against war while others accused her of political grandstanding, and most of the 'con' letters demanded she resign from her office.

Pacifists hardly were popular in the tear-soaked days after Pearl Harbor. But nobody became a target of public hate and ridicule to the extent of Jeannette Rankin, for the few grim horror letters written by people too cowardly to sign their names taught her how lonely dissent could be. One anonymous letter recommended she be spanked on the floor of the House: "That an old-fashioned hairbrush be used as per the good old days and be it specifically stipulated that there be no silk, rayon or any other fabric between the backside of the hairbrush and point of contact of Jeanette's [sic] anatomy."

She was called 'Pig Rankin,' told to pack her bags and go to Japan, and showered with oaths of fury. She was accused of ignoring the murder of her own people. Cold and unfeeling. Delightfully unimpressed with such slaughter. A surrogate for the fascist and imperialist interests in America. She bore such insults with dignity, preparing more than 3,000 form letters to reply to everyone who had written her.

Despite the loquacious anti-Rankin response, letters from Montana slightly favored her vote and letters from other states and Canada and South America overwhelmingly were in favor — by 10 to one — of her stand against war. "Your vote today should make you Montana's next senator," telegrammed Margaret Laughrin from Butte. "Montana women feel Japanese attack has long been administration provoked if not invited. Montana women will organize behind you to resent hoodlum hisses and boos on our woman leader."

The *Evening Kansan-Republican* saw the vote as the work of a martyr to an eternal principle — throbbing in the hearts of women — to oppose bloodshed and war. Wrote Lillian Smith, author of the books *Strange Fruit* and *Killers of the Dream*: "That one little vote of yours stands out like a bright star in the dark night." A letter from Lavinia Dock — the last of the old suffragists of the Susan B. Anthony style — spoke the best for them:

> *I can see the men crowding around you to urge your change from what appeared to them a hopeless and useless stand, but I can also look further and see that you were a symbol and type of the eternal hatred of war that is the heart and soul of downtrodden, oppressed, civilized, humane, forward-looking people of every nation, in every age, in every country.*

When declarations of war on Germany and Italy had come to a vote on Dec. 11, Jeannette stoically answered 'present,' deliberately confusing the tally clerk. This more subtle negative vote, however, passed with little notice while a massive influx of letters regarding the first vote kept Jeannette busy for more than two weeks. As she nibbled an apple and sipped milk in the cloakroom, America went to war with Germany and Italy.

Amid the confusion, she had the presence of mind to bundle up the most vivid letters and mail them to her niece in Virginia for safekeeping. Jeannette managed the pressure well, although she lost five pounds from lack of sleep and good food. Wellington, forever the watchdog for his enterprising sister, discovered one day she had addressed 4,000 Christmas cards to her Montana constituents with the greeting, "Peace on Earth," printed on the front, and was ready to take them to the post office.

Wellington immediately realized the irony of the Christmas greetings would arouse tremendous antagonism, and he firmly instructed Jeannette to destroy the cards.

The incident showed the tension building in her, for she normally was perceptive enough to avoid such a predicament. She travelled to New York to spend a few days with her old friends

Katharine Anthony and Elisabeth Irwin. They attended a few satirical Broadway plays, which distracted Jeannette from the realities and helped relieve the impact of the reaction of her war vote. By February, the flood of mail slowed, indicating the hysteria was subsiding. Americans were too busy obliging the pressures of mobilizing to continue chastizing what they thought was an aging, eccentric spinster from Montana.

Jeannette was anxious to forget the experience and she sought distractions of any sort. She complained sentimentally that the license plates her brother sent from Montana were not as pretty as the previous year. "Must we ask for pretty things in war?" she wondered.

But the critics had succeeded in registering their distrust with her, and she could not shake the feeling that she had failed in her mission.

In frustration, she complained to a friend: "Why people are so mad at me when they have the japs to hate and are now at war, I cannot understand."

Jeannette viewed World War II no differently than the First World War: a vicious cycle of hate in which only America would lose. She predicted that except for the growing confusion at home and the tragic deaths of young men abroad, the conflict would remain the same until America was able to claim victory by exhausting its foes. Then what remained of the dispute would be settled as it could have been before the war had begun, without the pathetic byproducts of crippling, death and racism. "I certainly feel sorry for the poor Jews and Negroes after this war," she observed.

Jeannette's bitterness was grounded deep in 25 years of intense commitment to the women's movement. Yet she was locked into her deep-seated psychological yearnings, and she knew she must drag herself into the fight again. She had been bent, beaten and dragged through tumultuous times. Her dreams had been shattered cruelly by vainglorious displays of the power of men. She had ridden the crest of fame and fashion in her election to Congress in 1917 and she had plummeted into the canyon of despair in 1941 as her single protest was swept under the tide of reactionary public opinion.

No Christmas benevolence was found among newspaper editors toward the wisdom of Jeannette's vote, although a few praised her courage to stand alone. One of those was William Allan White of the *Emporia Gazette* of Kansas: "When in a hundred years from now," White wrote, "courage, sheer courage based upon moral indignation is celebrated in this country, the name of Jeannette Rankin, who stood firm in folly for her faith, will be written in monumental bronze not for what she did but for the way she did it."

Her contemporaries generally tried to banish her from the mainstream of the peace movement with empty observations and eulogies for her tombstone, but she was not ready to quit.

Publicly oblivious of the criticism she had received, Jeannette declared she had spoken for millions of American mothers who did not want their sons to go to war. She took the liberty to conclude that in her political involvements she had learned facts about government's intentional entanglement in war. These facts, she said, were hidden from public view.

During the days Jeannette had invested with the National Council for Prevention of War, she had suspected that if America could blunder into war through financial commitments to foreign belligerents, it soon would learn the value of making war for its own benefit. As she matured to the awesome political opportunities inherent in the presidency, she broadened her view of the potential evil and abuse of the office. She realized as early as the late Thirties that the capabilities of the power structure allowed Franklin Roosevelt to manipulate American public opinion in favor of war.

Possibly Roosevelt had provoked Japan to attack America's Pacific Fleet at Pearl Harbor. But more blatant was propaganda from other American institutions striving to swing public opinion in favor of foreign aggression: a languid press refusing to dig into the facts, fanatical flag-waving by veterans organizations and hysterical rhetoric by politicians that war was honorable, glorious and patriotic. The atrocity of Pearl Harbor had served to distract attention from the causes and reasons of the attack, for the bombing, strafing and torpedoing had crippled a proud and democratic nation.

Jeannette had nothing to lose in seeking the truth, for her political future again had been destroyed. Through careful study and research, she assembled a thesis contending Roosevelt and Winston Churchill had plotted to thrust America into combat with Japan. Investigating moral overtones was an indiscreet thing to do in 1941, but Jeannette was not bound by discretion when the issues of war and peace were concerned.

On Dec. 8, 1942, to celebrate the one-year anniversary of her historic vote, Jeannette inserted a lengthy article entitled "Some Questions About Pearl Harbor" into the *Congressional Record*. Her remarks were the first attempt to explore the truth since sociologist Charles Beard in 1935 had prophesized such an attack.

Other Congressmen joined her in asking for an investigation, but the Naval Affairs Committee of the House of Representatives refused to discuss the issue while the nation was embroiled in world war. Jeannette ignored accusations that criticism meant treason. She bluntly accused Roosevelt of a conspiracy with Churchill to deprive Japan of badly needed raw materials until its people were near starvation. Her documents showed that Japan, unable to survive the economic blockade, was compelled to fight.

Jeannette suggested Churchill had duped Roosevelt into war to protect British imperialist interests in the Orient. The ambitious Japanese government — also an imperialist — had been threatening British colonialism with its aggression in China. Jeannette contended Churchill was worried he would be robbed of Britain's Far East possessions while the Germans bombed England. She insisted Churchill convinced Roosevelt during the Atlantic Conference of 1941 that American embargoes of exports to Japan would stall the enterprising Japanese from invading China. In Jeannette's opinion, Churchill hoped the Japanese would retaliate and attack America, drawing the King of Capitalism into the war as an ally to the British and their sagging war economy.

She wondered why Roosevelt might have acquiesced in the plan to cut off food and raw materials to Japan while continuing to export the principal war materials of oil and scrap iron. She asked:

> *Was it not strange that Mr. Roosevelt, who, by refusing for years to enforce the Neutrality Act of 1936 to prevent shipments of war supplies to Japan despite popular demand, had largely contributed to supplying that nation with the raw materials for the armament now being used against our troops?*

Painstakingly, Jeannette documented her argument. She made references to 16 published journals, comments or articles that pointed to a conspiracy. She insinuated Roosevelt expected an attack on Pearl Harbor, since for two weeks before the bombing the White House had sent almost daily warnings to the commander-in-chief of the Pacific fleet that the Japanese were expected to strike.

Jeannette attributed the early morning massacre to an unwillingness by naval commanders to take the cables seriously and an over-confidence that America never could be attacked. The moral implications of setting up innocent Navy men to die or be maimed in the interest of public opinion was immeasurable, she claimed, and far worse was that the severity of the attack was beyond Roosevelt's dreams and won his instant support for war. Observed Jeannette in her conclusion:

> *A year ago, one of my congressional colleagues, having observed for months the adroitness with which President Roosevelt had brought us ever closer to the brink of war in the Atlantic only to be continually frustrated in the final step by a reluctant Congress, seeing fate present the President on December 7, 1941, with a magnificent moral categorical, right out of the blue — a casus belli beyond all criticism — exclaimed in despair: 'What luck that man has!' But was it luck?*

Jeannette's suspicion of American conspiracy with the British eventually won her acclaim as the first revisionist to contest the facts of Pearl Harbor. Although she considered any armed conflict a heinous social crime, she could have condoned war if America was surprised with an invasion of its continental shores, making immediate defense imperative.

But she could not condone war as a method of economic aggression, feigned in the shroud of defense, as she interpreted the attack on Pearl Harbor. War in its very basic form, she believed, was unnecessary: strip the profits and the aggression, outlaw the luxurious lifestyles of military brass, expose the confused patriotism concept used to reinforce its evils and the entire thing would be unnecessary.

Although Jeannette raised some ugly possibilities concerning Pearl Harbor, Americans hardly stopped to listen. The White House avoided comment, and Roosevelt still was fuming over her indiscretions when Earl Godwin, a radio commentator on the Blue Network's Ford Hour, came to the President's defense. "Seems to me that it is about as low down a state of American mind as you could get without excavating pretty deeply," he broadcast to millions of Americans.

Jeannette got little credit for her work, but she was somewhat vindicated by 1952, when five major books had been written alleging a conspiracy. Although her credibility in Congress now was largely shattered, she kept her ideas attuned to the future.

Seventies feminist Gloria Steinem and the mystique of the women's liberation movement was decades away, yet Forties feminist Jeannette became more strident in her plea for women to unlock the door to peace. She was aware her teachings had enjoyed little impact, but she persevered in her campaign. While women had shown no discernable protest against war, Jeannette was convinced they would vote Roosevelt out of office in 1944.

> *I am still convinced that the women can prevent war if they put their minds on it. If the mothers cared as much for their sons as they do for their social position we would not have war. Alas, the parasitic life they have led has corrupted their emotional life.*

American women disappointed Jeannette when FDR was re-elected, although they at least attempted to steer the nation away from war by discussing peace among other 'gracious living' topics at their trendy 'in vogue' woman's clubs. Teenagers — including the young boys Jeannette was trying to protect — were locked into a social phenomenon of Army boots, bobby sox, slumber parties and jukeboxes, and Jeannette in her persistent dedication to peace suffered bouts of futility and depression and feared failure in the male world.

She finished her term in Congress in December 1942 sensing she could offer nothing more to the peace cause, and returned to Georgia to rebuild her home, which had burned in a kerosene fire a few years earlier. The unrest Jeannette encountered after leaving Congress signalled changes in her life by putting to death her notions that she could be a principal character in achieving peace. Although she frequently entertained thoughts of regaining public office, Wellington casually suggested her chances for re-election were nil. She mused:

> *It would take twice as much money as I have to make an easy race a hard one even more. Since there is no way to know about the war situation in the future im [sic] not willing to risk all I have.*

Jeannette enjoyed the prospect of becoming a student of the peace movement rather than continuing as a hard-fought leader.

As she contemplated her future, she toyed with the prospect of writing a book about peace organizations in America. Such a scheme was merely a fantasy; Jeannette hated to write, and her regret in not being more disciplined showed in her frantic attempts near the end of her life to document her history. More appealing to her sense of adventure was a trip to India, ostensibly to study its contribution to world peace. In 1946 she boarded a ship for an extensive world tour, but her intended target was India, where she sought a greater truth in the ideal of Mohandas Gandhi.

"Gandhi...was the greatest philosopher of our time. He had two things he taught people: truth and non-violence. If his philosophy doesn't hold, we are lost."

(Jeannette Rankin in a letter to a friend)

LEARNING FROM GANDHI
Chapter 10

Mohandas Karamchand Gandhi was renowned as a man of inner peace, mental strength and spiritual vision, and for this he was renamed Mahatma, meaning 'Great Soul.' Some people called him the Saviour returned, although more pragmatic minds admired him for his passive resistance to violence and his studied independence from oppression. Among his disciples of the latter was Jeannette Rankin.

After a short visit with her long-time friend, Harriet Yarrow, in Turkey, Jeannette entered India in the autumn of 1946 to seek out the famous Gandhi. Jeannette had great expectations of India. Since Wellington had paid for the trip — subsequently he would help her subsidize six more trips to India and world tours that included Russia, South America and South Africa — Jeannette could be frugal without being restrictive. The pursuit of knowledge was a pleasure she could enjoy, for education was a high priority in the Rankin family.

As the largest and richest landowner in Montana, Wellington easily could afford Jeannette's world adventures, and as his vast cattle ranches yielded huge profits, her travels yielded huge ideas.

When Jeannette arrived in Delhi, she was told Gandhi was 1,000 miles to the north in Bengal, trying to calm the rioting between the Hindus and the Moslems. The intrepid master of the Indian people was getting out of bed at 4 a.m. to walk to nearby villages to offer his consultation. Fearing she would be imposing frightfully to walk and talk with him while he was preoccupied with his work, she decided to wait until her next trip to India to visit him.

She regretted her decision.

Before she returned, Gandhi was shot to death at his home of retreat and prayer — his *ashram* — by a disgruntled Hindu newspaper editor. Although greatly saddened at his passing, Jeannette found in his life an immutable dedication to freedom, and such perseverance did not differ much from her own. He exemplified the Eastern concept, with its spiritualism and passive resistance, and she the Western concept.

They had little in common: Gandhi was a nationalist, Jeannette a social revolutionary; he was deeply religious, she a political philosopher; he fasted and sipped fruit juice to sustain himself, she was a skilled cook; he supported the British in World War I, but she was angered by America's commitment to what she considered a European war.

Yet Jeannette, forging ahead in her purposeful desire to free American women from the slavery of war, found the aging Indian pacifist the first real hero of her life. He represented to her the ultimate freedom: independence of the mind. Dutifully and nonviolently he had turned Indian public opinion against British colonial rule and was estranged as a criminal and branded a rebel by the British.

While Jeannette had voted 'no' amid the popular outcry for blood after Pearl Harbor, Gandhi was advocating passive resistance to the German and Japanese militaries. Jeannette understood his lonely, obstinate search for total independence, and she came to idolize him as she had no other human being.

Her burning desire to learn more about his teachings had smoldered since 1918, when in her second year in Congress she had urged that America recognize Irish independence from British rule. American leaders of the India community came to her office to inquire why she hadn't considered introducing a resolution to recognize the Indian struggle for independence. Jeannette subsequently met an Indian author named Lajpat Rai and read his books, *Young India* and *England's Debt to India.* They chatted about Gandhi for several hours until Jeannette realized he exemplified in many respects her concept of true freedom: one person using democratic rights for social change.

From that moment, she was sensitive to developments in India and was an avid student of Gandhi. She once wrote:

> *Gandhi got England — then the biggest nation in the world — out of India without the loss of life. In my opinion he was the greatest philosopher of our time. He had two things he taught people: truth and non-violence. If his philosophy doesn't hold, we are lost.*

Jeannette believed Americans who sought an intelligent substitute for war in settling international disputes might find in the methods of Gandhi a new knowledge and a new faith in power without violence. The significance of her India experience was not *because* Gandhi did things that interested her, but *how* he did it. She considered India far ahead of other Asian countries in the building of a new civilization attuned to the needs of its people, despite the extensive social misery propagated by its caste system.

Gandhi became one of two influences — the other being British sociologist Benjamin Kidd — who shaped Jeannette's thinking in the final decades of her life.

Gandhi, born in 1869, experienced a mediocre childhood fraught with disappointments in school, sports and social circles. Even when he graduated from London University with a law degree, he remained shy and withdrawn and withered from the crude personal attacks common in the courtroom. He signed a year's contract as counsel to an Indian firm in Natal, South Africa, and the oppression observed toward Hindus there started a new life for him. He became an activist with a penchant for inciting people to peaceful protest. As Jeannette Rankin was casting her historic vote against war with Japan in 1941, he had been jailed and ostracized for his beliefs, yet was considered the prophet of nonviolence in the 20th Century.

This vegetarian Indian in a loincloth showed how the public opinion of a nation could be vested against the government to secure a greater freedom. Personally, Gandhi's sacrifices were immense. He read deeply and compellingly, fasted, meditated and circulated quietly among the Indian people, breathing his gospel of passive resistance as a means of destroying oppression. Jeannette was Gandhi's Western counterpart; although she rejected the techniques of prayer, meditation and fasting as impractical in consumptive America, she made a similar dedication to her cause.

In letters to friends and relatives, "the Lady Rankin," — as Jeannette came to be known by Indians — said she was not advocating that America duplicate a program for peace from the Indian democracy, but that the country look seriously at the best of Gandhi's attributes and apply them to American society.

Jeannette concluded that India, with its stable democracy and fierce desire for independence, could become a model for world peace. "Civilization can be saved only by new ideas," she wrote. "If India has much to give us in the way of inspiration, we should receive it gladly. There is a new awakening in those old countries with their long backgrounds and we can profitably share in it, if we have the will and the knowledge to do it."

Although considered by many Americans to be an authority on nonviolent social change, Jeannette discovered she had much to learn if she was to match the Gandhi ideal. "One thing is certain," she wrote from India. "There will be ample opportunity for growth, and I hope I shall come back better prepared to face our own problems."

The Gandhi philosophy of passive resistance was conceived partly by America's Henry David Thoreau, who in checking out books on his Harvard University library card, began an extensive reading of Indian teachings. From that literature, Thoreau developed his principles of civil disobedience, in which he advocated a moral consciousness higher than civil law.

Gandhi integrated Thoreau's theories of civil disobedience into his philosophy of passive resistance, essentially a method by which Indian people could peacefully protest unjust laws.

Jeannette absorbed this knowledge as she brushed the lives of India's poor. While she mostly had tried to educate American women to pursue peace, rather than making herself an example of civil disobedience in the Gandhi ideal, her attitude changed with her first trip to India.

The wanderlust that had made her a champion of America's common people now was opening her eyes to the decadence of the Indian society, where 14 percent of the world's population was crammed into only two percent of the world's land. India was controlled by genteel British imperialists with no concern for the welfare of 'untouchables,' that vast populace too poor and too insignificant to be classed in the caste system.

Jeannette learned Gandhi had concentrated his work among the poor, encouraging them to become self-sufficient and to secure power for their destinies. His subtle but exacting protests of laws or practices he felt unjust carried great impact, because eventually his opponents withdrew, weary from fighting a foe who would not fight back.

During Jeannette's first visit to India, she saw this theory displayed in Gandhi's school for basic education at Sevagram, near the center of India. To Jeannette the school was the most thrilling thing she saw in India, a living demonstration of Gandhi's work. He perceived that England was buying natural resources such as cotton for a low price in India, processing it into cloth in England, and shipping it back to India to sell at a higher price. To correct these economic inadequacies, he taught self-sufficiency in his school, stressing that to provide for one's life lessened the chances of autocratic rule.

Jeannette saw in the school a reflection of Gandhi's love for ideas. Children were given responsibilities considered premature by American standards. The kitchen staff, for example, planned the menu, kept inventory of the pantry, and maintained a ledger of money spent. The children were encouraged to study in the library, and they listened to the headmistress give an account of the current affairs at the end of the day. The teachers showed the children how to plant a cotton seed. They explained how it grew, performing all the processes crudely so the children could understand. They watched the teachers take the seed from the cotton, and then spin it and weave it.

Eventually through this saturated training the children were expected to become masters of their destinies, being suitably informed of the world and capable enough in their crafts to defy the people who wanted to enslave them. Jeannette was enchanted with this theme, which encouraged her belief that humankind could anticipate the future and prepare for peace without being tied to the traditions of war.

During the summer of 1943 she had contemplated writing a book she thought could be entitled, "India's Contributions to the Peace of the World." She had planned to use the example of India to demonstrate how her peace ideas could be implemented, and outlined several chapters. In one she hoped to expose the reasons and causes of war, particularly how the American economy enhanced war. Another chapter would discuss the importance of public opinion in creating a state of neutrality. Other chapters included a review of America's defense purposes only; and a lesson on how to organize a peace plan, using Gandhi's protest tactics.

Jeannette scribbled extensive general notes in preparation for the book, but failed even to write the first page.

Yet she regarded Gandhi as the key to international understanding, believing his example of nonviolence to encourage change — *Satyagraha* in the Indian language — to be the flawless blueprint for world peace. She compared his teachings with the art of jujitsu wrestling, in which the wrestler overcomes his opponent not by pushing harder but by yielding faster, pulling the opponent off balance with surprise that he had not encountered violent resistance.

While Gandhi's love of peace was instigated partly by deep religious beliefs, Jeannette's was not. Gandhi had strong ties to the Hindu religion. Jeannette had rebelled from the strictures of the orthodox church as a youth, and generally was known to possess little patience with organized religion. Yet she found common ground with Gandhi in her pursuit of peace, much to her exhilaration.

This lesson proved to her that only the commitment to the ideal of peace — not religion — was a major issue in the movement. That the commitment of other pacifists had sprung from their religious beliefs made no difference to Jeannette. She neither encouraged nor discouraged the role of religion in the peace movement, preferring to judge the sincerity of the pacifist.

She remained agnostic throughout her life, although her brother Wellington and her sister Edna were strong Christian Scientists. Personal correspondence revealed Jeannette was knowledgable of religion; sometimes she freely quoted the Bible in references to peace, yet she was known to publicly accuse the church of being a tool of the war propagandists.

Throughout her life, she gave conflicting impressions of her beliefs to many people. At times she was mocking of religion. She once purchased a magnifying glass for Wellington, who because of his religion refused to admit his eyes were failing and declined to wear glasses. Despite her many preoccupations she maintained a brisk correspondence with Ethel Bielenberg, a Montana pioneer and long-time friend, whose greatest love was Christian Science. Many of Jeannette's letters to her were of a spiritual tone, and Jeannette left Mrs. Bielenberg's son, Donald, with the impression that much of her pacifism was founded on religious beliefs.

Yet Jeannette believed most churches tried to perpetuate war rather than prevent it, being locked in a deadly battle to assert their sectional philosophies through war. She regarded the 'holy' wars with scorn and wondered why religions continued to defy the ecumenical movement, which promised to unite world churches and become a stepping stone to world peace.

Jeannette substituted for religion an aggressive search for

knowledge, and she was rewarded during her first trip to India when she met Prime Minister Pandit Jawalarlal Nehru. En route from America, she had talked with the young son of Nehru's doctor, who promised Jeannette he would try to get her an appointment with Nehru. He did. She met the Prime Minister in his office in Dehli, and left impressed with his thoughts on the role of women in the world. Jeannette had read Nehru's auto-biography, *My India, My America*, in 1942, and her meeting with him only intensified her strong ties to India.

Nehru was considerably more hawkish than Gandhi, but prompted by Jeannette's seductive ability to loosen conversation, he talked with praise of the contributions of women to Indian life.

Staring absently at the wall, Nehru's eyes assumed a distant flicker and he talked intensely, never glancing at Jeannette. The moment was rómantic, with Nehru entranced meditatively and Jeannette watching him silently, her eager mind absorbing his words. In mentioning the contribution of India women to inde-pendence, Jeannette had asked the appropriate question, and Nehru, who had reinforced her old beliefs about the role of women in social change, had given the appropriate answer. Jeannette respectfully bowed out of his office, vowing to take back to America his message that women could make a difference in human equality.

Jeannette traveled to Montana to nurse her mother, who died in the spring of 1947. After attending to other personal business she returned to India to polish her expectations of what the world could do with a leadership bent on peace rather than war.

"India may yield a substitute for war," she said on the eve of her second departure in 1949. "Certainly the world needs one, in the face of the powerful weapons of destruction that are being de-veloped." The trip coincided with the World Pacifist Conference, which Gandhi had called before his death. Jeannette got her first real taste of the rigors of Gandhi's lifestyle when she was assigned a bed of hard boards. "All I had was a cotton saree and a wool blanket," she informed friends. "Someone found me a thin quilt and mat. I wished I had more cushion on my bones." Having taken her Ford automobile to India and hired a driver — who she promptly fired because he knew less than she — Jeannette drove from Madras in southeast India to Lahore (now Pakistan) in the northwest, to study the life of the common people. She was said to have a movie-like quality, always being met with humor, respect, sympathy and understanding from villagers and high officials alike. One of Jeannette's favorite places to stay was the Taj Mahal Hotel in Bombay. There she sipped tea and watched ships arrive on the Arabian Sea in front of the hotel. She spent summers at Almora in the Himalayas, always sharing life with the natives. She found Gandhi's influence everywhere.

While Jeannette studied Gandhi, the American war habit continued.

Alarmed by the alacrity toward military aggression displayed by a country still emotionally devastated by World War II, she had prophesized in 1947 during the Russian-American cold war that "definitely the United States is going straight to war unless we change our course. It will be as soon as we get another crop of men ready."

Jeannette met the Fifties with a worldly search for new knowledge about peace, as America entered the Korean War. President Truman had issued a statement from the Oval Office in September 1949 saying Russia successfully had exploded an atomic bomb, and a nation infatuated with the threat of communism and terrified that The Bomb would be dropped to end the new prosperity hardly noticed the expenditure of 25,000 men in Korea. Amid this new national hysteria Jeannette wrote Frederick Libby: "To my great disappointment, the warriors have succeeded in getting a good war started. It is hard to see the sad faces of the young boys who are having to face this war."

Jeannette's admiration grew for President Dwight Eisenhower, whom she credited with having the common sense to recognize the futility of war. After Korea, America found new distractions, however, in the glamor of sex symbol Marilyn Monroe, the commercialization of Davy Crockett, the Hula-Hoop fad and the Beat Generation's slang, guitars, poetry and coffee houses.

In accordance with America's lackadaisical political mood, Jeannette faded entirely from public view, preferring to expand her understanding of the world rather than instill ideas in other people.

She traveled to India again in 1951, 1956 and 1959, visited Africa and Indonesia in 1953, went to South America in 1956, and toured Ireland, Russia and Turkey in 1962. In these years of exile she absorbed the cultures and politics of those countries and was dismayed to find American corporate influence everywhere.

In the presidential race of 1960, Jeannette supported Richard Nixon, believing Eisenhower's ideas about peace had influenced him in eight years of the vice presidency. Opponent Sen. John Kennedy, meanwhile, had written a book entitled *Profiles in Courage*, in which he told of the achievements of American men. He was embarrassed by public pressure, however, that he had not included women. He quickly dashed off an article for *McCalls* magazine entitled "Three Women of Courage," one of whom proved to be Jeannette. Although the article contained several errors, he lauded Jeannette in observing: "Few members of Congress have ever stood more alone while being true to a higher honor and loyality."

The article coincided with the buildup of American military advisers in South Vietnam, and Jeannette, who had been silent publicly for a decade, was aroused to anger. "My views on peace have never changed," she warned in 1961. "I have always been an advocate of peace. I am fearful that warfare in this nuclear age will be the downfall of mankind."

Gandhi always had been foremost in Jeannette's mind, as she saw in his teachings the possibility of burying the war habit forever. Not without hard work, however, could this ideal be obtained, and Jeannette's incessant searching revived her spirit when she once again approached the pedestal of national prominence in her quest for peace.

"If I haven't had anything else, I've had freedom."

(Comments to a Georgia minister)

THE JEANNETTE RANKIN BRIGADE
Chapter 11

For 23 years after Jeannette Rankin's second term in Congress had ended, she avoided direct involvement in the peace movement, preferring to occupy herself with world travels and quiet summers at her brother's Montana ranch. Most Americans had forgotten this vibrant feminist, for she was no longer involved in public issues.

During the Korean War she had suffered frustration and depression, confiding to writer Katharine Anthony that her work had been futile and unserving: "I am not going to allow you to say that you are a futile person," Anthony promised her friend. "That just isn't true. And you mustn't ever say it again. With all that you have accomplished in life you should never let such a thought enter your mind."

Years of meditation, however, and the increasing tempo of the Vietnam War, convinced Jeannette she again was needed among the ranks of people protesting war.

In May 1967, she was invited to Atlanta by Georgia peace stalwart Nan Pendergrast to speak against the Vietnam War before about 100 members of Atlantans for Peace. Jeannette had read in a morning newspaper that 10,000 American men had been killed since the war began, and she suggested at the meeting that 10,000 women prepared to march in the memory of those dead men could stop the war.

"The time has passed for us to be nice. The army isn't polite when it selects a young man and says, 'come on and fight,'" she warned. The Associated Press wired the story nationwide, and the statement was splashed in newspaper headlines everywhere. In response to Jeannette's speech, Edith Newly of New Mexico wrote to thank her "for being the courageous American, the magnificent woman you are. That you go on in spite of the past is in itself stupendous bravery."

Vivian Hallinan, the wife of a prominent San Francisco attorney, learned of the first Congresswoman's comments and immediately flew to Georgia to meet Jeannette Rankin. Hallinan found the exuberant old feminist awaiting her at the airport in Atlanta. They made a contrasting pair: the young Californian, dressed in a camel-colored zipper suit, fishnet stockings and an orange sweater; and the spunky octogenarian with a comparatively mundane dress that most respectfully could be described as stylishy earth-toned.

As they bounced along the Georgia countryside — Jeannette holding the gas pedal to the floorboard of her Chevrolet with her foot inside a high-heeled shoe — the astounded attorney's wife asked whether Jeannette would allow 10,000 women to march on the United States Capitol in her name. By the time the marauding ex-suffragist had braked her car to a stop outside the renovated sharecropper's shanty she called home, she had agreed to participate in such a march.

Marching for peace on Washington would be more than a protest of war; it would be symbolic of everything Jeannette had advocated since she had joined the suffrage campaign in Washington state in 1910. Improving the status of women had been to Jeannette the all-inclusive reform that would foster government programs for mothers and children, help secure a more judicious system of electing a president, clean up decadent social conditions and most of all, calm aggression in foreign policy.

In 1918 she had read *The Science of Power*, a book by British sociologist Benjamin Kidd, which fortified her belief that men could not end war without a push from women.

Just as she had learned from Gandhi and Nehru that the uncompromising support of women was essential to peace, Kidd awoke her to the philosophical differences between men and women on the issues of war and peace. Men were the eternal aggressors; they loved to duel like gladiators because of their obsessions with material goods. This is what Kidd called 'force.' Women were the eternal procreators, always looking to the quality of life in the future. This is what Kidd called 'power.'

Coincidentally, Kidd's theories paralleled the structures of Jeannette's family. John Rankin had brawled with his fists for land, money and pride, which eventually built his reputation as an influential community leader. Olive Rankin had produced seven children from her womb in an era when behind the curtain of prosperity hid war, bigotry, job prejudice and other maladies. Although Jeannette subconsciously had derived from her father his shrewd drive for success, the influence of his violent temper was dulled by her mother's compassion for her children's future.

Olive Rankin was a dim figure influentially in Jeannette's life, but in outliving her husband by more than 40 years, she symbolized the eternal maternal influence of which Kidd spoke. John Rankin, however, had been a relatively short-term influence. But without the benefit of his gift for rugged individualism, Jeannette might have been just another mundane homemaker struggling for an identity as a thinking human being.

Yet she sensed oppression of her mother by her father, and was fearful that she, too, was vulnerable. This fear had motivated her to action, giving her an excuse to avoid what she dreaded most: marriage. This psychological urge to motivate was contagious with her brother and some of her sisters, such as birth control crusader Edna, who pursued unique and aggressive careers. Fortunately for Jeannette, this subconscious drive had not developed into an embittered condemnation of men. This would have betrayed total discontentment with her father's attitudes. Instead, she put her subliminal unrest to work positively, believing society through the promulgation of war had repressed equality of the sexes.

Jeannette had made *The Science of Power* her workbook for the role of women in peace, speaking of it religiously as the bible of her cause, and mailing copies to anyone expressing curiosity.

Kidd's thesis was that the future of the world depended heavily on women, for they had the power to develop what he called "the emotion of an ideal." This meant they could perceive and pursue an idea because thcy had a stirring love for it. Kidd concluded that the woman "is the creature to whom the race is more than the individual, the being to whom the future is greater than the present."

From Kidd's writings and Gandhi's teachings, Jeannette had polished her personal philosophy about the future of world civilization, believing women who carried children in their bodies for nine months had more concern for their environment than men, who forever were locked into the competition of might and force.

Jeannette's ideas about force and power surfaced publicly in 1967, when she realized she must revive her dovish principles. Gandhi had been walking to villages and townships to spread his word of freedom at age 77. Could not Jeannette, at 87, perform a similar feat?

She had been accused of being too idealistic in thinking women could stop war, for they had been stymied into silence by the 'war habit' of which she spoke: the American deed of rationalizing that killing and profiteering was a 'patriotic' obligation. Protest-lyricist Country Joe MacDonald was wailing in mockery of middle class America's baleful reluctance to view war as a grim horror with his words, "Be the first one on your block to have your boy come home in a box."

Yet as the Vietnam casualty figures sailed upward, the voice of female protest became louder. By early 1968, women were angry. Jeannette Rankin had been angry for decades, but few people had listened. Her attempt to build a peace epidemic had failed, and too often she had stood alone in her outrage of war.

Two voices were stronger than one, three stronger than two. Now women promised to rise in peaceful community protest of the Vietnam War. To Jeannette's exuberance, the march in Washington would satisfy Gandhi's ideal of passive resistance and Kidd's ideal of women using their power to secure their destinies.

All of the principles Jeannette had advocated since before World War I now were being accepted to a greater degree by American society.

The massive opposition to war she always had recommended grew daily after President Johnson in 1966 increased American military troops in Vietnam to 375,000. Revelations of military and corporate misdeeds abounded. Explosives dropped on North Vietnam each week exceeded the bomb tonnage dropped on Germany at the height of World War II. American taxpayers were paying $25 billion a year for human destruction: Vietnamese children savagely scarred by napalm, racial knifings in American camp shower tents, the machine gunning of civilian peasants, exploitation of Vietnamese coastal waters by Standard Oil and other oil conglomerates, the slaughter of American soldiers by their own misdirected 'friendly' fire.

Billowing public hate for American involvement in the Vietnam War had made people eager for leaders, and Jeannette rode its crest to national prominence. By October 1967, women were mobilized across the country and called themselves the Jeannette Rankin Brigade.

Shortly before dawn on Jan. 15, 1968, women and children began gathering at Union Station in downtown Washington, D.C. By 11:30 a.m. nearly 5,000 women were milling in hushed vigil, and squads of police lined the parade route. Actress Viveca Lindfors explained to news reporters that the brigade represented millions of people opposed to the war and oppressed by the persistent neglect of human needs in America. Then the procession stepped softly into the snow to begin the long hike up Louisiana Avenue to the Capitol.

Five thousand women dressed in mourning black, carrying placards and banners asking Congress to end the Vietnam War and bring a stop to the social crises at home, rambled silently through the snow, their procession extending for many city blocks.

Black-skinned linked arms with white-skinned, red-skinned with yellow, some eyes brimmed with anticipation, others showed tears. White-haired grandmothers shared the street with chic suburban housewives, and youngsters strapped papoose-style to their mothers eyed the cavalcade with fascination. The women were chilled with anxiety as they passed hundreds of police officers standing along the one-half mile route to the Capitol, whose curious stares never faltered.

At the forefront, undaunted, was Jeannette Rankin, the wise veteran of protest. The suffrage campaigns 50 years earlier had evaporated her fear of public dissent, and she fixed her bespectacled eyes calmly on the Capitol dome and pushed steadily ahead, invigorated with the pleasure of the task. The powerful body had shrunken, and the crisp white hair marking the lonely dissenter during the World War II Congress was covered with a brown wig. Yet Jeannette's eyes flickered with delight and her black gloved hands clenched a sprawling banner proclaiming her reason for being on that street.

Figuratively, Jeannette had walked a long way.

The march came nearly 51 years after Jeannette's first Congressional vote against war and more than 26 years after her landmark vote against American entry into war with Japan. Many of her parade companions had not been born by the time of the second vote; few had been born at the time of the first. Other women looked at Jeannette with astonishment and awe. The march had attracted famous women such as Coretta Scott King and Dagmar Wilson, founder of Women Strike for Peace. Yet Jeannette enjoyed an insatiable curiosity from her fellow marchers, which she gracefully and typically ignored.

How could she explain to them the dramatic ventures of fully half a century? The lonely vigils to distribute suffrage literature on street corners? The pandemonic lobbying on Capitol Hill? Holiday picnics where people preferred romping in the tall grass to listening to an anti-war speech? The American Legion's allegations of communism, the boos and hisses from the gallery at a vote cast in the negative, the thrill of hearing Hindu villagers talk of their love for the peace-seeking Mahatma Gandhi?

All of these experiences meant a lifetime commitment to peace, more so than the romantic notion of a silent street march through glistening snow by women dressed in black. Yet to Jeannette the spirit of those women pushing toward the Capitol embodied the spirit of the peace movement, for they represented her hope that American women, in nonviolent protest, could end war forever.

As they approached the Capitol, a young police officer scooted into the front line and gripped Jeannette's arm, presuming to escort her. Jeannette and other women immediately assumed he was making a condescending gesture. Was this frail old woman not capable of good behavior on the Capitol grounds?

"She can walk. You don't need to help her," he was told.

"Don't deprive me of that pleasure," he explained.

Interpreting his comment as sarcasm and anxious to crack the officer's arrogance, Jeannette lashed out. "You don't need to worry about us. We are unarmed and not at all threatening. Do you really need those great big guns to handle an old lady?"

An 1882 law forbade demonstrations on Capitol grounds, which miffed Jeannette and other organizers of the march. They had hoped to lead the procession directly to the Capitol steps to present their petitions to House Speaker John McCormack.

The Lyndon Johnson Administration had become fearful of anti-war demonstrations, however, and the women wisely concluded that the large police force had been dispatched to jail them if they tried to break the law. Most of the marchers knew detention centers had been prepared to imprison up to 500 of the demonstrators and a cordon of police was ready for mass arrest, and Jeannette observed dryly: "There is no reason why old ladies shouldn't be allowed to go into the Capitol."

The ugly prospect of crowded jails and hungry, neglected

women forced the organizers of the Jeannette Rankin Brigade to obey the law, although the march presented an opportunity to employ civil disobedience tactics to contest the seeming violation of the right to peaceful assembly, guaranteed in the First Amendment. At the Capitol, Jeannette and 16 representatives of the demonstrators broke away from the main body. The sky was darkly overcast as they climbed the great marble steps of the Capitol. Reporters and photographers huddled deeper in their overcoats.

As the remainder of the Jeannette Rankin Brigade moved to Union Square for a rally, Jeannette and her delegation presented Speaker McCormack with the petition:

We, the United States women, who are outraged by the ruthless slaughter in Vietnam, and the persistent neglect of human needs at home, have come to Washington to petition the Congress for the redress of intolerable grievances, to demand that:

1. Congress, as its first order of business, resolve to end the war in Vietnam and immediately arrange for the withdrawal of American troops.

2. Congress use its power to heal a sick society at home.

3. Congress use its power to make reparation for the ravaged land we leave behind in Vietnam.

4. Congress listen to what the American people are saying and refuse the insatiable demands of the military-industrial complex.

McCormack was not sympathetic, but he promised to refer the petition to the appropriate House committee. Then Jeannette turned her attention to Senate Majority Leader Mike Mansfield, who in 1943 had assumed her House seat from the Western Congressional district of Montana.

While folk singer Judy Collins stirred the hearts of women and children as she sang "This Land Is Your Land, This Land Is My Land" at the base of a statue of Ulysses S. Grant at Union Square, the gracious Mansfield reportedly tried to woo Jeannette to neutrality with a silver tea set. She considered the tea a ploy to distract from the urgency of the peace march, and she talked quickly, not giving him a chance to offer her a cup.

"We must bring the boys home from Vietnam," she told him.

"How are we going to do this?" he asked.

"The same way we got them there — by planes and ships," she replied.

When she left Mansfield's office, she was thronged by reporters demanding to know what had happened.

"He was very pleasant," Jeannette told them. "You know how politicians are."

The Jeannette Rankin Brigade received ho-hum coverage, and forever at odds with a news media failing to explore her attitudes and opinions, Jeannette accused newspapers and broadcasting of a "conspiracy of silence."

Although the march had coincided with the opening day of Lyndon Johnson's final Congress, both print and broadcast media reported that Washington had generated little news that day. The work of the many reporters who had covered the march was boiled into a few sketchy stories. America was denied a valid look at the reasons for the march, and women who had participated even began arguing among themselves. "The march was a farce," complained one disgruntled black nationalist only hours afterward. "The only part that was worth anything was the [radical caucus after the march] because it made people think."

Jeannette, typically, shunned factional squabbles, believing they divided women. She was not swayed by arguments from the radical caucus that the brigade should have been more militant in its approach to winning public opinion, possibly by committing acts of civil disobedience. Jeannette reasoned that militancy might have led to violence.

Militant leaders argued that widespread arrests would have forced Congress to study more closely the reasons for the march, but Jeannette concluded the impact was on women, rather than on Congress, and would encourage other women to express themselves.

As quietly as she had resisted the militancy of Alice Paul during the suffrage campaigns, she ignored the Sixties militants and envisioned the march of the Jeannette Rankin Brigade as a masterstroke in influencing American women. She simply was impressed that the gathering had transcended age, race and philosophy, forming a coalition of moderate and radical middle-class women. The march to Jeannette was more than an incident; it symbolized her life's work. "This tremendous number of women, expressing their deep emotion against war, can't do anything but help," she said.

The reality of 5,000 women and children banded together to chant for peace was an important milestone in Jeannette's life, fulfilling her interpretation of true freedom: freedom of lawmakers to enact legislation without the ghostly manipulation by corporations of government machinery. Freedom of the press to explore social issues. Freedom of women to cast off sexist shackles that had bound them since the beginning of life. Freedom of the American people to control their government and make their own decisions.

From the instant Jeannette conceived her ideal of peace, she was unimpressed with every single argument for war. She thought logic and diplomacy pre-empted by intelligence the hot-headed emotionalism of slaughter. Because the woman's political view traditionally was of little consequence to men, Jeannette continually encouraged women to revolutionize life in America, to question the status quo, to seek change.

Woman's power to bring social change had proven little to Jeannette in the years between the passing of the 19th Amendment in 1920, which gave women the right to vote, and the Jeannette Rankin Brigade in 1968. Yet she remained optimistic that the key to total freedom was peace. "The reason women haven't done anything in the last 50 years is because they have lost their freedom," she argued.

After the North Vietnamese and the Viet Cong launched the Tet Offensive, proving President Johnson's alibi that America controlled the war a lie, peace got a popularity boost. As Richard Nixon won the presidency and mumbled vague patriotic concepts about the honor of the American military, an end to war promised to be years away. Suddenly the ranks of war protestors were swollen with angry, embittered Americans.

Jeannette's public appearances became more dramatic, and she again was in the forefront of the movement for social change. By the time President Nixon was chanting, "peace with honor," Americans mostly accepted Jeannette's ideas and her lifestyles as trendy and plausible.

Yet Jeannette had not changed. In the Sixties she was the same Jeannette Rankin who had stumped the nation for suffrage in 1914. She had not grown up with America; America had grown up with her.

Jeannette adhered religiously to her self-imposed life of poverty in Georgia, struggling to retain her freedom despite her age. As a monk in exile, she combined humble living with an obsession for causes and ideas. She lived alone at her Shady Grove home with a dachshund named Sam, except for a brief platonic fling with a wayward law student who taught her the art of vegetarianism and became her personal secretary.

Vicariously, Jeannette was the prime of youth. Her vivacious mind had resisted the stereotypes of old age, although she was wrinkled and wore wigs to cover thinning hair. She had lived through the span of five American wars, yet her mind was fresh and searching, always grasping new knowledge.

Yet in tortured deliberance she drove herself to peace martyrdom, refusing to be committed to social rules and responsibilities that threatened to strip away her intellectual freedom.

She hated sexist titles, despising in particular the timeworn phrase, 'Lady from Montana,' which she thought should be 'Woman from Montana.' She preferred 'men and women' rather than 'ladies and gentlemen,' and thought 'Mrs.' implied, "You're married, too bad, sex." Jeannette had wondered as early as 1918 if the status of the husband also changed after marriage: "That marriage should change a woman's state is inconsistent and absurd. It is a relic of the old common law idea that held woman to be man's property."

Although nearing 90 years of age, she continued to devote more thought to the role of women in the peace movement than to the prospect of losing her physical capabilities: her house was laden with anti-war posters, Indian tapestries, magazines and newspapers of every description. The living room floor was of tamped earth, covered with plastic, tarpaper and Oriental rugs. The walls were cluttered with Indian memorabilia, much of it pertaining to Gandhi. She heated the room by tightly wrapping a Sunday edition of the *New York Times* into a log and rotating it on a contraption of her own invention in the fireplace. She pumped water from a nearby well and had no plans to install indoor plumbing. That would cost as much as a one-way ticket to India, and she preferred the ticket.

Wonder Robinson, a black sharecropper in his mid-20's and his wife Mattie lived in the comfortable brick house that was the main building on the property, although Jeannette as the proprieter should have lived in the house by Southern standards. The Robinsons helped with the heavy chores.

Throbbing in her little shanty was the heartbeat of the feminist movement and the peace cause. One young fan thought Jeannette epitomized "in one personality what Kidd is driving at for a coming generation of women who will allow the emotion of the peace ideal to totally possess them."

She had no practical reason for living so poorly, because her brother, before his death in 1966, would have paid handsomely for her to live in a modern house. She rejected his offers, however, continuing her love affair with the simple home life she had enjoyed in Georgia since 1926. Her indifference to material possessions and practical money matters had appalled her brother. After one summer in Montana, Jeannette was prepared to drive to Georgia. Wellington swiftly appraised her old Ford.

"You can't drive that old wreck back to Georgia," he told her.

"Why not?" she replied. "There's nothing wrong with it. It's a perfectly good car." In a few days, she had a new car, compliments of Wellington.

Wellington had arranged his sister's financial independence, having purchased a ranch and made other investments on her behalf. Although these strong-minded Rankins had battled philosophically for most of their lives, Wellington gave her the money without consternation. Jeannette used the money judiciously, spending most of her income for study trips, books, magazines or newspaper subscriptions, or bequests to needy friends or relatives. After Wellington's death she inherited $75,000 from his estate, which eventually she divided among her survivors.

Jeannette, in an unconscious parallel to Gandhi's work ethic, preferred the life of toil to the leisures of modern living. This was an idealogy rather than an old-fashioned notion, for she believed hard work created an awareness of a person's independence in the purest democratic fashion. Her disinterest in money and material goods was more of a studied determination, for she had proved early in life that her ingenuity for mechanical skills exceeded the interest of the average American woman. "If I haven't had anything else, I've had freedom," she told a minister who visited her cottage frequently.

Jeannette made of herself a living example of independence, telling women the only discrimination they faced they had imposed on themselves. If women would not make decisions about their futures, how could they expect to be free? Women could not wait for men to liberate them, and Jeannette admonished: "You can't throw out half the people of the country and say that their minds and feelings are inferior."

In a series of public appearances, Jeannette spoke fervently about the role of women in changing society, using anecdotes about their strength to color her argument that they were thinking, loving human beings who could make yet greater contributions to American living.

She spoke of a young man who had visited a Montana female doctor with a tale of courage. The man told the doctor of a woman several years earlier who had left her frontier cabin early in the morning by horseback and had ridden up a canyon, through a gulch, over a mountain, forded a river and crossed a plain, arriving late at night in a mining camp, having traveled 60 miles alone. Then her son was born.

The young man told the doctor, "I am her son. I heard you were working for the vote, and so I thought that I would tell you that I am for you."

This personable style won friends for Jeannette even among the distrustful, but many women rejected her arguments, suspicious they would be deprived of security and love from men if they tried to 'revolutionize' their lifestyles. Jeannette was impatient at this hesitation, and even needled her more liberal counterparts, accusing them of working only microscopically for liberation because they did not consider the oppression of war a major issue. Jeannette was ambivalent toward this sudden popularity among some women to consider themselves liberated, believing the mechanics of the movement were good but the goals were excessively timid. "I've been talking about these same things for 50 years," she said.

Change didn't occur fast enough for Jeannette. She saturated herself with the love of freedom, and she could not fathom the prospect of dying, without seeing America take a major step toward commitment to her peace ideal.

After six decades of political activism, Jeannette still viewed war as woman's greatest oppressor, for women had failed to subdue the male arrogance and brute force exemplified in war and sublimated in sex. She said the relationship between fear and procreation was shown in the substantial number of 'war babies' of the Forties.

"The modern male looks too much at woman as a sex object," she told feminists gathered on the steps of Georgia's Capitol in 1970. "In the animals sex is a matter of procreation." Jeannette viewed sex as the only creative pleasure remaining for Americans, contending they had resisted change for most of the century. "Most of it is for enjoyment," she observed in an interview in 1971, and with a smile, she added: "How would I know?"

Jeannette was distressed by this enslavement of women, and

during a cross-country tour she complained to a Tacoma, Wash., reporter: "If they're independent, talkative, and say what they think, they can't get a job or a husband. Look at me — unmarried and unemployed most of my life!"

Having been born into a close and proud family, Jeannette clearly was dismayed and angered that modern American families relied on commercialization, television and machines to entertain themselves, with the Vietnam War yet unsettled.

Although a woman without a son, she argued that war was ruining the American family. Jeannette in a single-minded sense slipped past — without great commitment — all the other facets of American living. She detested football, she thought light reading, television and movies were mostly superfluous, and she was not responsible for raising a family.

Yet she strongly thought the family to be the mainstay of American living, the human institution on which war inflicted the most harm. Every American soldier killed on foreign soil meant grief for a family, and Jeannette pleaded with women to spend less money for electrical conveniences such as can openers and dishwashers and contribute the dollars they had saved to the peace movement. She said modern appliances had made housework less challenging, depriving the woman of her purpose in life by devaluating her role as wife and mother. Jeannette told one interviewer: "It isn't a question of what she does. It's what she contributed to society as a whole."

President Nixon had condemned day care centers as a threat to the family, but Jeannette epostulated: "I don't think being separated from the children hurts them. I think it's what the mother does when she is with the child." Clearly, she believed the first responsibility of a mother was to teach her children the attributes of peace and the truth about war. But sometimes her optimism faded, for in 1969 she had said bluntly: "Women still raise the boys and men take them off to war and kill them."

Jeannette related two anecdotes illustrating her growing concern of the mindless impact of military propaganda on women and children:

Some children visited her home in Georgia and alarmed her when they began singing about wanting to be soldiers. Sensing they did not understand military life beyond the romanticism of the uniform, Jeannette had them substitute the word 'slave' for 'soldier,' explaining a soldier knew no glamor for he did only what he was ordered. The children sang the tune with 'slave' as lustily as they had sung with 'soldier.'

In another instance, Jeannette had seen a kindergarten teacher telling children to march with the instructions, "Raise your knees like soldiers." In complaining that in a peaceful environment children should not learn the indoctrination of war, she termed the kindergarten lesson "the most awful propaganda you could think of."

Jeannette was popular with the children, for bursting from her wrinkled exterior was the absolute joy of living and an incarnate kidishness shining in a disarming smile. She was like a magnet to children everywhere; and her charm with young people was shown in a letter from youthful Jennifer Robinson, the black girl who lived over the hill from Jeannette's Shady Grove:

> *Dear Jeanette Rankin*
> *You is coming home tonight   I did miss you and I no you miss*
> *me   Stanley Wonder and Mattie Jeff and me miss you   We*
> *wrote you a letter   did you Right us a letter   We send you*
> *some picture   and we send you a letter   Miss Rankin I did*
> *miss you   I love you   all of us Love you*
> *from Jennifer*
> *Love you*

While Jeannette romanced with being young, she schemed a plan to help other elderly women be independent. Sailing to America from the Orient in the mid-Sixties, she had thought of building a cooperative home for aged women. She envisioned the home to be a place where women could prosper and share, and learn through caring for themselves how to be socially and financially independent.

After returning to Georgia, Jeannette designed what became known as the Round House, constructed from cement blocks and built atop a hill overlooking her cottage. Ten wedge-shaped bedrooms surrounded a common room, which had cooking facilities. Three bathrooms were built to one side of the building. Jeannette planned a lake for boating and swimming and a large vegetable garden. Carloads of people were attracted to the curious building, but nobody accepted a room.

Many — such as Elizabeth Winburn Sinclair — had good intentions of joining the commune, but their enthusiasm withered. Some conceded to the pressures and responsibilities of their families, while others discovered belatedly they were afraid to trade the security of their homes for this new venture.

Dejected, Jeannette turned her interest to other projects while the Round House suffered the indignities of a brawling fraternity party and a roaming gypsy band. The house stood mostly idle until her death, and her last will and testament revealed that she still saw hope in the project. A clause read: "Five acres of said land surrounding the round house for women workers and the house shall be distributed to such charitable foundations as shall be selected by my Executrix, to be used for the benefit of unemployed women workers as a home...."

Jeannette never gave up wanting women to be free.

However idealistic she was in her theories about women's contribution to the peace movement, she demonstrated the perseverance of one woman committed to a cause and a zest for making attempts to stop the rambling cessation of war. As she neared her 90th birthday, people who knew her well realized the true milestone of her life was not her age, but the feasibility of her progressive thought.

"If only we could get more women to follow in your footsteps," wrote a New York woman who just had read a feature article about Jeannette in *Ramparts* magazine. "Not merely to have won the vote is enough; that to take one's public stand for what is right and just is more important."

In a telegram congratulating Jeannette on her 90th birthday, Coretta Scott King observed:

Your dauntless courage as a leader for equal rights for women and as a champion of peace have immortalized you in the hearts of millions at home and abroad. It has been a privilege to support your efforts and to have my efforts supported by so great a woman. You have brought honor to yourself, America and womanhood.

The accolades sketched a portrait of an American woman who had defied convention to make her appeals heard, but Jeannette was not finished with her blueprints for peace. One major segment remained, and that was the reinstitution of democratic government.

> *"Miss Rankin ... is a future directed person who throws herself into her cause. If aging is the erosion of one's ideals, then Jeannette Rankin is young forever."*
>
> (Consumer Advocate Ralph Nader in the *Washington Star*, September 1972)

PEOPLE POWER
Chapter 12

Three thousand people massed in New York's Carnegie Hall.

They were New York's affluent, dressed in fashionable furs, evening gowns, tuxedos and top hats. The great hall darkened, leaving a patch of light on the main stage. When Jeannette Rankin's slender, chiffon-clad figure approached the podium, the people applauded loudly, and the nation's first Congresswoman smiled in friendship. The audience gawked in wonder at this petite spellbinder, this crusader for social causes, this tough, rebellious maverick with a penchant for womanly charm and persuasion. Eagerly, and without fear — for speaking to 3,000 fashion-conscious New Yorkers could be an intimidating experience — Jeannette unveiled her argument:

> *Each day we feel the question asked why, with our improved means of production resulting in such splendid material products, have we failed to increase the products of human happiness? Is it necessary to have so much poverty, misery and crime? With these questions the demands of the people for a controlling voice in their destiny will be imperious. This*

means we must have democracy in government, in industry, in social life if we are to have social growth.

An apt description of the Watergate Era?

Perhaps.

The speech, however, was delivered in March 1917, just one month before Jeannette's debut in Congress. Her timeless ideal-ogy concerning 'people power' in governmental affairs proved as apropos 50 years later, when she revived old ideas to crest a new movement. Jeannette considered her scheme for people power to be a last-ditch effort for peace, for it involved the rudiments of democracy in their purest form. She simply wanted to restore government to the people.

She had proposed such principles before 90 percent of today's Americans were born. To Jeannette, the question of election reform was simple: either elected representatives supported democracy, or they did not.

She sought several simple democratic changes throughout her lifetime. They included the initiative, which enabled voters to petition to put legislation on the ballot; the referendum, to repeal legislation undesirable to voters; the recall, providing a chance to end the poor performance of an elected official by voting him out of office; multi-member Congressional districts, to place more candidates before the electorate; a unicameral Congress, to be more representative of the people and prevent gerrymandering of districts; and the preferential direct election of President, to downplay the presidential primary, remove candidate selection from the power of the two major political parties, and provide the voters with a broader selection of candidates.

"What good is the vote if you have no one to vote for?" she asked, regarding preferential voting as a natural extension of suffrage.

Under Jeannette's plan, the Electoral College would be abolished. She believed the President, if more dependent on public opinion and less on corporate money to win, would be more inclined to serve the people instead of the men in corporate boardrooms.

These ideas were challenged by some people as subversive, but Jeannette argued that the Constitution implied the power of Americans to determine their destinies through election reform. Her opinion, however, was that the balance of power in the legislative and executive branches was controlled by the military-industrial complex.

By 1969 she almost exclusively criticized the military as the worst threat to democracy. She told 1,500 students in a speech at the University of Georgia moratorium rally on Oct. 15 that the Vietnam War was being kept alive by mercenary interest groups with tremendous influence on federal lawmakers. "We waste our money on the military," she complained. "We spend over half of our peacetime money getting ready for the next war. We give military aid to countries that have no need of it and say we're settling a dispute. Day after day..., we say that we've got to be strong enough to dominate the world, and the people do not have a vote."

Determined to exercise her constitutional rights, Jeannette joined every anti-war demonstration she could and eagerly used the press to ridicule the military mind. "War is nonsense. Bring the boys back forthwith," she told a reporter from the *San Francisco Examiner*. The reporter asked if that meant surrender, and Jeannette replied, "Surrender is a military idea. When you're doing something wrong, you stop." The anti-war demonstrations intrigued, even captivated her. She was thrilled that many hundreds of thousands of Americans were expressing their beliefs in street protests and public rallies, although she was sure their might was small compared with that of the military.

Jeannette's high profile was romanticized by youth; a portrait photograph for *Ramparts* magazine was made into a color poster and hung in bookstores stocking counterculture literature, for example. But she, too, gained something new. She read current anti-war books, such as *Armies of the Night*, Norman Mailer's nonfiction tale about peace demonstrations at the Pentagon, and called moratoriums "a marvelous expression of opinion...the most spontaneous thing that has happened."

Although Jeannette hinted at her ideas about democratic government through decades of outraged attacks on the war establishment, only during the moratorium of the late Sixties did she unveil an educational campaign to try to alert voters to what she thought was a deliberate military takeover of the United States. Jeannette was convinced a military-induced conspiracy already was planning a sequel to the Vietnam War. She anticipated that her life had nearly run its course, and she frantically and elaborately outlined the methods she thought would be most helpful to bring Americans closer to democracy. By 1972, consumer advocate Ralph Nader had concluded that her ideas were sound and prophetic, and he said if aging was the erosion of a person's ideals, the 92-year-old feminist was young forever.

Although a national magazine in 1963 had spoken of her as "the late Jeannette Rankin," her indomitable spirit remained alive and intense, her ideas polished to a glistening clarity. As the Vietnam War stumbled to a pathetic finish and Jeannette neared the end of her life, she worked in the interest of youthful generations, who faced the prospect of other wars.

Futuristically, Jeannette felt obliged to leave the children of the Seventies with a legacy of hope, and in a flurry of public activity she presented her principles of people power during national television talk shows: TODAY, the Dick Cavett Show, the David Frost Show, and at meetings of women's political caucuses in Georgia, New York, Arkansas and Tennessee. She addressed the Constitutional Convention in Montana in 1972, and prolifically distributed information sheets nationwide, telling of her ideas on democratic reorganization. Radio broadcasts and newspaper columns were filled with her ideas, and national news magazines heralded Jeannette Rankin as the heroine of the feminist counterculture.

Life magazine's Elizabeth Frappollo, for example, wrote: "In a national election year, Jeannette Rankin's political experience and phenomenal energy are helping to make her one of the most popular — and surprising — figureheads of the women's movement."

Deeper research would have eased the necessity of being surprised about Jeannette's public acceptance. Her view of the American political economy was based on the principle that human rights transcended property rights, dating to her years at the School of Philanthropy in 1908 and her friendship with settlement worker Jane Addams. Of the humanitarian's contribution to peace through reform, Jeannette noted:

> *I am sure that if she were living today she would recognize how important it is to perfect the machinery through which the people may voice their wishes. It is difficult for me to see what one can accomplish for peace unless one recognizes that even in times of peace one-half of our tax money is spent to promote the war establishment. Day by day we become aware of the fact that our government is not carrying out promises to curb the war machinery.*

Jeannette thought if war was eliminated, taxes could be cut drastically and people would have more money to spend, stimulating the economy. She figured a liquid money system would redistribute wealth and decelerate the struggles and misery caused by class consciousness.

Having plunged conveniently into the brouhaha of Progressivism in 1910, Jeannette learned to view with disgust the corporate influence of government. She disdained the thinking of President William Howard Taft and other 'big money' advocates, who believed the uneducated strata of Americans was incapable of running the government machinery and needed the guidance of a big brother.

Jeannette concluded that corporations manipulating Congressmen also regulated the intent and direction of legislation, which meant Americans had nothing to say about their destinies. If Congress wanted to propel them into war, how could they stop the momentum? If social legislation was shelved, who could be their advocate?

Jeannette believed the inevitable consequence of corporate control of government was war. If federal time and money were devoted to economic investments abroad — and huge sums of money were appropriated to a questionable defense plan — Americans would suffer. In a nation of plenty, people would go hungry. "With all our ingenuity, skill and devotion to progress, why have we hungry people in the United States?" she had asked the congregation of the Prince Avenue Baptist Church in Athens, Ga., in 1932. "Is it because we don't care? Is it because of our inability to overcome the obstacles? Is it because of failures in the past?"

She remembered only too well when America was in the midst of the Great Depression and unemployment had caused unprecedented numbers of broken homes and unhappy people. She regarded the Depression as the unsavory aftermath of American investments in World War I. Economic suffering would provoke other aspects of social misbehavior, such as crime and welfare abuse, and Jeannette believed the government would find difficulty in policing the problems it inadvertently caused by its negligence.

Her solution in its purest form was to return government to the masses.

Although Jeannette's ideas about direct democracy were embedded in the history of Twentieth Century America, only in the Sixties and Seventies with a new awareness in politics did they become popular. This awakening enhanced her public usefulness in the final eight years of her life, enabling her to dovetail the lessons of the past with the optimism of the future. As a democratic, future-oriented person, Jeannette believed she should speak loudly and forcefully about inequities in the American government system. The idea of philosopher John Stuart Mills that a true democracy is "a government of the whole people by the whole people represented," was a favorite with her.

Because Jeannette's call for broader representation endangered special interest groups and the Congressmen they had elected, she was not popular with the conservative business-oriented sector. Among progressive legislators, however, she found new friends and allies.

One of them was Rep. Emanuel Celler, a New York Democrat

who had been in Congress when Jeannette was elected in 1940. He had invited her to testify on democratic government and election reform before the House Committee on the Judiciary on Feb. 26, 1969.

She was a big attraction, for the mysticism that had drawn thousands of people to her lectures in 1917 persisted. People simultaneously praised and were awestruck by this woman, and as Jeannette entered the committee room on Capitol Hill, she again discovered such an atmosphere.

Several men rushed to the door to escort her to a chair, but Jeannette indignantly brushed past them. Although she was nearly 90, she was remarkably energetic. Her mannerisms betrayed a youthful exuberance and a modern thinker. A wide, brown leather watch band was strapped to her right wrist and a string of 'hippie' beads encircled her neck. As she spoke, she rose out of her chair. But Chairman Celler interrupted her and urged her to sit, fearing she thought she was obliged to stand despite her age.

Jeannette was unimpressed. "May I stand?" she asked him. "I fight better standing."

Anyone knowledgable in the issues of election reform knew for what Jeannette Rankin stood. She advocated, supported and pursued the principle of 'people power,' which in her humanitarian ideal meant a voice for everyone: not just the rich, the intelligent, the influential and the conspiring; but the poor, the uneducated, the apathetic and the innocent. "I can trust the people," she told the committee.

Jeannette by 1968 had taken a fresh look at the role of the presidency. With America deepening its involvement in the Vietnam War, she threw her support behind the Democratic populist Eugene McCarthy. When McCarthy was destroyed in the primary, however, she cast her vote for Richard Nixon, resurrecting her belief that he'd learned the value of peace from Eisenhower. "Ike seems to be really in ernest [sic] about preventing war," she had written during the Fifties. "It is the only way his name can live in history and he knows it." Just how wrong

Jeannette's choice in 1968 proved to be was reflected in the election of 1972, when she voted for George McGovern and his antithesis of Nixon's foreign policy and his personal and presidential lifestyle.

She had lost faith in Nixon, particularly incensed about his flaccid statement, "peace with honor," which she believed was a statement of his link to the military-industrial complex and not to allegiance with the American people. She believed that while Lyndon Johnson had been stampeded out of office by a nation sick of war, the election machinery ineffectively prevented Americans from carrying their will further. "The 1968 political year demonstrated ... we can throw a President out, but we cannot elect one," she said.

Jeannette thought the only way America could be exonerated from presidential misconduct and corporate influence was to elect a president truly representative of the people. First, the Electoral College must be abolished, a method of election Jeannette regarded as an archaic ritual that went against the will of the people. Previous presidential elections, such as that of Benjamin Harrison in 1888, substantiated this contention. President Grover Cleveland had won more popular votes but Harrison had the benefit of the Electoral College.

Jeannette's more innovative scheme, however, was preferential voting. This idea was linked to her premise that political parties did nothing useful; her intermingling attitudes on economics and politics made her less than a party advocate. She detected no major differences between the Republicans and the Democrats, believing they adopted platforms only to entice the mood of the people they were trying to sway without taking a firm stand on any issue.

In the months before Jeannette had entered Congress for the first time, Theodore Roosevelt wrote from Sagamore Hill, admonishing her to make and keep the Republican Party loyal to the spirit of Abraham Lincoln. Roosevelt thought Jeannette symbolized the power of change and innovation, and he asked that she always be conscious of the rights of each American.

Roosevelt asked Jeannette to remember that the Republican Party must "make this nation the land where love and justice go hand in hand; which stands for fair play within our own borders." By the time she celebrated her 90th birthday, she had little regard for his worship of the Republican ideal, but she had heeded his advice on democracy.

Political parties were to her but roadblocks to real issues, and she had proved in both of her elections to Congress that only the issues on which she campaigned made the difference in her being elected. In 1916 she was elected as a Republican in a Democratic landslide. As Woodrow Wilson was elected president, he carried the Democratic tide almost to the precincts, but Jeannette had been elected on the nonpartisan issue of equal suffrage. In 1940 she was elected to Congress when Montana Democrats swept the state with huge pluralities; a blatant peace candidate shadowed by war. With the inhibiting threat of party politics removed, Jeannette argued, candidates could pursue their beliefs.

Jeannette's plan for preferential voting provided for the opportunity of pure democratic representation. She viewed the ideal presidential election as a horse race, in which each participant in the field had widely varying abilities.

Her plan was to circumvent the primary elections where minority candidates were ripped apart by big party politics, and place on the general election ballot the name of every candidate who legitimately desired to become president. Candidates would be required to prove a genuine following to prevent the list from becoming outrageously lengthy. The ballot might contain the names of several Democrats, several Republicans, and a handful of minority candidates, but they would not be designated as such.

Following Jeannette's arrangements, a voter in the 1972 presidential election — and this is the author's interpretation — could have had a choice among Shirley Chisholm, representing blacks and women; Henry Jackson, a Western financial conservative; George Wallace, representing the white South; Edmund Muskie, a New England liberal with a respected Congressional background; George McGovern, a blatant anti-war candidate with

Populist leanings; Richard Nixon, a domestic conservative with friendly ties to the military and industrialists; Hubert Humphrey, a liberal champion of labor; Fred Harris, an anti-war liberal representing the poor and the Indians; and Eugene McCarthy, representing students, the poor, the working class and the anti-war movement.

Jeannette believed names should be rotated on the ballots among states, since psychology revealed people often voted alphabetically.

The order of the candidates' names in Montana, for example, would differ from the order on the Minnesota ballot, and also from the New Mexico ballot. The essence of the open ballot was two-fold, in Jeannette's opinion. Anyone with a large following could be a candidate, through petitions or preferential primaries.

Jeannette anticipated voting would be more complex but not beyond any American's intelligence. A ballot sheet would list all candidates, and voters would mark the order of their preference. A voter who wanted Richard Nixon to be president, for example, would mark a blank after Nixon's name as his first choice. If Henry Jackson was the voter's second choice, he would mark it accordingly.

Votes would be tabulated by computer. A person with a majority of first place votes would become president. Lacking a first place majority, the candidate with a majority of second-place votes would become president. The process would continue in this manner until a candidate won. Votes for the vice president — insuring a candidate properly prepared for office, unlike the old system of party politics — would be conducted likewise.

Jeannette justified the direct preferential vote as the method of election most in accord with American democracy, believing it returned to the American people the sovereign power of choice and made the president directly responsible to the voters. "It would increase the possibility of each vote having the same value," she had said at Carnegie Hall. "True democracy demands that each man has a vote and one man one vote."

Anticipating an outcry from the old convention party-goers

that she was destroying the two-party system, Jeannette sarcastically footnoted her overtures by assuring these people they still could wave their banners and balloons in the new system.

By 1972, American concern for the environment, the Vietnam War, alternative lifestyles and energy had revived interest in greater voter influence. Jeannette Rankin appealed to national public opinion makers to explore these surfacing ideas. She urged CBS News commentator Mike Wallace, who had reported on the issue of voter dissatisfaction in America, to air some of the constructive alternatives. To David Brinkley, the NBC News commentator who mentioned the crying need for election reform as he covered the 1968 Democratic convention, she proposed the same. Walter Lippman, who wrote a story about election reform entitled "The American Predicament" in *Newsweek* magazine, was told the fundamental idea of 'people power' represented progress for America.

Ralph McGill, publisher of the *Atlanta Constitution*, was informed that change was not new to the election process, and Jeannette reminded him that the United States Senate once was a "rich gentleman's club" of men chosen by state legislatures.

She appealed to pollsters George Gallup and Lou Harris to conduct a scientific analysis of voter habits and the voters' opinion of her preferential vote scheme, and she asked them whether she could adapt such a polling technique to the national peace organizations.

Jeannette's plan for multiple-member districts in electing members of Congress was only a more sophisticated method of taking the profits out of war. More Congressional candidates on a state ballot meant less inclination to align with special interest groups, presuming financial backing would not be required for success. This proposal was reminiscent of her suffrage work, when she had argued to convince men of the power of their vote and the significance of giving women the ballot.

To gain a broader representation of talents, backgrounds and viewpoints in Congress and to teach candidates to be responsible to the people to whom they were indebted for their election,

Jeannette proposed to pare to a minimum the number of Congressional districts in each state. New York, for example, which had 41 districts in 1972, could have six districts with 41 members. This meant each voter could cast more votes for representatives, insuring a greater base of loyalty among Congressmen. Therefore, one district could not be gerrymandered by special interest groups whose desire was to control the behavior of their representative to Congress.

By 1972 Jeannette had become a staunch proponent of a unicameral legislature, which she had admired and witnessed during her visits to India. She questioned why America must duplicate the expense of elections, research, salaries and committees if the House of Representatives consciously responded to the needs of the electorate. The Senate, then, only would be a rubber stamp, in her opinion.

Controversy, she argued, had been incompatible with the traditional American political process because elected officials were too preoccupied with the procedures of being re-elected.

"When I went to Congress in 1917, a kindly old hand asked me if I knew what my concern should be," she said. "Before I could open my mouth to tell him what I felt to be the burning issues, he smiled and said: 'Working for your next election.' The implication was that I should remain passively placid and not stir up any bears. Unfortunately for my Congressional career he was right."

But in Jeannette's love for the emotion of an ideal, she had outlasted many of the 'old hands.' In a lifetime of work, she had stated her case for freedom, and as she contracted a throat ailment and began to lose her voice, she involuntarily stopped her public appearances and rented a retirement apartment in Carmel, Calif.

One problem remained, however. Decades of work had shown one woman's proposal for a path to peace. Now, Jeannette's blueprint was complete. But true fulfillment would come in recognition for and an appreciation of her work, and in that she would be judged by history, by the masses for whom she had worked. Would she be remembered, or had she struggled in vain?

> *"When others were swept away in the tides of pas-*
> *sion, she stood her ground and gave an example of*
> *moral courage which has continued to inspire all*
> *those who love peace."*
>
> (A plaque presented to Jeannette Rankin in 1958 from the
> War Resisters' League)

JEANNETTE'S LEGACY
Chapter 13

"What can I, one person, do?"

Jeannette Rankin asked herself this question in 1910, when under the auspices of the Washington Equal Suffrage League she apprenticed the painstaking task of learning how to seek change when people resisted.

In 1973, Jeannette knew the answer. Seeking change was deliberate, tedious, unrewarding work, but she never lost sight of the emotion of her ideal: freedom. Her unflagging commitment to this goal made America readier for social change. Her work was the example to millions of people; no less to men than to women, no less to hawks than to doves, no less to conservatives than to liberals.

And she was a free thinker who made an example to women everywhere. She said of her first Congressional vote for peace:

> *I had not planned to make that speech. All my life, I have*
> *worked harder for freedom than the average person, but I*
> *knew that the first woman in Congress had to vote against*
> *war.*

And from that brief moment in 1917, she knew if she wanted to be free she had to protest war. "I believed then as I do now that women are the ones who must be concerned with the needs and development of the human race," she noted in a self-produced pamphlet. "I have always fought for the dignity of all human beings — for those of the present as well as those of future generations. I will continue to struggle as long as I live."

In nearly six decades of social activism, Jeannette Rankin had avoided a life of sex stereotypes, successfully putting her mind to a better use. And while the pacifist Jeannette exuded eternal confidence that women could stop war, the feminist Jeannette shivered with apprehension that women were being pushed through history by the moods and whims of men, and she doubted whether women desired to crack the male world of war.

She had proved by her own life, however, that a loud stir could be made by one woman who raised her voice against oppression, and she wondered how war would fare if thousands — or millions — of American women joined in the same dedication for peace and freedom. While she was disappointed that women as a political bloc had not figured prominently in the century's anti-war movement, she began to see hope in feminism. "The women's movement is going to take forward steps beyond anything we envision today," she told the *Spokesman Review* of Spokane, Wash. "I'm quite thrilled with what they're doing."

One morning in February 1972 Jeannette carried her mail into the living room of her Georgia home and tore open an envelope from the National Organization for Women. She was asked to board a plane for New York, for she had been chosen the first member of the Susan B. Anthony Hall of Fame, which had been established to recognize the superstars of women's rights. At the presentation, she was honored as "the world's outstanding living feminist," and among those applauding were other sisters of liberation: Gloria Steinem, Bella Abzug, Betty Friedan and Shirley Chisholm.

This honor came at a time in Jeannette Rankin's life when she needed a boost of morale, for in her final three years she feared she would leave the mortal earth without having cast an impression of her existence in American history.

In some respects she was a pathetic figure as death crept closer.

Almost belligerently she demanded of children: "Have you ever heard of Jeannette Rankin?" and predictably they replied negatively. She eagerly scanned the index pages of new reference, history and political books for her name. Mostly, it was absent. This was the only glimpse Jeannette allowed herself of her past, and with regret she wondered why she didn't realize the historical value of her life earlier.

But the equanimity of Jeannette's personality made her a noble, inspiring, positive thinker through the last moments of life. This was her public side, the person who sparkled with a zeal for better living and a love for humanity. This was the Jeannette Rankin who had waved banners for suffrage and weathered the hostility of a nation at war. This was the Jeannette Rankin who feared nothing and saw in the darkness of despair a flicker of encouragement to work toward a better life.

Jeannette was regarded as one of the few great humanitarians of the century, a trailblazer who hurdled generations with her ideas. Learning was an obsession with her, and she had earned her prestige. Anyone who had visited her apartment understood why. Tables were littered with books, magazines and letters. The joyous love of learning emanated from this humble setting; visitors who expected a teacup and small talk were surprised with a vigorous handshake and a discussion of American foreign policy.

Jeannette celebrated her 90th birthday on June 11, 1970, and a celebration commensurate with her status was scheduled at the Rayburn House Office Building in Washington, D.C. Hundreds of people waited for the proud old suffragist to stride into the banquet room in her reputed manner.

Three months earlier, Jeannette had fallen on the steps of a drug store, fracturing her hip. Try as she might, she was unable to regain her strength to walk. A fighter should be standing, and Jeannette suffered a loss of self-esteem being confined to the wheelchair.

Her peers, however, took no notice.

This timeless woman was known among them as a person of dedication and conviction, a woman who had frontiered a path for peace and justice before many of them were born. Sen. Margaret Chase Smith of Maine described Jeannette as "90 years young, tall as a giant in statesmanship that is unparalleled in American history. She broke the way for me by being elected in 1916. I salute her for being the original dove in Congress."

Clad in a gold-tinted silk dress she had sewn while living in India, Jeannette was a prominent presence in the room. More noticeable, however, was her quick wit and her keen knowledge of current affairs. Seated between Senators Lee Metcalf and Mike Mansfield of Montana, both of whom had started their political careers in the same district that had elected her to Congress in 1940, Jeannette saw decades of social change reflected in members of the audience.

Rep. Patsy Mink of Hawaii represented the continuing role of women in Congress. Former Sen. Gerald Nye of South Dakota had fought vigorously against war profiteering in the Thirties. And former Sen. Burton K. Wheeler of Montana, a liberal lawyer, had championed human rights.

They and many others, such as Metcalf and Mansfield, had worked to broaden the base of political control in government, but inevitably the acknowledgements focused on Jeannette's work for peace, and she listened attentively to their arguments.

Metcalf spoke the most articulately and consciously of Jeannette's contribution to humankind. He heralded her as one of the most prominent women in the world: a spokeswoman for peace, freedom and the consumer, for child welfare and industrial and labor problems, against economic maladjustments, social injustice and racial prejudice.

This resembled the calendar of issues before Congress in the Seventies. He explained further:

> Such is only a bare outline of a truly incredible career which has extended for 60 years.... I have dwelt on what Miss Rankin accomplished in her long life. They say, better than I

*can, what she is: a saver with a great heart, a builder, a trail
blazer and an example to all legislators who would have the
courage of their convictions.... I salute Jeannette Rankin for
her effective interest in Western problems that have influenced global civilization. It was easier to represent the First
District of Montana independently because of her example.*

The greatest message, however, was the subtle reprimand in
Jeannette's own comments. "We'd be the safest country in the
world if the world knew we didn't have a gun," she said. "Men are
not killed because they get mad at each other. They're killed
because one has a gun."

The impact of the late Jeannette Rankin's example upon the
American consciousness will, of course, show itself only in the
debate on the issues of war and peace. Without her presence,
possibly her ideas never can be expressed as clearly or enthusiasti-
cally. A personal magic made Jeannette beam. She was the
saleswoman of her cause and she found in her adversaries a
respect for her plight.

"She had such charm and a special style of beauty that her
opponents respected, even loved her," remembered American
Civil Liberties Union founder Roger Baldwin in 1978. The
spunky Baldwin, himself a vigorous opponent of war, believed
Jeannette's sense of humor, her wit and her common sense
appealed to everybody, whether conservative or liberal, man or
woman. "Miss Rankin's special distinction was her political courage, her fidelity to a pacifist conviction..., her integrity, her courage, her charm, and her broad appeal to women especially."

As a dissenter, Jeannette realized she never would benefit from
the public prestige and attention directed toward flamboyant
eccentrics such as George Wallace or establishment liberals like
John Kennedy, but her contribution would persevere, being the
substance of deep thinking in the absence of public acclaim.

She persisted with her beliefs regardless of their popularity, for
she was certain they were unbound by time or incident and would
lie dormant until the sleeping American consciousness awoke to
them.

Jeannette viewed war much like the predicament faced by a retarded child, who was tested for his learning ability by dipping water out of a barrel being filled from a faucet. "How do you know when he is feeble-minded?" Jeannette was asked. "They who aren't feeble-minded turn off the spigot," she replied. In this example she said that when Americans awake to the simplicity of peace they will shut off the spigot of war.

To Jeannette, peace was the ultimate recognition by civilization that humankind could exist in harmony and understanding without the influence of hate and discord. Problems could be shared and solved; hungry people could be fed, and ignorant people could be taught. Freedom truly was Jeannette's "emotion of an ideal," as the British sociologist Benjamin Kidd had advocated, for in her opinion the pleasure of human rights superseded all other commitments. She had said in a prayer in 1942:

God grant us the courage and wisdom to insist that the abundance we have here today may be shared with all mankind; that freedom, justice, righteousness, brotherhood and everlasting peace be established throughout the world.

Friends, relatives and acquaintances knew no weak side to Jeannette, except for a flaming temper that showed when the work of other people failed to meet her expectations. She was to most people the bastion of self-assurance and confidence, absolutely fearless that she might be assassinated or injured by someone opposed to her views. She believed the power of progressive ideas transcended all other earthly considerations.

When Jeannette was 90, for example, she contemplated campaigning for Congress again. Had she won a seat she would have been the oldest person ever to sit in Congress, but the possibility of such an unprecedented situation did not excite her. She was more interested in the ideas she had to offer. Perhaps with the experience and other credentials she had amassed, she would have done well as a candidate for the presidency. Such a novelty would not have bothered her; she had been several steps ahead of American innovation for more than 60 years.

Death was promising to interfere with those plans, however,

and Jeannette faced the reality that her active involvement in American politics was limited to years, maybe months. Her contribution to American living had been etched in history, the work of an inspired woman committed to her dreams of peace. Jeannette's mission was complete, and now she would be judged by what she had accomplished.

She was disappointed that her work for peace showed few results as the world's superpowers competed in a maddened race for nuclear superiority and greater military sophistication. Privately, she blamed herself that she could not have cut deeper into the national consciousness with her peace plan.

Such self-degrading thinking was futile, however, since Jeannette had sacrificed every moment of her adult life to the pursuit of peace. She had deprived herself of marriage, a family and anonymous personal happiness. She was robustly healthy and alert in old age. The exuberance of her life; the thrill of having a social cause to work toward, showed in her general health.

She wanted Americans to have a better understanding of the causes and antecedents of war and the sweetness of peace. If Jeannette Rankin gained anything in her tenure as a feminist, she convinced the world that freedom and justice were not empty words. She demonstrated that war was not the glorious and patriotic institution it was portrayed; war was a multi-faceted social problem that thrived on ignorance and lies to survive.

Jeannette believed peace was an attainable goal because it appealed to the progressive nature of humanity; unfortunately, she had no measuring stick with which to gauge the effect of her work, and she was greatly disappointed she did not witness the signing of a world peace pact and the abolition of war as a means to settling disputes.

As a crusader, however, she hardly was qualified to be objective toward an issue that enveloped her totally.

While Jeannette preferred to see her efforts come to a supreme conclusion, her contemporaries recognized her as a flesh-and-blood statue of human progress, to whom the American public could look for guidance when it truly decided to pursue the peace ideal. Sen. George McGovern, for example, piloted a bomber plane during World War II, yet he remains a strong admirer of Jeannette for her "absolute devotion to principle and for her rare courage."

Jeannette spouted ideas until the last months of her life, when her throat ailment stole her voice altogether. For the first time in her life, she felt truly alone, for communication had been her lifeblood. She viewed news programs and documentaries on television, but that was not enough. Her friends were bewildered at the garble coming from her mouth; they could not understand what she was saying.

Frustrated and alone, Jeannette begged her doctor to withdraw her medicine and put her to sleep forever. He refused. But she died in her sleep in her California apartment on May 18, 1973, only a few weeks short of her 93rd birthday.

When the news of her death reached the wire services, teletype click-clacked in newsrooms across the world. The news aroused ambivalent memories for hundreds of thousands of people, as Jeannette's body was being prepared for cremation. By 5:30 p.m. the day of her death, her remains were scattered at sea, three miles west of Point Lobos, near Carmel, Calif.

But she would not be forgotten. Four years later, Ambassador to Japan and former Sen. Mike Mansfield wrote of Jeannette Rankin:

> *She was a remarkable woman who has left her imprint upon history and who strove consistently to achieve a more peaceful world. We will miss her, but she has made her contribution and she will be remembered for decades to come.*

BIBLIOGRAPHY

BOOKS

Addams, Jane, *Twenty Years at Hull House* (N.Y., MacMillan, 1938)

Beard, Charles A., *The Devil Theory of War* (N.Y., Vanguard, 1936)

Catt, Carrie Chapman and Schuler, Nettie Rogers, *Woman Suffrage and Politics* (N.Y., Charles Scribner's Sons, 1926)

Chamberlin, Hope, *A Minority of Members: Women in the U.S. Congress* (N.Y. Praeger, 1973)

Chatfield, Charles, *For Peace and Justice, Pacifism in America* (Knoxville, University of Tennessee Press, 1971)

Dykeman, Wilma, *Too Many People, Too Little Love: Edna Rankin McKinnon, Pioneer for Birth Control* (N.Y., Holt, Rinehart and Winston, 1974)

Glasscock, C.B., *The War of the Copper Kings* (N.Y., Grosset and Dunlap, 1935)

Engelbrecht, H.C., and Hanighen, F.C., *Merchants of Death* (N.Y., Dodd and Mead, 1934)

Fleming, Alice, *Ida Tarbell: First of the Muckrakers* (Crowell, N.Y., 1971)

Flexner, Eleanor, *Century of Struggle, the Women's Rights Movement in the United States* (Cambridge, Belknap Press, 1959)

Fox, Mary Virginia, *Pacifists, Adventures in Courage* (Chicago, Reilly and Lee Books, 1971)

Grimes, Alan P., *The Puritan Ethic and Woman Suffrage* (N.Y., Oxford University Press, 1967)

Harper, Ida Husted, editor, *History of Woman Suffrage* (N.Y., National American Woman Suffrage Association, 1922)

Hofstadter, Richard, *The Age of Reform* (N.Y., Alfred A. Knopf, Inc., 1955)

Josephson, Hannah, *Jeannette Rankin: First Lady in Congress* (N.Y., Bobbs-Merrill, 1974)

Karlin, Jules A., *Progressive Politics in Montana* (N.Y., Lewis, 1956)

LaGuardia, Fiorella, *The Making of an Insurgent* (N.Y., Capricorn, 1961)

Lawson, Don, *Ten Fighters for Peace, an anthology* (N.Y., Lothrop, Lee and Shephard, 1971)

Libby, Frederick J., *To End War* (N.Y., Fellowship Publications, 1969)

Malone, Michael P. and Roeder, Richard B., *Montana: A History of Two Centuries* (University of Washington Press, 1976)

Melosi, Martin, *The Shadow of Pearl Harbor: Political Controversy over the Surprise Attack, 1941-1946* (Texas A and M University Press, 1977)

Millis, Walter, *The Road to War: America 1914-17* (Boston, Houghton Mifflin Co., 1935)

Norris, Frank, *The Octopus* (N.Y., Bantam, 1901)

Park, Maud Wood, *Front Door Lobby* (Boston, Beacon Press, 1960)

Richey, Elinor, *Eminent Women of the West: Jeannette Rankin, Woman of Commitment* (Berkeley, Howell-North, 1975)

Riis, Jacob A., *How the Other Half Lives* (N.Y., Hill and Wang, 1957)

Rutland, Robert A., *The Newsmongers: Journalism in the life of the Nation* (N.Y., Dial Press, 1973)

Sinclair, Upton, *The Jungle* (N.Y., Heritage Press, 1906)

Slayden, Ellen, *Washington Wife, Journal of Ellen Maury Slayden from 1897-1919* (N.Y., Harper and Row, 1962)

Solomen, Louis, *America Goes to Press* (London, Crowell-Collier, 1970)

Spargo, John, *The Bitter Cry of Children* (N.Y., Garrett, 1970)

Toole, K. Ross, *Montana: An Uncommon Land* (Norman, University of Oklahoma Press, 1959)

Toole, K. Ross, *Twentieth-Century Montana: A State of Extremes* (Norman, University of Oklahoma Press, 1972)

Waldron, Ellis, *An Atlas of Montana Politics Since 1864* (Missoula, MSU Press, 1958)

Wheeler, Burton K., *Yankee from the West* (N.Y., Doubleday, 1962)

PERIODICALS

American Historical Review, July 1920, "New Light on the Origins of World War," by Sidney Fay.

_____, October 1970, "Preparing the Public for War; Efforts to Establish a National Propaganda Agency, 1940-41."

Atlanta Constitution and Journal Magazine, June 21, 1959, "Rebel With A Cause," by Gregory Favre.

_____, May 7, 1967, "First Woman in Congress Still a Pacifist," by Lucy Justus.

_____, Feb. 13, 1972, "She Campaigns for Change," by Lucy Justus.

Atlanta Journal and Constitution, Nov. 24, 1953, "Pioneer Lady Solon a Georgian," by Frank Daniel.

Brenau Bulletin, February 1935, "The Chair of Peace."

Bulletin of Friend's Historical Association, 1954, "An Early Example of Political Action by Women," by E.B. Bronner.

Christian Century, Nov. 20, 1940, "Congresswoman Rankin Returns to House."

_____, Sept 4, 1940, "First Congresswoman Seeks to Return."

Christian Science Monitor, April 15, 1932, "Women to Put Masses Power Back of Peace."

Collier's Weekly, April 21, 1917, "Jeannette of Montana," by Peter Clark MacFarlane.

Commercial West, July 27, 1918, "Worthy Tribute to Miss 'Congressman' Rankin."

Current History, July 1924, "American Women's Ineffective Use of the Vote," by M.W. Willey.

Current Opinion, December 1916, "Portrait."

Fortune, March 1934, "Arms and the Men."

Georgia Historical Quarterly, Spring 1974, "Jeannette Rankin in Georgia," by Ted C. Harris.

Harpers, Dec. 5, 1914, "Motherhood and War," by F.W. Pethick-Lawrence.

_____, May 1933, "Our Quarreling Pacifists," by Marcus Duffield.

Independent, Nov. 20, 1916, "Portrait."

_____, April 2, 1917, "Lady from Missoula," by Donald Wilhelm.

Independent Woman, December 1940, "Who's Who in Elections."

Journal of Modern History, March 1951, "The War-Guilt Question and American Disillusionment."

Life, March 3, 1972, "Feminists' New Heroine," by Elizabeth Frappolo.

Literary Digest, Nov. 18, 1916, "Portrait."

_____, Nov. 25, 1916, "Member from Montana."

_____, Aug. 11, 1917, "Our Busy Congress-woman."

McCall's. April 1917, "Our First Woman Congressman," by Bertha Filer.

_____, 1917 "What We Women Should Do," by Jeannette Rankin (ghosted by Katharine Anthony).

_____, January 1958, "Three Women of Courage," by John F. Kennedy.

Montana Business Quarterly, Autumn 1971, "Montana's First Woman Politician — A Recollection of Jeannette Rankin Campaigning," by Mackey Brown.

Montana: the Magazine of Western History, July 1967, "The Lady from Montana," by John Board.

_____, Winter 1973, "Montana Women and the Battle for the Ballot," by T.A. Larson.

_____, Summer 1974, "Mother Was Shocked," by Belle F. Winestine.

Nation, May 31, 1917, "Lady from Montana," by The Tattler.

_____, Nov. 2, 1918, "Politics in Montana," by Louis Levine.

New Outlook, November 1933, "Deaf and Dumb Ships," by Wayne Francis Palmer.

New Republic, March 9, 1918, "The Legal Status of War," by S.O. Levinson.

_____, Nov. 18, 1936, "Pacifism: It's Rise and Fall," by Bruce Bliven.

Newsweek, Feb. 14, 1966, "Woman Against War."

Outlook, Nov. 22, 1916, "First Woman Elected to Congress."

Pacific Northwest Quarterly, January 1964, "The Montana Woman Suffrage Campaign, 1911-1914," by Ronald Schaffer.

Peace Action, March 1936, "Emergency Peace Campaign Is Planned."

Public Opinion Quarterly, April 1937, "Organizing American Public Opinion for Peace," by Elton Atwater.

_____, March 1940, "Influences of World Events on U.S. Neutrality Opinion," by P.E. Jacob.

_____, September 1940, "America Faces the War: A Study in Public Opinion."

_____, December 1940, "The Peace Groups Join Battle."

Ramparts, February 1968, "History of Rise of Women to Power in the United States, 1961-68," by W. and M. Hinckle.

Scribner's Commentator, November 1941, "Woman Against War."

Scribner's Magazine, February 1935, "National Politics and War."

Suffragist, Jan. 16, 1915, "Woman's Movement for Constructive Peace."

_____, March 31, 1917, "An Impression of Jeannette Rankin," by Winifred Mallou.

Sunset, November 1916, "First Woman Elected to Congress," by Belle Fligelman.

Survey, July 21, 1917, "Political Power in the Hands of a Woman."

_____, Feb. 1, 1919, "Federal Mothers' Aid."

_____, December 1920, "National Consumer's League."

Survey Graphic, February 1937, "Who Wants Peace?" by Dorothy Thompson.

Union Printer, May 5, 1945, "Social Progress Moves on the Feet of Women."

Woman Citizen, July 2, 1917, "What a Congresswoman Has Done for Working Women," by Ethel Smith.

Woman's Home Companion, July 1926, "Our Gypsy Journey to Georgia," by Katharine Anthony.

_____, August 1926, "A Basket of Summer Fruit," by Katharine Anthony.

_____, September 1926, "Living on the Front Porch," by Katharine Anthony.

Woman's Journal, Nov. 11, 1916, "Miss Rankin Gives New Turn to Old Ideas," p. 365.

_____, Nov. 25, 1916, "The Press on Jeannette Rankin," p. 384.

_____, Dec. 23, 1916, "G.O.P. Bowed to Woman's Spirit," p. 415.

_____, Jan. 6, 1917, "Quiet Life for Congresswoman," p. 1.

_____, March 10, 1917, "Jeannette Rankin Addresses 3000," pp. 55-56.

_____, March 17, 1917, "Breezy Bits from the Capitol," p. 4.

_____, March 17, 1917, "Miss Rankin Aids Suffrage Hearing," p. 63.

_____, March 24, 1917, "Miss Rankin Speaks in N.J.," p. 67.

_____, March 31, 1917, "Congresswoman Opens Office in Washington," p. 73.

_____, April 7, 1917, "Jeannette Rankin Takes Place in House," p. 79.

_____, April 14, 1917, "Miss Rankin Kept Busy," p. 89.

UNPUBLISHED MANUSCRIPTS

Board, John C., *Jeannette Rankin: The Suffrage Years and Before*, graduate paper, undated.

Board John C., *The Lady from Montana: Jeannette Rankin,* master's thesis, University of Wyoming, Laramie, 1964.

Harris, Ted Carlton, *Jeannette Rankin, Warring Pacifist,* master's thesis, University of Georgia, 1969.

Harris Ted Carlton, *Jeannette Rankin: Suffragist, First Woman Elected to Congress, and Pacifist,* doctoral dissertation, University of Georgia, 1972.

Lindquist, Adah Donovan, *A Study of Jeannette Rankin and Her Role in the Peace Movement* (Hanover, Ind., 1971), Honors Paper, Swarthmore College, Pa.

Oral History Project, The Bancroft Library, University of California, Berkeley. *Jeannette Rankin Transcript.*

Schaffer, Ronald, *Jeannette Rankin, Progressive Isolationist,* doctoral dissertation, Princeton University, 1959.

Ward, Doris Buck, *Winning of Woman Suffrage in Montana,* master's thesis, Montana State University, June 1974.

Wilson, Joan Hoff, *Peace Is A Woman's Job... Jeannette Rankin's Foreign Policy,* fellowship paper, Arizona State University, 1977.

MANUSCRIPT COLLECTIONS

Belle Fligelman Winestine Papers, Montana Historical Society Library, Helena.

Jeannette Rankin Papers, Montana Historical Society Library, Helena.

Jeannette Rankin Papers, National Council for Prevention of War files, Swarthmore Peace Collection, Swarthmore College, Pa.

Jeannette Rankin Papers, Arthur and Elizabeth Schlesinger Library on the History of Women in America, Radcliffe College, Cambridge, Mass.

Wellington D. Rankin Papers, Montana Historical Society Library, Helena.

PUBLIC DOCUMENTS

House Journal of the Twelfth Session of the Legislative Assembly of the State of Montana. Helena, Montana: Independent Publishing Co., 1911.

Senate Journal of the Thirteenth Session of the Legislative Assembly of the State of Montana. 1913, pp.110, 138, 159.

National American Woman Suffrage Association, 45th Annual Report, 1913, p. 80.

U.S. *Congressional Record,* 65th Congress, First Session, 1917.

U.S. *Congressional Record,* 65th Congress, Second Session, 1918.

Hearings, "Right of Suffrage to Women," House Committee on Woman Suffrage, 65th Congress, Second Session, on H.J. Res. 200, Washington, 1918.

Report of the International Congress of Women, Zurich, 1919. Women's International League for Peace and Freedom, 1919.

U.S. *Congressional Record,* 67th Congress, Vol. 61, 1921. Pp. 3141-3146, 4206-4217, 7926-7950, 7979-8014, 8034-8037.

Hearings, "Public Protection of Maternity and Infancy," House Committee on Interstate and Foreign Commerce, 66th Congress, Third Session, on H.R. 10925, Washington, 1920.

Hearings, "Exportation of Arms or Munitions of War," House Committee on Foreign Affairs, 72nd Congress, Second Session, on H.J. Res. 580, Washington, 1933.

Hearings, "Construction of Certain Naval Vessels," Senate Committee on Naval Affairs, 73rd Congress, Second Session, on S. 2493, Washington, 1934.

Hearings, "Taking the Profit Out of War," House Committee on Military Affairs, 74th Congress, First Session, on H.R. 3 and H.R. 5293, Washington, 1935.

Hearings, "American Neutrality Policy," House Committee on Foreign Affairs," 75th Congress, First Session, on H.J. 147 and 242, Washington, 1937.

Hearings, "American Neutrality Policy," House Committee on Foreign Affairs, 76th Congress, First Session, 1939.

U.S. *Congressional Record,* 77th Congress, First Session, 1941.

U.S. *Congressional Record,* Vol. 87, Part I, 77th Congress, First Session, pp.791-793, 813-814, pp. 9520-9530, Washington, 1941.

U.S. *Congressional Record,* "Some Questions About Pearl Harbor," 77th Congress, Second Session, Dec. 8, 1942.

Hearings, Joint Committee on the Pearl Harbor Attack, 79th Congress, First Session (38 parts), Washington, 1946.

Report of the Joint Committee on the Pearl Harbor Attack, 79th Congress, Second Session, Senate Document 244, Washington,1946.

U.S. *Congressional Record,* 91st Congress, Second Session, Vol. 116, Parts 15-16, June 22, 1970.

ORAL INTERVIEWS

Brown, Dorothy McKinnon, taped interview for the author, Jan. 29, 1978, Del Mar, Calif.

Brown, Dorothy McKinnon, taped interview for the author, July 5, 1978, Del Mar, Calif.

Elge, Frances, personal taped interview with the author, Dec. 10, 1977, Billings, Mont.

Galt, Louise Rankin, personal taped interview with the author, Oct. 6, 1978, Helena, Mont.

Rankin, Jeannette, taped interview with John Board, Aug. 29-30, 1963, Missoula, Mont.

Rankin, Jeannette, television interview with Dick Cavett, April 17, 1972, Los Angeles, Calif.

Ronhovde, Virginia, personal interview with the author, Oct. 11, 1978, Helena, Mont.

Winestine, Belle Fligelman, personal taped interview with the author, Aug. 17, 1977, Helena, Mont.

Winestine, Belle Fligelman, personal taped interview with the author, Dec. 14, 1977, Helena, Mont.

Winestine, Belle Fligelman, taped interview with George Cole, undated, Lewis and Clark Library, Helena, Mont.

Winestine, Belle Fligelman, personal taped interview with the author, July 21, 1978, Helena, Mont.

PERSONAL CORRESPONDENCE

Baldwin, Roger, personal letter to the author, Aug. 23, 1978.

Mansfield, Mike, personal letter to the author, Sept. 18, 1978.

McGovern, George, personal letter to the author, Nov. 1, 1978.

McKinnon, Edna Rankin, personal letter to the author, Oct. 10, 1977. Mrs. McKinnon died in 1978. She was Jeannette Rankin's sister.

Ronhovde, Virginia, personal letter to the author, Nov. 1, 1978. Mrs. Ronhovde is Jeannette Rankin's niece.

NEWSPAPERS

Anaconda Standard, (Montana), Aug. 15, 1917, pp. 1, 7.

Athens Banner-Herald (Georgia), Feb. 10, 1928, p. 4; Sept. 28, 1934, p. 1; Oct. 18, 1934, p. 1; Oct. 26, 1934; Dec. 8, 1941.

Athens Daily Times (Georgia), Nov. 4, 1934, p. 5; Dec. 20, 1934; Jan. 28, 1972, p. 1.

Bismarck Tribune (North Dakota), May 19, 1967.

Boston Advertiser, March 9, 1925.

Butte Daily Bulletin (Montana), Oct. 24, 1918.

Butte Daily Post (Montana), Oct. 30, 1940; Nov. 4, 1940; Nov. 7, 1940.

Chicago Evening News, May 19, 1919.

Chicago Sunday-Herald, Jan. 9, 1917; Feb. 11, 1917; Feb. 18, 1917;
   May 13, 1917; May 27, 1917; June 3, 1917; June 10, 1917;
   June 17, 1917; June 24, 1917; July 8, 1917; Aug. 5, 1917;
   Oct. 21, 1917; Nov. 11, 1917; Dec. 3, 1917; Dec. 10, 1917;
   Dec. 17, 1917.

Cleveland News, March 27, 1925.

Cleveland Plain Dealer, March 26, 1925.

Daily Missoulian (Montana), Jan. 15, 1914, p. 6; Feb. 15, 1914, p. 1;
   March 23, 1914, p. 3; April 3, 1914, p. 4; May 26, 1914, p. 1;
   Nov. 6, 1914, pp. 1, 7; Nov. 8, 1914, p. 8; Nov. 14, 1914, p. 1;
   May 18, 1916, p. 2; July 9, 1916, p. 2; July 29, 1916, p. 5; July
   30, 1916, p. 2; Aug. 23, 1916, p. 1; Aug. 30, 1916, p. 4; Sept.
   27, 1916, p. 8; Oct. 23, 1916, p. 8; Nov. 2, 1916, p. 1; Nov. 6,
   1916, p. 1; Nov. 7, 1916, p. 12; Nov. 10, 1916, p. 1; Nov. 18,
   1916, p. 10; Jan. 12, 1917, p. 5; March 31, 1917, p. 1; April
   6, 1917, p. 1; April 17, 1917, p. 8; June 4, 1917, p. 1; Aug. 22,
   1917, p. 1; Aug. 23,1917, pp. 1, 5; Jan. 6, 1918, editorial p. 1;
   Aug. 24, 1917, p. 4; April 20, 1918, p. 6; July 6, 1918, p. 1;
   Aug. 29, 1918, p. 1; Nov. 3, 1918, p. 8; Nov. 6, 1918, p. 1;
   Nov. 7, 1918, p. 6; Oct. 22, 1940, p. 5; Oct. 23, 1940, p. 6;
   Nov. 6, 1940, p. 1; Jan. 4, 1941, p. 3; Dec. 11, 1941, pp. 1, 4, 5.

Des Moines Register (Iowa), April 15, 1917, p. 4.

Emporia Gazette (Kansas), Dec. 10, 1941, p. 4.

Gainesville News (Georgia), Oct. 31, 1934.

Great Falls Tribune (Montana), June 20, 1934; April 6, 1937; July
   7, 1940, p. 5; July 12, 1940, p. 1; July 19, 1940, p. 1; Nov. 7,
   1940; July 12, 1941; Dec. 12, 1941, p. 7; Sept. 29, 1949;

June 3, 1951; Oct. 5, 1959; June 6, 1951.

Helena Independent (Montana), Feb. 2, 1911; April 3, 1917, p. 4;
   April 26, 1917, p. 4; Aug. 9, 1917, p. 6; Oct. 5, 1917; Jan. 17,
   1918, p. 4; Jan. 22, 1918; April 18, 1918; April 19, 1918; May
   21, 1918, p. 4; June 23, 1918; June 26, 1918; July 7, 1918;
   Nov. 3, 1918, p. 4; July 16, 1940; Dec. 9, 1941.

Helena People's Voice (Montana), Oct. 30, 1940; Dec. 10, 1941,
   p. 1; Aug. 11, 1967.

Knoxville News-Sentinel (Tennessee), Feb. 13, 1972.

Louisville Courier-Journal (Kentucky), April 8, 1917, p. 4.

Macon Evening News (Georgia), Feb. 11, 1930, p. 1; Dec. 10,
   1934, p. 4; Oct. 10, 1935, p. 4.

Macon Telegraph (Georgia), June 2, 1928, p. 4.

Minneapolis Tribune, Dec. 10, 1941, p. 4.

Montana Progressive, Jan. 14, 1915.

Montana Record-Herald, July 12, 1916, p. 2; March 3, 1917, p. 7;
   April 11, 1917; Aug. 16, 1917; Sept. 12, 1918, p. 1.

Montana Standard, Dec. 10, 1941, p. 4.

Nashville Tennessean, Feb. 13, 1972.

New York American, Jan. 10, 1918; Jan. 11, 1918; March 17, 1918.

New York Herald-Tribune, Jan. 24, 1947.

New York Times, Aug. 14, 1913, p. 6; Nov. 18, 1916, p. 10; Nov.
    21, 1916, p. 10; Feb. 21, 1917, p. 14; March 3, 1917, p. 4;
    April 3, 1917, p. 4; April 6, 1917, p. 1; April 7, 1917, p. 4;
    April 8, 1917, II, p. 2; April 14, 1917, p. 12; May 29, 1917,
    pp. 1, 4; July 2, 1917, p. 7; July 16, 1917, p. 9; Aug. 3, 1917,
    pp. 3, 16; Aug. 31, 1917; Nov. 9, 1917, p. 13; Nov. 17, 1917,
    p. 4; Dec. 13, 1917, p. 19; Aug. 3, 1918, p. 16; Aug. 10, 1918,
    p. 5; April 10, 1919; May 18, 1919; Dec. 16, 1934, IV, p. 6;
    Feb. 10, 1938; Feb. 6, 1940; June 9, 1940, IV, p. 2; Dec. 9,
    1941, p. 8; Dec. 12, 1941, p. 8; Jan. 16, 1968; Jan. 24, 1972, L,
    p. 24; May 20, 1973.

New York Tribune, Feb. 25, 1917, p. 7.

St. Louis Post-Dispatch, Dec. 10, 1941, p. 2C.

Washington Daily News, April 6, 1937.

Washington Evening Star, Dec. 8, 1941; Jan. 16, 1968.

Washington Post, May 6, 1917, p. 3; April 2, 1917, p. 1;
    April 8, 1917, p. 4; Dec. 12, 1941; Jan. 12, 1968.

Washington Times, April 2, 1917, p. 3; Aug. 8, 1917, p. 2.

FILM

Fisher, David, "Jeannette Rankin: First Lady of Peace," a film pro-
    duced for WGTV in Athens, Ga. On file at the Arthur and
    Elizabeth Schlesinger Library on the History of Women in
    America, Radcliffe College, Cambridge, Mass.